Toward an African Theology of Fraternal Solidarity

african christian studies series (africs)

This series will make available significant works in the field of African Christian studies, taking into account the many forms of Christianity across the whole continent of Africa. African Christian studies is defined here as any scholarship that relates to themes and issues on the history, nature, identity, character, and place of African Christianity in world Christianity. It also refers to topics that address the continuing search for abundant life for Africans through multiple appeals to African religions and African Christianity in a challenging social context. The books in this series are expected to make significant contributions in historicizing trends in African Christian studies, while shifting the contemporary discourse in these areas from narrow theological concerns to a broader inter-disciplinary engagement with African religio-cultural traditions and Africa's challenging social context.

The series will cater to scholarly and educational texts in the areas of religious studies, theology, mission studies, biblical studies, philosophy, social justice, and other diverse issues current in African Christianity. We define these studies broadly and specifically as primarily focused on new voices, fresh perspectives, new approaches, and historical and cultural analyses that are emerging because of the significant place of African Christianity and African religio-cultural traditions in world Christianity. The series intends to continually fill a gap in African scholarship, especially in the areas of social analysis in African Christian studies, African philosophies, new biblical and narrative hermeneutical approaches to African theologies, and the challenges facing African women in today's Africa and within African Christianity. Other diverse themes in African Traditional Religions; African ecology; African ecclesiology; inter-cultural, inter-ethnic, and inter-religious dialogue; ecumenism; creative inculturation; African theologies of development, reconciliation, globalization, and poverty reduction will also be covered in this series.

SERIES EDITORS

Dr Stan Chu Ilo (St Michael's College, University of Toronto)
Dr Philomena Njeri Mwaura (Kenyatta University, Nairobi, Kenya)
Dr Mwenda Ntaragwi (Calvin College, Michigan)

Toward an African Theology of Fraternal Solidarity

UBE NWANNE

༄

IKENNA U. OKAFOR

Foreword by Kurt Appel

PICKWICK *Publications* · Eugene, Oregon

TOWARD AN AFRICAN THEOLOGY OF FRATERNAL SOLIDARITY
UBE NWANNE

African Christian Studies Series 7

Pickwick Publications
An Imprint of Wipf and Stock Publishers
199 W. 8th Ave., Suite 3
Eugene, OR 97401

www.wipfandstock.com

ISBN 13: 978-1-62564-593-7

Cataloguing-in-Publication Data

Okafor, Ikenna U.

Toward an African theology of fraternal solidarity : UBE UWANNE / Ikenna U. Okafor ; foreword by Kurt Appel.

xviii + 218 p. ; 23 cm. Includes bibliographical references and index.

ISBN 13: 978-1-62564-593-7

African Christian Studies Series 7

1. Christianity—Nigeria. 2. Igbo (African people)—Religion. 3. Solidarity—Religious aspects—Christianity. 4. Church and social problems—Nigeria. I. Appel, Kurt, 1968–. II. Title. III. Series.

BR1463.N5 O37 2014

Manufactured in the U.S.A.   09/29/2014

This work is dedicated to the loving memory of my father,

Wilfred E. M. Okafor,

and in appreciation to

Most Rev. Dr. Valerian Maduka Okeke,
Archbishop of Onitsha, Nigeria

"Ọ naghị anyị m alọ, ọ' nwanne m."

She is not a burden to me, she is my sister.

Contents

Illustrations

Foreword

It is in accordance with the earliest Christian tradition to attribute the signature of universality inmostly to the *Logos*. This theologoumenon has become in a whole new way in our time the *kairos* for the Church and theology. The question of a universal horizon of thought and action is not accidental but rather constitutes arguably, in view of global risks and global interdependence, the challenge which the churches and theologies, as well as societies and politics today must unavoidably confront.

One of the first theologians who drew attention to this new urgency of a universal horizon was Karl Rahner. In his essays on *The Future of the Church*, he proposes a theological division of Church history, which differs from the profane Eurocentric division of history into ancient, medieval, and modern periods. In Rahner's view, a short period of Jewish Christianity was followed by a very long "period of the Church in a particular cultural milieu, namely, the Hellenistic and European culture and civilization," which will eventually be overtaken by a "period in which the living space of the Church will primarily be the whole world."[1] Two councils, namely, the Council of Jerusalem in apostolic time and the Second Vatican Council marked the turning points between the respective periods. What is remarkable about this partition is that it does not merely evaluate history retrospectively, but rather connects it with an open vision that is oriented toward the future. Since the Second Vatican Council the Church is confronted with the task of becoming the real Universal Church and no longer merely European-exported Universal Church. There are no immediate available guidelines about how this can take place; rather it requires a long process of transmissions, a search for encounters and convivial exchanges in which it will be successful, perhaps, to begin a mutual interpretation and appreciation of each other's different cultural experiences.

1. Rahner, *Schriften zur Theologie*, 14:294.

ix

Thus is the room for discourse marked out, in which Ikenna Okafor's work tries to make some laudable steps. The work takes its point of departure from the Igbo idiom, *Ọ nụrụ ube nwanne agbala ọsọ*, which he at the beginning matter-of-factly applies in the work without explanation and attempt at translation. In this way the motif, which Ikenna Okafor describes as a basic experience from the Igbo context, is shielded from any premature and presumptive tendency to subject it to in-depth discussion or immediate interpretation, as if it could simply be classified under traditional European categories. It must first of all be left in its uniqueness and untranslatability. And not until in an encounter with Latin American liberation theology, African theologies and (secular) liberation movements, the theology of the books of Exodus and Deuteronomy as well as in Lucan and Johannine theologies and the diverse experiences of the African context that it became possible to explain this idiom and to develop thereby a "theology of fraternity."

The work ends with the creation of a city under the title of "*Philadelphia in Ecclesiae.*" If Ikenna Okafor takes Philadelphia to mean a "city of brotherly love," this is reminiscent of the last image of the Apocalypse of St. John—the story of the open, hospitable city whose source of light is God Himself (Rev 21f.). Thus, in addition to universality, another *kairos* for Church and theology is underscored today, namely, the relationship between religion and city in view of massive urbanization, which has taken place in the last decades and has led to a new type of centerless megacity that we still call a "city," only because we do not have a better term for the phenomenon.

What can be the contribution of a "theology of fraternity" for a Church that has no choice but to become a Universal Church in a universal horizon and faced with the challenge of urbanization? This is the question that the author poses from the experience of the Igbo culture, and from the experience of inhabiting two worlds, the African and the European. The examples and attempts at answers which he offers, are capable of inspiring readers of different worlds to a deeper exploration of Christianity and of our world today.

Prof. Dr. Kurt Appel
Professor of Fundamental Theology
University of Vienna, Austria

Acknowledgments

Such a challenging academic project cannot be accomplished without being indebted to many who directly or indirectly are instrumental in making it a success. My first gratitude goes to God Almighty in whom we live and move and have our being, and He who endows us with the necessary intellectual gift and health of mind and body to think and write.

I thank my bishop, Most Rev. Dr. Hilary Okeke, with whose permission and moral support I undertook my doctoral studies. And in a special way, I thank my former Rector, Most Rev. Dr. Valerian Okeke, Archbishop of Onitsha who hand-picked me to be one of the beneficiaries of the scholarship to pursue higher theological education in Austria. To him I also humbly and gratefully dedicate this work. I thank His Eminence, Christoph Cardinal Schönborn, whose benevolence made the scholarship possible, and who assigned me as a pastor in his diocese and thus provided me all the necessary logistics, environment and resources that facilitated my work. Similarly, I am very grateful to Msgr. Mag. Franz Schuster, Vicar General Emeritus of the Archdiocese of Vienna, whose humane assurances and brotherly assistance, whenever I needed his help, were a source of moral encouragement.

Every student needs a mentor in order to discover the genius in him/herself. It is on this note that I thank in a special way my Professor, Dr. Kurt Appel who, as one might say, midwifed the birth of this work. His friendship and encouragements are very motivating for me. Similarly, I am grateful to Dr. Helmut Jakob Deibl who also read this work and commended it. His generous comments were encouraging. Also deserving exceptional thanks is Professor, Dr. Elochukwu E. Uzukwu, one of the most prominent Igbo theologians, whose willingness to appraise this work is a great honor to me. His theological evaluation and suggestions were a valuable help to me.

There are also some good friends whose remote influence on the outcome of my academic endeavors cannot be ignored. To them I owe profound gratitude for enriching my life in general through their moral and/

or financial support. Among them are: Jutta Wiesenhofer, Rev. Dr. Joseph Ibeanu, Rev. Fr. Jude C. Okeke, Rev. Dr. Victor Mbanisi, Rev. Mag. Annistus Njoku, Rev. Dr. Jacob Nwabor, Rev. Dr. Ndubueze Fabian Mmagu, Rev. Dr. Peter Okeke, Rev. Dr. Moses Chukwujekwu, Rev. Fr. Damian Umeokeke, Rev. Fr. Matthew Ugwuoji, Rev. Fr. Charles Anedo, Rev. Dr. Stan Chu Ilo, Rev. Dr. Humphery Anameje, Members of Nigerian Priests and Religious Association (NIPRA) Austria, Dr. and Mrs Walter and Ilse Neumayer, DI Harald and Marthina Seifert, Mrs Rita Okechukwu and family.

Exceptional thanks also goes to the catholic communities of Großenzersdorf, Raasdorf, Franzensdorf, Rutzendorf, Mühlleiten, Atzgersdorf-Wien, Breitensee im Marchfelde, Lassee, Schönfeld, Markthof and Schlosshof. The friendship of the Christians I encountered in these parishes gave my pastoral engagement in Austria a meaning that invigorates. I appreciate in a special way the humble invaluable assistance of Rosalia Böck, Maria Reuckl, Alexandra Kernbauer, Elisabeth Brandstetter and Brigitte Hemmelmeyer, whose tireless engagements in my parishes helped to relieve me of enormous pastoral burden and thus enabled me to study. I appreciate the healthy, humorous environment of the rectory in Leopoldsdorf where Mag. Robert Ryş, Mag. Jérémie Bono, Marlies Goldstein and Anja Zyş-Ochrymovicz strengthened me with a lot of laughter.

Finally, I acknowledge with deep love the indispensable role of my relatives: my mother, Mrs. Beatrice A. Okafor; my sisters, Amalachi Ojukwu, Nkechi Momoh, Chika Ifechukwu, Chima Ndụbụisi, and their respective families; and my brothers, Ilechukwu and Obinna, whose love is, in fact, the soul of this work. I commend all to the mercy and providential care of our LORD and Brother Jesus Christ.

Abbreviations

ANC	African National Congress
AT	Altes Testament
AZAPO	Azanian People's Organization
BCM	Black Consciousness Movement
CBCN	Catholic Bishops' Conference of Nigeria
CCC	*Catechism of the Catholic Church*
CELAM	Consejo Episcopal Latinoamericano (Latin American Episcopal Conference)
CIV	*Caritas in Veritate*
CIWA	Catholic Institute of West Africa
CSN	Catholic Secretariat of Nigeria
DCE	*Deus Caritas Est*
EATWOT	Ecumenical Association of Third World Theologians
EC	European Community
GS	*Gaudium et Spes*
JCA	Joint Church Aid
LG	*Lumen Gentium*
LN	*Libertatis Nuntius*
NE	*Nichomachean Ethics*
NF	National Forum
PP	*Populorum Progressio*
RM	*Redemptoris Missio*
RN	*Rerum Novarum*
SM	*Sacramentum Mundi*
UDF	United Democratic Front
WCC	World Council of Churches

Maps of Africa, Nigeria, and Igboland

AFRICA

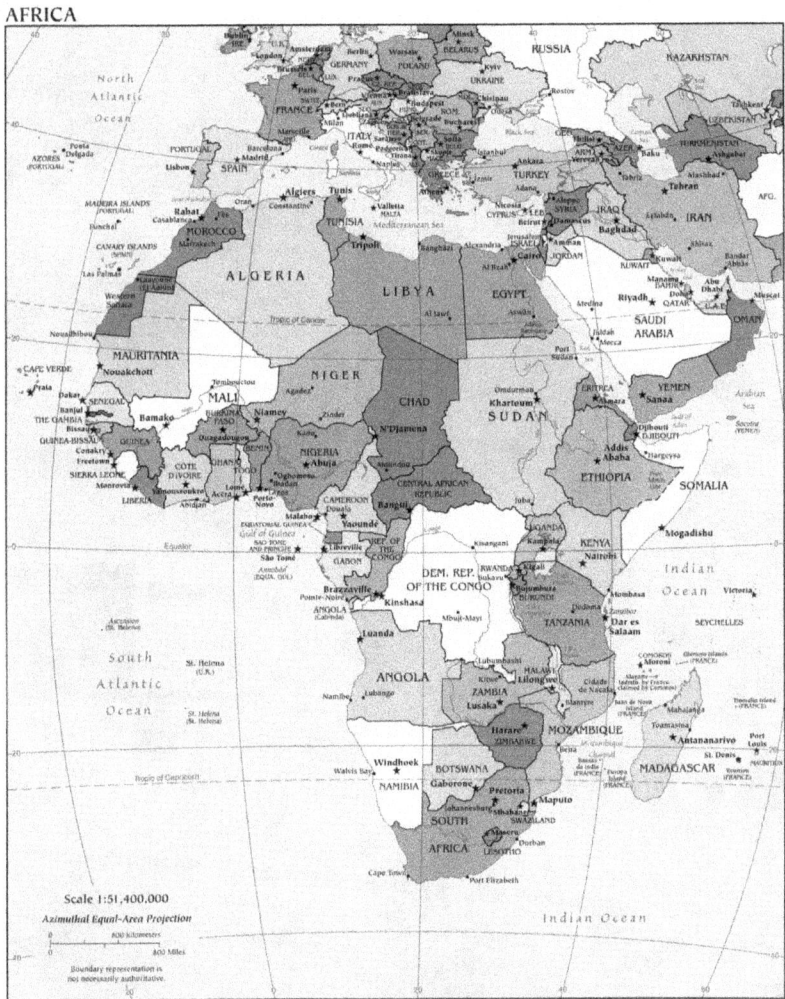

Figure 2: Map of Africa

Figure 3: Map of Nigeria

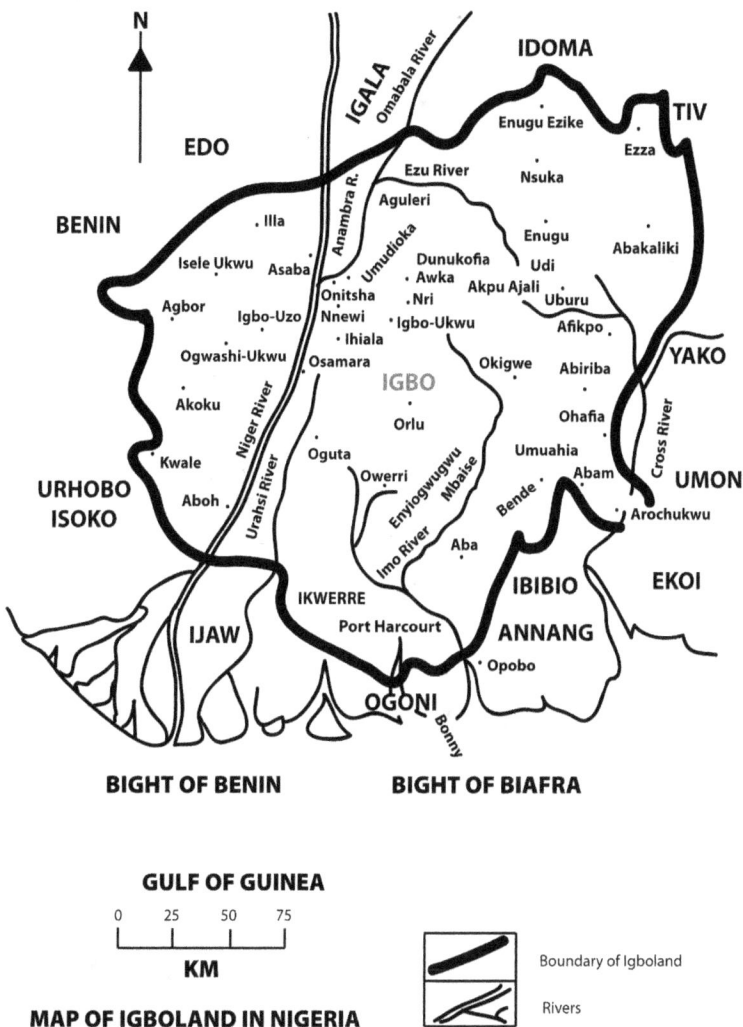

Figure 4: Map of Igboland

Introduction

THE SOCIAL RELEVANCE OF theology today will always depend on its ability to nourish itself from those life's daily encounters that provide essential raw materials with which theology engages the human project of building the kingdom of God on the academic level. The significance of such daily experiences of theological expressions is apprehensible in a memorable encounter I had with a Nigerian boy in March 2001. I was driving home after having concluded a series of transactions in the city of Onitsha. It is usually the hottest season of the year and the tropical sun was really scorching. People who travel by foot under such temperature always reckon with blisters from the hot sandy soil, and no one grows used to such intolerable heat. In spite of my air-conditioned car, I was sweating behind the wheel as I drove back to the parish rectory located on the countryside. I desperately needed a cold shower to soothe my nerves. The road between Onitsha and my residence was seemingly desolate at that time of the day. Such was the circumstance which made me feel obliged to offer help to a boy of very tender age (about 6 or 7 years old) who was carrying his younger sister (about 3 years old) on his back and trekking the lonely road to what must be probably a long distance for both. The children were perhaps on their way homewards after visiting an old aunt or grandmother in a neighboring village. I pulled up gradually to a halt beside them and called out to offer them a lift to their destination. Then I realized that I have frightened the young lad.

As I beckoned on him to enter my car so that I could transport them to their destination, the boy panicked and made to flee. The young girl on his back started crying. Guessing that they may have been warned by parents to beware of strangers who pretend to be generous and kind to little children, I tried to reassure him that I meant no harm but simply wanted to help them. My effort to convince him, that under the circumstance it must be too burdensome for him to trek a long distance on the hot soil with his sister as

1

a load on his back, was in vain. However, the short conversation that took place between us that afternoon became the beginning of a series of theological reflections which stuck in my mind like super-glue, and which will eventually give birth to the theological discourse articulated in this work.

> "She must be too heavy a burden for you to carry and trek," I persuaded, referring to his sister (the load on his back), but the little boy retorted in Igbo:
>
> "Ọ naghị anyị m alọ, ọ' nwanne m," which means,
>
> "She is not too heavy for me (or a burden to me), she is my sister."

After the unsuccessful attempt to help I continued on my way, with the brief encounter appearing actually uneventful at first. But the boy's words have struck a chord that generated a symphony of thought in my mind as I continued on my way home. I thought of so many things: of ethnic and religious conflicts; of various forms of exploitations in the world; of the insecurity so rife in Africa; of many children who are dying of hunger and diseases; of slavery and colonialism; of sexism; of bigotry in politics and public square everywhere in the world; but above all of the tenacity of this young courageous boy who is gladly carrying a load that is more than half his own weight under such an extremely hot weather. Unknown to him, he has sown in me the seed of a theology that has immediately begun to germinate in my mind—a seed of thought that I have increasingly come to appreciate in homilies as I began to analyze the implications of the boy's statement. I ended up likening it to a latent mineral deposit that must be explored. In fact, it is a latent theological deposit for the exploration of "a theology of fraternal solidarity." The polite rebuff was surely motivated by the little boy's sense of filial responsibility to guard his sibling. His words, however, were packed full with a sublime message that did not cease ringing bells in the ears of my memory. And since that fateful day of March 2001, I never stopped pondering at the depth of theological lesson which is apparent in that spontaneous, simple, but profoundly sublime, thought-provoking wisdom from a young and innocent intellect: "she is not a burden to me, she is my sister." It was expressed so matter-of-factly as if to demonstrate that the principal reason why the little girl is not a burden is precisely because she is his younger sister. And indeed no other reason could be advanced, for it is obvious that the boy could not have been willing to carry any other type of load that weighs exactly as his sister. Turning down what for him may be an enticing but risky offer of a free ride, one can still bet on how joyfully contented this boy will be on reaching his destination, tired but satisfied for having carried his younger sister home to safety. His tenacity and spirit of sacrificial endurance is impressive and very instructive, because it is in the consciousness of having intimate fraternal ties with one another that human beings discover an incalculable inner strength capable of making heavy burdens seem light, simply by virtue of an innocent sense of responsibility that is purely motivated and nourished by love. In fact whenever love enlivens our actions, carrying one another becomes a beautiful and pleasant experience.

This love has both human and divine countenance, and the purpose of Christian theology is to ensure that the countenance of fraternal love is reproduced in the hearts of most, if not all, women and men of this world. In other words, it is one of the transformative functions of theology to bring women and men to learn the virtue of seeing one another as real sisters and brothers and consequently be prepared to carry one another on this journey of earthly life whenever the need arises. The little Igbo boy's demonstration of this virtue is perhaps instinctual, but at the base of that humanistic instinct looms a fundamental question for theology today, namely: "Who is my sister or brother, to whom I am indebted in love and solidarity?" Jesus' answer to this question breaks the boundaries of consanguinity (cf. Matt 12:48–50) and of nationality (cf. Luke 10:29–37). It recommends for us a new way of perceiving one another—a way that also requires in our time a new theological hermeneutic. The following pages are devoted to exploring this new hermeneutic and using it to analyze a variety of historical contexts that have irrevocably impacted African and Igbo history.

The basic question with which theology confronts men and women today is: Cain, where is your brother Abel? In asking this question, the attention of this work focuses at illuminating the biblical as well as Christological matrix for a theology of solidarity that is not only *bona fide* Christian but also truly Igbo in its cultural expression. The Igbo idiom that serves as the vehicle for the transmission of thought here brings to light how African understanding of life and relationship enriches theology in general. Latin American liberation theology, European political theology, and the Church's social teaching, however, serve as essential dialogue partners insofar as their respective perspectives also provide African theology with resonant theological, historical or social-analytical resources that enrich the theme of our discourse.

In the African context, theologizing and philosophizing are essentially idiomatic. African moral and intellectual pedagogy is essentially built on idioms, proverbs, folklores, and other forms of cultural expressions that are lived out on a daily basis, rather than on the method of abstract rationalization that is comprehensible only to a few elite scholars. The latter has been disparaged by liberation theologians as "academicism."[1] *Ọ nụrụ ube nwanne agbala ọsọ* is a simple pithy saying, but it is no less a theological treatise, in which an idiomatic perspective to liberation and fraternal solidarity is compactly and profoundly articulated. It confirms the view "that God speaks into the African context in African idiom, and that it is through hearing in African mother-tongues "the great things that God has done" (Acts 2:11), that African theology emerges to edify not only the African Church but the Church world-wide."[2]

Speaking to African bishops gathered in Kampala on 31st July 1969, Pope Paul VI said, "*[Y]ou possess values and characteristic forms of culture which can rise up to perfection such as to find in Christianity and for Christianity a true superior fullness, and prove to be capable of a richness of expression all its own and genuinely African.*"[3] Making Christ and the Christian message intelligible and socially relevant to Africans should not ignore the need and importance of excavating those inconspicuous cultural treasures that illuminate African humanism. This requires telling the complete story, especially the beautiful stories of our children, who Jesus has declared the heirs of the kingdom, and who teach us by their innocent examples that it is in carrying one another that human life finds its fulfillment. There are also other less beautiful stories, whose re-telling is important in identifying the root-cause of the African cry. With this approach this book goes beyond a liberation-oriented hermeneutic in order to address the deficiency that lies at the root of social injustice—a deficiency that is rooted in an aberrant perception which human beings in the opposing sides of the economic, social, sexual, religious and racial divides often have of each other. African and global communities are confronted with an exhortation to recognize the essential vocation of living together in the world as a call to reach out and grasp the *kairos* presented by the Gospel of Christ, to shun parochialism and to rediscover the spirituality of the well-sung conviviality that is touted as the distinctive mark of the African culture and temperament. The kairotic nature of salvation history obliges men and women of today to see in the ethnic, cultural, and religious diversity of our world an invaluable treasure; an opportunity that compels us to be willing to perceive, embrace, and cherish one another as true brothers and sisters and thus cooperate in building a civilization of love in which exploiters, oppressors and bigots no longer have room for active roles.

1. Segundo, *Liberation of Theology*, 25.

2. Hans Visser and Gillian Bediako, Introduction to Kwame Bediako, *Jesus and the Gospel in Africa*, xi

3. Paul VI, "Le Voyage de Paul VI en Ouganda," 64–66. Cited by Arinze, *Lenten Pastoral Letter.*

In order to achieve this in the African context; in order to be able to enter into solidarity with the suffering, the Church in Africa needs to fertilize those "values and characteristic forms of culture" of which Pope Paul VI spoke about in Kampala, and which will continue to remain the driving force behind African theology. They are values for which Africans must be grateful to God, and which indicate that God is not so disdainful of Africans as to be incommunicable in their languages.[4] In the effort to promote those values, it is incumbent on the Church to deepen her preoccupation with the harrowing conditions of the life of the poor in Africa, with the forces and processes that exploit and oppress them, and with actions and struggle for their liberation. How is this going to happen? The proclamation of the Gospel of Christ on African soil is an evangelical mission that must at once address the social and cultural situation of the people while giving them assurance of hope here and hereafter. It must be a proclamation that tries to modify, enrich and regenerate autochthonous values. It must also seek collaboration beyond religious, denominational and ethnic boundaries. Josiah Young rightly noted that in a continent where people are abused at alarming rate (at work, on the streets, in the homes and schools, even in churches, etc.), African theologians' creative and courageous commitment to liberation and the insightful explorations of the meaning of African culture define an option for the poor that goes to the heart of liberation theology. For theology must address injustice, and theologians must be close to the misery of its victims, if they are to have credibility in the light of Christianity's dominant emblem—the Cross.[5] However, liberation theology should not be seen as the final destination; it can be an important "bus stop," where the vehicle of Christian mission endeavors to carry along many passengers who are left at the margins of the society, but it cannot be the end station.

The cross as the symbol of suffering and self-sacrificing love is essentially also a symbol of inclusion and not of exclusive religious identity. As Miroslav Volf argues in *Exclusion and Embrace*, no one can be in the presence of the God of the crucified Messiah for long without overcoming the double exclusion of the enemy and of oneself; that is, without transposing the enemy from the sphere of monstrous inhumanity into the sphere of shared humanity and oneself from the sphere of proud innocence into the sphere of common sinfulness.[6] Within the context of liberation as a mere "bus stop" theology teaches that the mission of Christianity is to propagate this message of inclusion. The "good news" or "gospel" of salvation advo-

---

4. Sanneh, "Horizontal and the Vertical in Mission," 166.

5. Young, *African Theology*, xiii.

6. Volf, *Exclusion and Embrace*, 124.

cates the "freedom of the children of God" by which humanity is to be rid
of all divisive factors, and influences that inhibit the perfect realization of
the human vocation on earth and ultimately in the eschatological future.
The life of Christ, the God who became a perfect human being, testifies to
and brought about this salvation of man's nature in the objective sense. The
CCC distinguishes between the objective and subjective senses of salvation
by making clear that the saving work of Christ is paradoxically both perfect
and uncompleted at the same time.[7] In his teachings Christ showed what
salvation entailed for man subjectively, and in his often volatile encounters with elements oppressive of humanity, be they persons (e.g., Herod),
institutes (e.g., Pharisees, the Sanhedrin), laws and customs or spiritual
forces (e.g., demons, sin, etc.) he taught his followers (the Church) how to
deal with spiritual and structural evil. The Church has increasingly come to
acknowledge the existence of structural evil in the society as morally unacceptable. This has not always been the case. With the dialectic of liberation
theology the Church has come to recognize that exercising the mandate to
preach the kingdom of God is inseparable from dealing with both spiritual
and structural evil in one's own private life and in the society at large. Juan
Luis Segundo rightly observes that "the prophetic content of Jesus' proclamation moves and revolves around the words; kingdom, salvation, the poor
and good news."[8] And Jesus declares himself a brother to all who are attentive to this proclamation (cf. Matt 12:46–50; Mark 3:31–35; Luke 8:19–21).
Therefore, to be Church, to belong to the family of Jesus Christ is to have the
compassion and gentle sensitivity of Jesus for the multitude.

In 2005 one of Africa's foremost new-guard liberation theologians,
Jean-Marc Ela, expressed a view shared by many theologians and students
in Africa. His famous book, *African Cry*, which has inspired many African
scholars, has indeed awakened my interest in liberation theology. *African
Cry* was very lucid in articulating the contemporary theological challenges
presented by the miserable situation of Africans. The context in which Africans toil and strive to de-alienate their brothers and sisters, *to give them
back their voice and their soul,* to permit an entire people to rise up and
share in the conduct of collective existence, constitutes for Ela the backdrop
of all reflection and activity of the Church in the African context.[9] Presumably, there is a sense in which the situation presents a picture of Africa

7. *Catechism of the Catholic Church*, 609. Hereafter cited as *CCC*. The objective
sense of salvation refers to the paschal mystery as a mystery of a free sacrifice offered in
perfect obedience to and love for the Father. The teachings of Christ, however, outline
how individuals should work out their salvation subjectively.

8. Segundo, *Historical Jesus of the Synoptics*, 87.

9. Ela, *African Cry*, 77.

that has lost voice and soul. This is apparent in the protracted denial or marginalization of her arts and history; subjugation of her culture; and imposition of a predominantly negative narrative on her. Recovering this lost voice is an arduous task that has motivated a spate of African scholarship in various fields of knowledge, like history, anthropology, politics, religion, and philosophy, in the past twentieth century.

Among these disciplines, African theology is understood as one of the mouthpieces of the African soul. Battered by poverty, diseases, exploitation, and racial denigration the African soul has consistently cried out and with that anguished cry advocates for the lowliest, the disinherited and alienated in every continent, thereby challenging the Church and the entire world to enter into solidarity with all who hunger and thirst for social justice, following the footsteps of Christ who died on the cross to liberate us human beings by the testimony of his love for us who are his brothers and sisters. The challenge of the African liberation project cannot be met without an inclusive cultural model that does not neglect the aspirations of African women and minority groups in African society.

This liberation project recognizes that the poverty and sufferings that yoke African society today are man-made and scandalous; they are brought about by the undeserved affluence of a few corrupt elite in Africa and the world. So are also the sufferings caused by various forms of exclusions that are oppressive and parochial. These forces that afflict and victimize many Africans and other poor people in developing countries have again and again been deplored by theologians and humanists in many ways. Ethical disgust against the structural injustice that produces and perpetuates such sufferings through violence, oppression, exploitation, and marginalization in human society has led to a sustained reflection on the Christian tradition and spirituality. The poverty and human misery that plague developing countries have thence given the theology of liberation a particular urgency and distinctive outline that tremendously energized its discourse within the second half of the twentieth century. Hence, liberation theology's concern with temporal well-being and its understanding of the Church's mission in terms of practical measures for alleviating human suffering has earned it enormous influence and attention in our time. As a result many African theologians found it pragmatic to welcome the hermeneutic of liberation in the theological engagements with the African situation. However, the perceived reluctance of the Church to endorse liberation theology and appreciate its merits has led to a declining profile that exasperates many Latin American liberation theologians. These theologians attributed the Church's stance to the influence of a Marxist phobia[10] which betrays her doctrinal position on libera-

10. Karl Marx and his followers have been very suspicious of religion, which they

tion discourses as one affected by ideological prejudice that gives credence to the Marxist assumption that the chains of the oppressed are obscured by the flowers of ideology. Tearing down the walls of such obscurity has been seen as a major challenge by liberation theologians. To liberate Christian teaching from ideological prejudice requires, however, a balance of approach between a dubious neutrality and a controversial, overzealous compassion—a balance that rests on a constant theological re-examination.

The African theologians' interest in liberation theology has been that of persistent drawing of attention to the African cry. It expresses itself often in demands for a "listening ear" from the Church and the global community. Convinced that God speaks into the African context in African idioms and that it is through hearing in African mother-tongues (cf. Acts 2:11) that African theology edifies not only the African Church but also the universal Church, African theologians have been united in their refusal to accept the negative views of African religion held by western missionaries. Most of the new responses, however, are no longer preoccupied with the apologetics of African primal religion but rather focus on locating the cries of the poor, the oppressed and marginalized individuals and groups whose sighs of distress grow increasingly louder every day. These cries lay a burden on the narrative of Christian love and promise. Hence, conceptualizing the theological models that give adequate answer to the numerous and varied contexts of the African experience in human society today is a task that obliges African theology. This involves, above all, an attentive listening to the message of indigenous cultures with a view to appropriating the authentic values of those cultures in the service of evangelization. "Toward an African Theology of Fraternal Solidarity: Ọ nụrụ ube nwanne agbala ọsọ," re-examines, in the light of African and Igbo historiography, those problems that constitute the subject-matter of liberation theology in the African context, and draws attention to an African (Igbo) idiom that gives valid and plausible hermeneutic clues to addressing these problems. The work appraises liberation

---

see as an obstacle to the revolutionary change in human society. Marx described religion as the opium of the masses, the sigh of the oppressed creature, the heart of a heartless world, and the soul of soulless conditions. See Marx, *A Contribution to the Critique of Hegel's Philosophy of Right* (1843). Therefore, Karl Marx sees in religious institutions the perpetuation and legitimation (even when not deliberate) of oppressive status quo. To achieve the change Marx envisaged, religion and all ideologies of hierarchy must be abolished. This is almost impossible, as the history of Communism has proven true. Hence, critics see in Communism the most fatal weakness of Marxist philosophy.

Liberation theologians, however, claim that they prefer not to throw the baby out with the bath water. They sift out and borrow from Marx ideas that are helpful in making a social analysis of their theological contexts—a method that has become highly controversial since its inception.

theology as well as critiques the Church's social teaching, and proposes a new perspective that provides a "hermeneutic torchlight" in contemporary theological discourses. Tapping from indigenous knowledge, the book aims at a synthesis of inculturation and liberation in the African context, a context that necessitates a culturally authentic and prophetic theology, bearing in mind that theological hermeneutics in Africa should have a unitary perception of both inculturation and liberation.

At the twentieth anniversary of the social Encyclical of his predecessor, Paul VI, on the progress of peoples, *Populorum Progressio,* John Paul II, admitted that "in a world divided and beset by every type of conflict, the conviction is growing of a radical interdependence and consequently of the need for a *solidarity* which will take up interdependence and transfer it to the moral plane."[11] What this moral plane is remains to be named in concrete terms. But what we know is that globalization has made the theme of fraternal solidarity very significant and central in the new theological dispensation. In this new dispensation, this work argues that a new form of relationship between rich and poor, women and men, black and white, Christians and Muslims, etc. in Africa and in the world is possible and should be fostered. The scandal of poverty in a world blessed with superabundance of goods; the plight of the exploited and the oppressed in a world where might is right; the hatreds and violence by bigots etc., are all effects of a lack of appreciation of one another as sisters and brothers. What is really wrong is the selfishness in lives that are closed off from true concern for others—a lack of concern which becomes then institutionalized and systemic. As a continent battered by numerous malaises, Africa is a veritable specimen for the analysis of social evils. She is also the locus where the answers are to be found presumably in a theology of solidarity that is capable of avoiding the controversial and ideological pitfalls that dogged the steps of liberation theology. This is done through attention to a holistic perspective that addresses the problems of poverty, women's subordination, and all other forms of exclusion in public life using the hermeneutic of fraternity. Tapping from African contributions to Christian theology, which is particularly exemplified in the ecclesiology of the Church as family, I want to offer here a perspective that is helpful in evaluating the theories and praxes of the option for the poor. Docile to the dialectics of liberation theologies and Social Teachings of the Church, the Scriptures are read from a new point of view that morally indicts the present structures and cultures of human relationship.

Demonstrating that African indigenous knowledge (preserved in folks' sayings) is a relevant tool of theologizing that makes revelation more

---

11. John Paul II, *Sollicitudo Rei Socialis,* 26. Hereafter cited as *SRS.*

comprehensible to the faithful and makes theology less abstract and obscure for the ordinary men and women is very important. Albeit the task of communicating in-depth systematic theological knowledge in African languages still remain an intractable challenge, theological truth must, nevertheless, be seen as already present and accessible in the worldviews and thoughts of the people, for theology is in many ways idiomatic. The theologian is merely tasked with helping the ordinary folk discover this truth in their own God-given treasury of knowledge and adapt it to life's situations. Hence, appropriating *Ọ nụrụ ube nwanne agbala ọsọ*[12] as a popular Igbo exhortation, this work appreciates the extent to which profound meaning is concealed in some of those folks' sayings we often overlook.

The work contributes to an African Christian theology within an analysis embedded in the context of the facticity of African historical experience as seen through an Igbo perspective. If a poor African woman, for example, were to suffer discrimination in America based on a fourfold factor that she is a woman, African, black, or poor, it is true that the primary cause of such discrimination is a mental construct that must first of all be dismantled before one could effectively address the problem of structural injustice in human society. No structural reform will be able to prevent such discrimination without a change in people's attitudes in relating with others who are perceived to be different. Humankind has apparently not yet learnt to look beyond the differences in order to see the similarities and the unity. *Ọ nụrụ ube nwanne agbala ọsọ* is in this sense a thesis not only of Igbo ethics but also of Igbo phenomenology. As ethics, it is an awakening call to join in building a civilization that is worthy of the human vocation—the civilization of love; and as phenomenology, it is a new vision of otherness and sameness. Being labeled in the past as primitive, savage, underdeveloped etc., Africa and Africans have often been victims of a human hubris that has sneered at the phenomenology of "being with." Africans have also hubristically exploited and oppressed their own folks. In the analysis of the world of victims and villains, therefore, the scope of this discourse can only be delimited by the hermeneutic of inclusive fraternity. The book oscillates in scope between the particularity of the African context, on the one hand, and the universality of social ethics, on the other.

Theology of fraternity impugns against the privileged members of the human family who dwell in the false comfort of being rich simply because others are poor and because they have the power to preserve that poverty. Human beings are not fishes that must swallow the others in order to grow

---

12. This pithy saying was made popular in Igboland by "High Life" musician Bright Chimezie and his Zigima Sound with the song "Ube Nwanne." See http://www.youtube.com/watch?v=qO4ZR1xjvzI.

fatter. Hence, the egotistic human agency that has brought African society to her knees is repeatedly critiqued in the light of the alternative of fraternal charity. The place, which God and the Church occupy in this reality, is of great significance and remains a point of constant reference. I have adopted the method of looking at Africa's historical experiences, for salvation history, which theology deals with, is God's involvement with and concern for mundane history. And every human experience contains within itself a transcendental element of historical development and the personal experience of self is also in its total extent the history of the ultimate experience of God itself. In the light of the historical data collated, structural and semiotic analyses are used in making theological critique of historical experiences. And by semiotic analysis, I mean an analysis of the covert and overt attitudes of human beings in their relationship with one another. Hence, prejudicial perception of other human beings, who are seen as not belonging to one's own group, is identified as the principal cause of social injustice. Such prejudicial perception is responsible for attitudes of nepotism, exploitation, condescension or downright hostility.

In the Church, the utopia of harmonious living is normally what every theologian and christian will call the "Kingdom of God." The major emphasis of liberation theology is the biblical notion of this kingdom of God as a vision of societal existence marked by justice, peace, and loving collaboration. Identifying this kingdom in human terms as one that should be characterized by congeniality, I applied the method of hermeneutic interpretation of Igbo ethical concepts that bring to light the profound and relevant theological proposition which Igbo wisdom in this sense communicates. They are concepts which help us to retrieve the authentically biblical spirituality that offer insight into that type of egalitarianism (which ought to be present in Igbo and every other culture) that is worthy of the kingdom of God.

Albeit the poor, the oppressed, the marginalized etc. are the main subject of discussion, I am less concerned here about statistics and poverty or human development indices than about simply identifying the obstacles to social justice. A theology of fraternity makes no pretense of discarding liberation theology. On the contrary, most of the tenets of liberation theology are viewed through an African (Igbo) perspective that is committed to inclusiveness; through a synthesis of culture, Scripture and a passion for integral human development.

This work is structured into three main parts. Part I deals with the significance, challenges, and limitations of liberation theology in the African context. Chapter 1 highlights liberation theology's heuristic value for African theology and how it has enabled the voices from the "underside of history" to be heard in theological discourse. It shows how theology was reborn in a tale of many narratives and what this entails for African historiography. Chapter 2 tackles the question of the centrality of Christ in theology, the hopes and opportunities as well as the obstacles and controversies arising from conflicting Christologies. Chapter 3 deals with the ambivalent notion of poverty which exposes the weakness of liberation hermeneutic. It goes further into the study of selected documents of the Church in order to distinguish between two important aspects of liberation: liberation as justice, and liberation as service of charity.

Part II focuses on the African historical experience of need for liberation. In chapter 4 I delved into a long excursus of the African crucibles, which are identified as the Trans-Atlantic slave trade, Western racial denigration, colonialism, ethnic wars (represented by the Biafran story), and bad governance by corrupt leaders. Chapter 5 then investigates the secular as well as theological struggles that generated various liberation initiatives for Africa's political and theological independence. Each problem is analyzed in terms of its relation to or negative impact on fraternal solidarity.

Part III focuses on the shift in hermeneutic from liberation to fraternity. A good deal of biblical hermeneutic is used to authenticate the theology of fraternity in this part. Chapter 6 begins with a hermeneutic of the key Igbo word "*nwanne*," which is used to articulate an ecclesiology of fraternity that shuns selfishness and apathy. Chapter 7 continues on the heels of the *nwanne* hermeneutic with an Igbo Christology of Jesus as *Brother* of the marginalized. Chapter 8 establishes a link with European political theology viewing the pithy saying "*Ọ nụrụ ube nwanne agbala ọsọ*" in terms of a mysticism of compassion, which also sees the passion of Jesus as the seal and ideal paradigm of fraternity. It defends the methodological validity of the idiomatic perspective and also anchors the theological efforts of the book on the vision of *Gaudium et Spes* of the Second Vatican Council.

Finally, in chapter 9 the book concludes with an anticipation of a city of brotherly love, *Philadelphia,* which is laid on the cornerstone of *philia* with the Church as its sacramental "light house" and the temporal manifestation of the kingdom of God. This city is the utopia of the kingdom of God which is the goal of the Christian vocation and spirituality—the goal of authentic life. The utopia of the city of brotherly love is supposed to epitomize the perfection of the human response to the cry of the suffering brother through a social commitment to the elimination of prejudice and hatred. For "If anyone says, 'I love God,' but hates his brother, he is a liar; for whoever does not love a brother whom he has seen cannot love God whom he has not seen. This is the commandment we have from him: whoever loves God must also love his brother" (1 John 4:20–21).

PART I

General Critique of
Liberation Theology

1

History and Tenets in African Liberation Theology

Understanding African Liberation Theology

SINCE I HAVE CHOSEN liberation theology as my point of departure in this book, it is only fair to recognize its Latin American roots. As Fiorenza rightly states, historically and specifically liberation theology refers to a theological line of thought within Latin America that focuses on the political, economic, and ideological causes of social inequality and makes liberation rather than development its central theological, economic, and political category. It analyzes the concrete Latin-American situation, but also argues that all theology should begin by analyzing its concrete social situation and by returning to its religious sources for means to rectify it.[1] Note that liberation theology focuses on the "political, economic, and ideological" causes, but after studying liberation theology's tenets for some time I have come to observe that these factors do not actually exhaust the causes of social inequality. Such a psychological factor like the way we think about others in relation to ourselves play important role in determining how we value them. Such judgments of values which normally occur at the private personal level of human interactions always have multiplying effects that significantly impact on politics, economics, and ideology. If our judgment is impaired by lack of knowledge, for example, the fear of the unknown might trigger some negative attitudes that will create an unjust social environment. This is why I speak of "aber-

1. Fiorenza, "Liberation Theology," 544–46.

rant perception" of others as the major impediment to social justice and equality in the world today. It is from this perspective, therefore, that the concrete situations of Africa are analyzed historically and theologically.

Inspired by the Latin American context, it was such analyses of concrete social situations in Africa which led to the discourse that eventually came to be known as "African Theology." This term was allegedly used for the first time in 1955 when a group of African and Haitian priests studying in Rome met to discuss the problem of relating the Christian message to the life and thought of their people.[2] Hence, the conscious and systematic efforts to build such a theology were not earlier than the 1960s. With less than hundred years of evangelization African missions were still concerned with the questions of how the Christian message could be "incarnated" in the African culture. The economic and political situation then in the 1960s and 1970s, as portrayed by Patrick Masanja, was characterized by the underlying struggle between imperialism in its neocolonial form and real economic and political independence. It was a struggle between, on the one hand, foreign multinationals allied to local dominant classes who want to continue the exploitation of the natural resources and wealth of African countries, and, on the other hand, the workers and peasants who would favor social transformation and real economic independence.[3] The multinational companies have invested in Africa with the intention of reaping great benefits. Agricultural and mineral industries were largely foreign-owned or foreign dominated. Commerce and transport were monopolized by western countries and the pricing system as well was determined by these foreign market forces. So-called foreign aid, foreign investments and loans, through which capital inflow was always exceeded by profit outflow, were examples of forms of foreign domination. There were also more subtle forms of exploitation by multinational corporations in joint "partnership" with local private capital or even state investments, designed to guarantee them monopoly control of the market as well as control of the labor force.[4] The capitalist exploitation and colonization went hand in hand with racial oppression.

Such was the situation in Africa when the Catholic Church convoked the Second Vatican Council (1962–1965). The situation inspired across Africa national liberation movements, which were understandably anti-colonial and anti-imperialist. The cry was for independence, but it was not yet clear what kind of society would emerge after the political independence. Eventually, due partly to the colonial legacy and partly to the invitation of

2. Ukpong, "Theological Literature from Africa," 68.

3. Masanja, "Neocolonialism," 15.

4. Ibid., 10

foreign companies, the indigenous governments became agents of foreign capital in their own countries but the exploitation and oppression of peasants continued. African churches soon realized, with the illusion of political independence, that they are faced with new tasks and responsibilities, which include cultural adaptation of the gospel to African cultures. Hence, African theology was born and, as its name indicates, it is meant to signify an otherness that edifies Christian thought, thus implying that Africans have broken away from Eurocentric theologies which virtually ignore the unpleasant legacies of slavery and colonization that afflict African people. From its inception, therefore, what is known today as African theology has always been a theology of liberation, emerging from the "underside of history" in order to give expression to the social and religio-cultural analysis of the African world in the light of the gospel. African theology is, in fact, part of the history of Christianity in Africa. Even though to talk of the history of African theology would actually mean to go back to the time of ancient Christian traditions which recorded the contributions of no less eminent theologians as Clement of Alexandria (third century), Origen (185–254), Athanasius (296–373), Tertullian (160–220), Cyprian (200–258), and Augustine (354–430). Although these church Fathers rightly belong to the history of theology in Africa, African theology is taken here to refer to the more recent history of the post-Vatican II theological reflections in Africa.

The spirit of aggiornamento, which pervaded the Church and led to the Second Vatican Council, actually laid the foundation for the theology of liberation in Latin America as well as in Africa and Asia. No doubt, dominant on the list of themes discussed in the Council were the concerns and problems of the European Churches. However, the Council opened the doors and windows of the Church so that all regional and local Churches would ask themselves how the Gospel is to be proclaimed in the light of particular situations. It offered opportunity for Latin American and African theologians to engage themselves with their situations and cultural *facticity* in the light of the Gospel. From 5th to 12th August 1976, a theological summit took place in Dar es Salaam[5] where the best theologians from Asia, Africa and Latin America had the opportunity to meet each other and discuss the situations of colonialism and oppression, which their people suffered or were still suffering. This became the birth of Ecumenical Association of Third World Theologians (EATWOT), an organ through which liberation theology was integrated into the wider context of the theology of the *so-called*[*6] Third World. African theologians thus entered into dialogue

---

5. Torres and Fabella, *Emergent Gospel.* (1978).

6. *I use the term Third World with the emphasis *"so-called"* in order to make clear

and mutual sharing of perspectives with their Asian and Latin American colleagues.

Now it has become obvious that after a long period of European influence and domination of the Christian tradition a new demographic phenomenon has emerged, which has been recently described as a modern shift of the center of gravity of Christianity from the northern to the southern hemisphere. This shift, which began after the Second Vatican Council, has been accompanied by an intellectual movement in Africa that struggled to define the African self no longer from the categories of the "white man." African theology, emerging out of this intellectual movement, seeks to reinterpret Christianity from the point of view of African narratives, myths, and idioms. Having inherited a Christianity that was heavily dressed in European garb and motivated by colonial independence, African theologians began to see the incongruity of a "good news" of salvation which was transported in the language and culture of perceived oppressors. The coming to maturity of the gospel in Africa, therefore, inspired also a strong desire for de-europeanization of Christianity, for it was no longer possible to ignore the cultural alienation that the western-oriented Church imposed on African religious mind. Hence, inculturation and acculturation became dominant themes of a theology that understood itself as a liberation theology. Borrowing Oduyoye's distinction, acculturation pertains to the efforts of Africans to use things African in their practice of Christianity, whereas inculturation refers to the manifestation of changes that have come into the African way of life as a result of the Christian faith.[7] Such changes include the recognition and acknowledgement that God has indeed revealed himself to Africans in a new way in Jesus Christ whose story stirs hope and exceptional devotion in the African soul. Although Africans were barely present at the Second Vatican Council, the Council has prepared a fertile ground for Africans to give both liturgical and intellectual witness to their own specific joy of welcoming the gospel. So it was that a theology with an African character began to take root. And as it did, it became obvious that African theology of inculturation cannot avoid being also a theology of liberation.

The necessity of the link between African theology and liberation is already underscored by the situation of exploitation that heralded its birth. Barnabas Okolo affirms this intimate relationship all the more when he

---

that I do not share the idea of such a nomenclature that classifies human societies in a presumptive hierarchical structure. However, I am not able to renounce the use of this term entirely for reasons of academic precision especially when some literatures I work with get somewhat fixated with the terminology.

7. Oduyoye, *Hearing and Knowing*, 454.

suggests that the Christian meaning of liberation in Africa is made clear through inculturation. This is to say that the gospel takes root in Africa as it plows through and uproots the injustices that oppress the poor, creating free space for them to reap the gifts of racial and economic justice.[8] In other words, the gospel cannot be seen as truly inculturated in the African context if it does not liberate. Okolo, however, admits that while liberation is to be defined in African terms—coincident with African realities and in accordance with African cultures—Latin American theology has great heuristic value for African theology. Particularly edifying in the Latin American context is the discovery that liberation involves a praxis in which theology is the second step.[9] According to the Latin American understanding liberation theology is seen as a reflection on the basis of praxis, within the ambit of the vast efforts made by the poor and their allies, seeking inspiration in faith and the gospel for the commitment to fight against poverty and for the integral liberation of all persons and the whole person.[10] Therefore, the essential and critical step toward God's kingdom and inculturation is the activist's commitment to struggle with the poor against the inhumane and ungodly structures that oppress them. The originality of liberation theology does not consist in its theme, method, addressee or language, nor does it consist in its finality, but rather in its readiness to intervene concretely on behalf of the poor and oppressed, and as such actively taking part in the historical process of their liberation. It is all about holding on firm to the conviction that any theology that does not base itself in the context of a faith-experience runs the risk of becoming a kind of religious Metaphysics—an automobile wheel that rotates in the air without moving the vehicle forward.[11] In this sense, liberation theology is understood as a *second act*, which presupposes a *first act* as the object of its reflection. This first act is the faith-experience— i.e., a prerequisite spirituality, what South African liberation theologian, Allan Boesak, calls "authenticity." Because of the peculiar circumstances of the African encounter with Christianity, African counterparts in the field of liberation theology insist on such authenticity, understood as resisting the temptation to yield to uncritical accommodation, becoming a "cultural theology" or a "religion of culture." For Boesak, "an authentic situational theology is prophetic, critical, not merely excavating corpses of tradition, but taking critically those traditions from the past which can play a humanizing and revolutionizing role in our contemporary society. It is taking from the

---

8. Okolo, "Liberation Theology and the African Church," 314.

9. Ibid., 352.

10. Boff and Boff, *Introducing Liberation Theology*, 8.

11. Gutiérrez, *Aus der eigenen Quelle trinken*, 103.

past that which is positively good, thereby offering a critique of the present and opening perspectives for the future."[12] Liberation theology as a second act thus follows behind the first act (faith-experience). And it is actually this faith-experience or authenticity that is contextualized in the form of engagement or commitment for the other. This faith experience raises a lot of question about how we understand ourselves in relation to others.

African liberation theology shares this common goal with its Latin American antecedent, namely, to correct the ahistorical interiority of classic spirituality, its elitism, and its deficient sense of the presence of the LORD of history in liberative social processes.[13] It contrasts from classical theology of the classroom insofar as it makes itself understandable only through an active and personal involvement in the real and historical process of liberating the oppressed. It dedicates itself to a committed retrieval of biblical spirituality of justice in the reenactment of God's intervention in history. Leonardo and Clodovis Boff maintain that "the Scholastic theology of the eleventh to the fourteenth century made undeniable contributions to the precise and systematic presentation of Christian truth, but liberation theology criticizes it for its overbearing tendency to theoreticism, to voiding the world of its historical character . . . , showing precious little sensitivity to the social question of the poor or their historical liberation."[14] Similarly, African theology indicts western theology for its dubious silence on the slavery, colonization, and the racial ideology that nourished these oppressive phenomena.

It is the conviction of all liberation theologians that "Commitment to the liberation of the millions of the oppressed of our world restores to the gospel the credibility it had at the beginning and at the great periods of holiness and prophetic witness in history. The God who pitied the downtrodden and the Christ who came to set prisoners free proclaim themselves with a new face and in a new image today. The eternal salvation they offer is mediated by the historical liberations that dignify the children of God and render credible the coming utopia of the kingdom of freedom, justice, love, and peace, the kingdom of God in the midst of humankind."[15] As its name imply, liberation theology is a theology which assigns primacy to the liberation of the poor thereby positing liberation "as that part of the content of theology around which all of theology can be organized—all questions of who God and Christ are, what grace and sin are, what the church and society are, what

---

12. Boesak, "Coming in out of the Wilderness," 83.

13. Boff and Boff, *Introducing Liberation Theology*, 8.

14. Ibid., 36

15. Ibid.

love and hope are, and so on."[16] It is thus understood as a "Theology of practical Faith." It is a theology that emerges from praxis and at the same time reflects about the praxis of engaged Christian communities. As a systematic theology, it is the theological reflection that accompanies and assists the people on the communal promenade to liberation. In fact, since there are liberation movements of peoples, there is also a theology of liberation. In this sense faith does not become a mere narrative about history, but rather a practice in history about which theology is called to reflect upon.

Now reflecting on the practice in history, we may ask what the primordial motivation of the activist in the first place is. What animates her actions? What compels her to move beyond the spirituality of almsgiving in order to take a decisive stand in solidarity with the poor, even risking her own life in the process? Does she see what the oppressor did not see; or what the oppressor is willing to ignore? Has she recognized in the poor and oppressed the countenance of suffering sisters and brothers? What role can theology play in the struggle for liberation and social transformation in Africa? These questions, which go to the heart of the liberation struggle as a necessity, define the outline of a theology of fraternity that seeks to articulate a new way of Christian discipleship. The passion behind the activism of the theologian finds explanation or meaning in its similitude with the virtuous and praise-worthy acts of children carrying their younger and weaker siblings. As Gustavo Gutiérrez notes, "the question . . . will not be how to speak of God in a world come of age, but rather how to proclaim God as Father in a world that is inhumane. What can it mean to tell a nonperson that he or she is God's child?"[17] If liberation theology is a critical reflection about human praxis *seen in the light of the practice of Jesus* and the demands of the faith,[18] then it is in the identification of themselves with the person of Jesus of the Scripture that Christians come to appreciate themselves as sons and daughters of God and invariably, as brothers and sisters who ought to carry each other. The challenge of an inhumane world is already anticipated in the challenge of the world that crucified Jesus and persecuted his followers. And in order to confront this challenge adequately one must be inspired by a new vision of fraternity and solidarity without which liberation activism will be nothing but another class struggle with an illusory hope. In their contribution to the world synod of bishops held in Rome in November 1971, the Peruvian bishops stress, for example, that "the salvation of Christ does not stop at political liberation, but the latter has its

16. Ibid., 39

17. Gutiérrez, *Power of the Poor in History,* 57

18. Boff, "Rezeption des II. Vatikanums," 640.

place and true meaning within the total liberation incessantly announced by sacred Scripture, fulfilling in human beings their true dignity as sons and daughters of God."[19] Liberation hence implies, on the one hand, the rupture with all that keeps persons from self-fulfillment as an individual and in community, and on the other hand, the construction of a new society which is more human and fraternal.

The Tenets of Liberation Theology

Liberation theology is credited for having given the poor a voice in a world in which the phenomenal victory of the powerful has installed the unhappy principle that might is right—a principle that entrenches violence and manipulation as the vices of success. The poor and the defenseless are forced to accept this principle like a bitter cup of vinegar down their throat. But *if might is right, then there is no place for love in the world.* This is what makes liberation theology to anchor its tenets on compassion and an emphasis on the *kairotic* character of the kingdom of God as proclaimed by the prophets of the Old Testament and Jesus himself (cf. Mark 7:37; 12:2–6; Luke 4:16–21; 7:18–23; 11:20).[20] The programmatic proclamations of Jesus demands conversion, faith, and discipleship (cf. Mark 1:16–20), understood in terms of a commitment to struggle under the banner of love against the opposition of the anti-kingdom. According to Jon Sobrino, "God's reign" is the positive action through which God transforms reality, and "God's Kingdom" is what comes to pass in this world when God truly reigns: a history, a society, a people transformed according to the will of God.[21]

Basing its argument on the *kairos* and the call to commitment in discipleship, liberation theology posits and defends the right of the poor to justice and a fair share of this world's goods for which they tirelessly labored, as well as a fair hearing as they narrate their joyous and painful experiences, their hopes and disappointments (cf. GS, 1). The theological content of the experience of the poor lies precisely in the fact that God reveals himself in the poor. And the kingdom of God finds its sacramental expression in the historical process of human society. Liberation theology, hence, advocates that the perceived losers of this world must be enabled to rewrite their history. It is a constant refrain of all liberation theologies that the perspective

19. Bishops of Peru, "Justice in the World." 128.

20. Jesus' answer in Luke 7:18–23 to the disciples of John the Baptist who came to query whether he is the "One who is to come" is particularly remarkable. It evokes the idea of a "kingdom of God" that is already present and at the same time should be made present by the liberating actions of healing for the mind and body.

21. Sobrino, *Jesus the Liberator*, 71.

of the poor and marginalized offers another story, an alternative story to that told by the wielders of power whose story becomes often the "normal" account. It is in telling the stories from the underside of African history that theology rediscovers Africa and her trampled humanity. Remarkable in relation to Igboland is the infamous account that has been chronicled in British colonial historiography as "the pacification of the Lower Niger." Elochukwu E. Uzukwu is an Igbo theologian who gives us a new and better insight into this story, and I would like to quote him at length here:

> At the dawn of the colonization of southern Nigeria, the Onitsha Igbo wanted to protect their economic, cultural, and religious interests and to negotiate on terms of equality with the missionaries and their British trading partners (the West African Company), whose trading terms and trade monopoly were against the best interests of the Onitsha community. At a meeting organized between the Onitsha chiefs and Bishop Adjai Crowther, the head of the Church Missionary Society mission, the chiefs made their interests and objectives clear: the missionaries should change their style or quit bag and baggage; missionary preaching was doing harm to traditional practices and loyalties; they should stop introducing an alien lifestyle, such as giving T-shirts to their members, because it was creating a social dichotomy; the bishop should intervene with the West African Company in favor of the Onitsha community for better trade terms. However, to ensure prolonged cooperation with the immigrants and to protect the benefits accruing from the relationship, the chiefs proposed to seal the relationship with a marriage pact. According to Crowther, the chiefs demanded, 'that an agreement should be entered into for intermarriage between the children of the settlers and those of the natives of Onitsha that all may become one people, or else they could not see how we could profess to be their friends without such arrangement.'
>
> Bishop Crowther, who was asked to negotiate the pact, was not receptive to the Onitsha wisdom. The Onitsha chiefs were convinced that the sealing of such a relationship with marriage pacts would ensure the elimination of violent or inimical acts from one or the other. When Crowther turned down all their requests, the chiefs decreed a boycott of the missionaries. The relationship deteriorated. Between 1868 and 1880, living together became very tense. British trading interests became more intolerant of competition (especially from the French). The militarily weaker Onitsha community was on the receiving end of unfair trade relations and missionary propaganda. Finally,

on October 28, 1879, after British citizens had been carefully evacuated, Onitsha was brutally bombarded by a British gunboat. A similar bombardment took place in 1880. Such *gunboat diplomacy* as witnessed in Onitsha was popularly known in the British colonial dictionary as 'pacification.'[22]

In the light of the above, the task of liberation theology in Africa is then to tell from the vantage point of the weak the untold stories that debunk the single narrative of the powerful. In fact, it should promote a method of theologizing that enables Africans tell their own stories. Whoever hears that story is then obliged to contemplate it in the spirit of discernment, to rethink the meaning of Christian discipleship, and to make a personal decision to play an active role in shaping the future, both of theology and of society in general. Therein lies the significance of the Igbo exhortation that is encapsulated in the saying, *"Ọ nụrụ ube nwanne agbala ọsọ."* In the course of history, the colonial "gunboat diplomacy" may have been substituted with other types of insidious diplomacies that are cleverly devised to conceal the harm they intentionally harbor. Having discarded the outmoded formula of "direct occupation and colonization," imperialist countries have resorted to the neocolonial formula whereby countries have all the outward manifestations of independence ("flag independence"), but the economic and political systems of these countries are tied to and dominated by the imperialist countries.[23] Theology faces the challenge of unmasking the new formulas and the harms they harbor. And as a result of the progress made in the past decades in this respect, we now know that there has been a greater appreciation of gender and race alongside poverty as factors that need to be taken into account in any liberation theology. Women and minority groups who are stripped of their rights and human dignity are now getting a hearing, or better said, making themselves be heard.

More importantly liberation theology holds that human society is a social construction, not a fixed creation of God or nature, and thus can be reconstructed in ways that promise greater justice and participation. As Peter Scott would say, "theology must reflect upon and be directed to determinate situations. Theology is concerned with the particular and not the general, the ambiguities of the real history of people in struggle, with commitment to the struggle for liberation. In particular, the commitment to theological thinking in a specific context raises the issue of the location of theology: what is the 'place' of theology? To what pressures is it exposed?"[24]

---

22. Uzukwu, *Listening Church*, 39

23. Masanja, "Neocolonialism and Revolution in Africa," 10

24. Scott, *Theology, Ideology and Liberation*, 10

It is precisely in addressing this question about the place of theology in social life that one of the major theses of liberation theology, namely, the critique of ideologies, is illuminated. Feminist theology, for instance, describes how masculine language and patriarchal images have specified the religious understanding of God and how anthropological misconceptions have become institutionalized as religious taboos. Black theology, on the other hand, not only uncovers how the oppression of blacks has been legitimated in church history, but also shows how fundamental images of blackness and whiteness have led to this oppression. In each liberation theology, therefore, the experience and analysis of injustices has led to a critique not only of the present but also of the past with its cultural and religious traditions.[25] In its task of social reconstruction, black theology discovers in black experience, history, and cultures the resources to overcome alienation. It reinterprets traditional conceptions of divine providence, suffering, and salvation. Feminist theology retrieves images of the femininity of God and views of the equality of the sexes within the history of religions and Christianity. It also reinterprets traditional religious symbols and beliefs. In urging that sexist language be excluded from biblical, liturgical, and theological texts, it seeks to revise dominant images of God.[26] At last it seems as if we are finally having a family tête-à-tête, but until the conversation is divested of power tussle; until each party is listened to in the spirit of fraternal charity that is based not only on the idea of justice and equality but above all on gratuity, then we cannot hold that liberation has been achieved. The kingdom of God is more than freedom from constraints; it is a communion of saints who are brothers and sisters of Christ.

The feminist orientation to the liberation struggle in Africa, eloquently represented by Mercy Amba Oduyoye with her mythopoeic discourses, consists in voicing the exigency of a critique of ideology in dealing with theological hermeneutics, even with Scripture itself. Myths, including biblical myths, Oduyoye maintains, inform social activities, shape men's and women's lives and attitudes, and give expression to people's fears. Creation myths, for example, are replete with imagery that echoes how society functions, of the nature of social relations relating to families, the economy, the running of the community. They help us see, at times, the society's attempt to think through the paradoxes of life. And awareness of this function helps liberate us to some degree from the negative effects of myths. Myths then cease to function as "Canon Law" and become a source in the search for

25. Fiorenza, "Liberation Theology," 545.
26. See ibid.

meaningful community.[27] In recapitulating Isidore Okpehwo's[28] story of an African woman's retelling of the Adam and Eve story, Oduyoye observes that in this version, Eve's burden reflects the woman's own experience. And in accepting the myth of the Hebrew Bible, this African woman appropriates what it means to be a woman in her own culture, and accepts it as a punishment. This internalization of the Church's teaching, according to Oduyoye, shows its negative effects on the self-image of African women.[29]

I shall later come back to the issue of how biblical myths are exploited in imposing and seeking to perpetuate structures of injustice in human society. Meanwhile let me quickly point out that myths are used to explain the imbalance that exists rather than resolve such imbalance. But the solution to this imbalance cannot be achieved through a power-sharing ideology of equality, but through a transcendent vision of humankind as children of God. It is only through such a theistic anthropology that purifies our mutual perceptions that liberation theology, or in fact, theology of fraternity will be able to unmask and discard all possible ideological garbs theology may have obscured in inherited myths. The challenge of theology today is to ensure that myths are no longer used to legitimize abuse of power, for the purpose of power is service. Just as the little African boy (mentioned in my introduction) feels obliged to carry his younger sister, so are all persons or groups of persons in powerful positions expected to use the advantage which destiny have placed at their disposal in the service of humanity without any discrimination. The books of Exodus and Deuteronomy in the Old Testament exceptionally help us in appreciating the messianic dimension of human history and of the role of human agents in bringing about the liberation and egalitarianism that God wills for his children.

Liberation and the Oppressor: Exodus and a Critique of the Magisterium

The book of Exodus unquestionably provides us with a very significant biblical matrix for a theology of liberation and the hermeneutic of oppression. Narrating the story of an organized plot to thread upon the rights and freedom of a people and to decimate them, it tries to portray an injustice which God could not pretend to ignore. It then narrates the great deeds

27. Oduyoye, *Daughters of Anowa*, 21.

28. Okpehwo, *Myth in Africa*, 112–13. It reads: "You will weed. The rain will beat on you there. The sun will burn you there as you think of your husband's soup. For that is what you choose."

29. Oduyoye, *Daughters of Anowa*, 9.

wrought by God to liberate the oppressed as well as punish the oppressor. Indeed, for Israel the entire Bible is simply a rereading of the exodus, when the people of the covenant became aware of the crucial moment when God genuinely created them as a people. Exodus-event is hence the central event through which God is revealed as intervening in people's history. The whole Psalter seems driven by Miriam's refrain after the passage through the Red Sea (Exod 15:21–22). There is no psalm without an echo of *In exitu Israel de Egypto . . .* (See Psalms 105; 66; 78).[30] As one of the most important biblical narratives, Exodus establishes how salvation history is inseparably bound with the socio-political history of the human race.

Exodus' close relationship to Deuteronomy is also an indication of the close relationship between liberation and fraternal solidarity, which the latter espouses in a special way. Indeed a re-reading of the book of Exodus is essential to any revision of the Church's christological position hitherto. While offering reasons for the necessity of a new Christology of liberation, Jon Sobrino reminded us that one must not forget how the Latin American continent has been subjected to centuries of inhuman and anti-Christian oppression, without Christology giving any sign of having noticed this and certainly without it providing any prophetic denunciation in the name of Jesus Christ.[31] The same is true of Africa. Theology must not forget the stories of African children, like Olaudah Equiano, who were abducted, literary cut off from their root and shipped to Latin America where they had to toil as slaves in the plantations under the yoke of unprecedented cruelty in human history. Officially, the Church often tends to avoid creating a dichotomy between the rich and poor as rival groups opposed to each other. Even when this is sometimes done to temper social unrest, it unwittingly compromises the Church's prophetic message with an ideological prejudice that favors the strong. Apartheid South Africa is a good example, although the Catholic Church was not directly implicated.

Ideological prejudice on the part of the Church cannot, as a result, be seen as deliberate. However, what liberation theology has revived in our time is the book of Exodus' sharp distinction between the oppressor and the oppressed, and the partial stance of an impartial God. According to this stance, the only middle way in an unjust world is to take side with the weak. The staff of Moses should be made to swallow the staff of Pharaoh's magicians in a world that is ruled by unbridled cupidity and materialism; a world where selfish interests are aggressively superimposed over the common good; a world where unscrupulous consciences debase humanity

30. Ela, *African Cry*, 31–32.

31. Sobrino, *Jesus the Liberator*, 3.

and distort the *imago Dei*. It is not at all gratifying to behold the Church responding in such circumstances only with impotent communiqués. Jean-Marc Ela is point blank on the opinion that the times in which we live call for a certain aggiornamento to the radicalism of the gospel: that we listen to Africans who live in harrowing conditions; that we accept a basic challenge to our experience of faith. What must mobilize us, in this sense, is a Christianity seeking to redefine itself totally in relation to the struggles of the people in their resistance to the unjust structures of domination.[32] The action of the Church should, therefore, be analogical to that of the *"Goël"* in all ramifications of the meaning of that word—"an uncle," "a redeemer," or "an avenger," in fact a brother who is moved by the cry of a sibling. Regrettably, the African Church today is a typical example of the marginal fruitfulness, if any, of the bishops' approach to the problems of the society. One can hardly identify anything that changes in society as direct or partial results of ecclesiastical exhortations. Speaking about the Nigerian situation, Orobator correctly pointed out that "as a way of gauging the effectiveness (or the lack thereof) of the exhortatory approach, we might note how the bishops relentlessly emphasize the fact that they have 'spoken before' and will continue to do so, even while admitting that their words fall on 'deaf ears.'"[33] It is easy to read the discernible note of frustration and obvious resignation which marks the Catholic Bishops' Conference of Nigeria's declaration of September 11, 1993: "We *insisted, pleaded and urged* that democratic procedures be allowed to prevail. Although our advice was not accepted, we still even now, stand by the position we have taken on the basis of principles. This is our duty as religious leaders and *we have done our duty*."[34] With the failure of exhortations, the bishops resorted to appeal for hope: "As Christian leaders, we are, however, apostles of hope. We urge the people of Nigeria, especially the youth, the poor and the lowly who have had to bear the great burden of the protracted political crisis not to despair. The God we serve is a compassionate, loving and saving LORD. . . .. We believe that He will soon see us out of the dark tunnel."[35]

As could be seen, Orobator concludes, the kind of hope that the church leaders preach repeatedly manifests itself as a call for patient endurance of the burdens of life in a traumatized Nigerian nation. Calm, patience and perseverance, coupled with the rejection of violent means of effecting change in

32. Ela., "Christianity and Liberation in Africa," 152.

33. CBCN, *Save the Family and Save the Nation*, Communiqué. Cited by Orobator, *Church as Family*, 84; Orobator's emphases and mine.

34. CBCN, "Nigeria in Distress," Communiqué (September 11, 1993).

35. CBCN, "Prolonged Distress of the Nigerian Nation," Communiqué (September 16, 1994).

society, constitute the recurring themes in the bishops' statements.[36] Hence, the attitude of the church has been that of tolerating oppression while praying and hoping that God will usher in a better future. This contrasts sharply with Exodus' message of radically challenging oppression and demanding freedom and justice.

Surely, there is a violence that is irrational no matter what its intent pretends to be. But one should not as a result jettison every use of violence to achieve liberation goals, for it is sometimes necessary to use the "whip of righteous wrath" to drive away the money changers who abuse the temple (cf. John 2:15–16) and thus tame the "beast" that is making the child cry. This may be an unpopular view in Christian theology, and of course is not meant to advocate violence, but rather to argue for a more eloquent sign of protest against established corruption and oppression. Nigerian bishops, for example, could have organized protest-marches similar to what the Christian Solidarity International (CSI) is doing annually in Austria, in order to make it clear that they are on the side of the oppressed. One must not lose sight of the fact that the essence of the liberation struggle consists in revolutionizing the mutual perception of human beings as brothers and sisters of a cosmic family. Yes, to bring to the awareness of the self-complacent rich with a prophetic rebuke that the poor children and adults who languish and die on the streets are their sisters and brothers. To realize this truth is to grasp the knowledge of the primordial "*Ipseity*" of life about which Michel Henry[37] wrote. According to Henry's phenomenology of Life, the prescriptions of the Christian ethic result "from the fact that the Being-in-common of Sons is their Being-in-God and their belonging to a 'chosen race,' to a 'royal priesthood,' and a consecrated people (1 Peter 2:9)."[38]

> The self-givenness of absolute phenomenological Life, in which each Son is given to himself, is the Being-in-common of Sons, the pre-unifying essence that precedes and preunites each of them, determining him a priori both as a Son and as sharing in this essence, potentially, along with all conceivable Sons, and in this way as "members of God's household" (Ephesians 2:19), "a people belonging to God" (1 Peter 2:9). Access to the other is only by way of the access of a Son to a Son, in the transcendental

---

36. Orobator, *Church as Family.* 84.

37. I use the word *ipseity* also with Michel Henry's nuance. This word can hardly be defined. However, in an attempt to explain it, Henry summarizes it as "the concrete phenomenological mode" by which the process of life's self-generation is produced as its own self-revelatory process. See *I Am the Truth,* 57.

38. Ibid., 257. Note that Henry uses the term "Son" in an inclusive sense, that is, as representing sons and daughters.

birth of both, in the self-givenness of absolute phenomenological Life in its essential Ipseity—only in God and within the
Arch-Son: "So in Christ we who are many form one body" (Ro-
mans 12:5).[39]

Henry, commenting on Jesus' injunction of universal love, explains
further: "That one should love the other is a prescription any ethic could accommodate, as uncertain as its foundation might be . . . But that one should
love the other who is your enemy, even if he is depraved, degenerate, hypocritical, or criminal, is in effect only possible if this other person is not what
he appears. . . .. It is only if, as Son, the other carries within him Life [*ndu*]
and its essential Ipseity that he may, in his depravity, be the object of love, or
rather not him—in the sense of a person, the one whom other people call a
person—but the power that gave him to himself and constantly gives him to
himself even in his depravity. The command is to love the other insofar as
he is in Christ and in God, and on this condition alone."[40]

In the above sense, one should also understand that the Exodus-
event and the liberation of Israel do not tantamount to God's hatred of the
Egyptians, but rather a radical removal of an evil that vitiated humanity
and tainted the *splendor of life—mma-ndu*.[41] Hence, it is not the person of
Pharaoh that is being destroyed in the process, but the evil despotism which
the Pharaoh personifies. And one owes the effort to remove this evil as a
brotherly obligation to the weak, the oppressed, and God, for "blessed is
the servant who his master will find, when he returns, doing the work,"
namely, taking charge of his master's household and giving them food at
the proper time. "But if the servant is dishonest and says to himself, 'My
master is delayed,' and sets about beating his fellow-servants and eating
and drinking with drunkards. . ." (Matt 24:46ff.), the consequences will be
unpleasant to that servant. The consequences of Pharaoh's tyranny were the
plagues which culminated in the death of all first born male Egyptians and
the destruction of Pharaoh's army at the Red Sea.[42] However, those Egyptians
who disapproved of Pharaoh's cruel agenda and secretly dissented, like the
midwives, Shiphrah and Puah, were blessed by God (cf. Exod 1:15–20). The
point here is that power and authority are given by God to establish justice

39. Ibid.

40. Ibid.

41. The Igbo term for human being is *mmadu* (compound of *mma*, "beauty," plus
ndu, "life"), which means "beauty and splendor of life," implying the acme of existence.

42. I very much acknowledge that this biblical account is arguably a mythic narrative. But it has a didactic significance in the sense that the punishment of a whole nation
for the fault of one tyrant is justified on the basis of the people's overt approval of the
tyranny.

on earth and to protect the weak, and wherever this duty is flouted, whether in private (e.g. in domestic homes) or in the public (e.g. in Politics and institutions), it stands to be conscientiously and vehemently opposed by all who have a sense of justice. God used the hand of Moses to oppose such intransigence in Egypt and continues to call theologians, church leaders, and men and women of goodwill to stand up against the "Pharaohs" in every age. The human person, known in Igbo language as *"mmadu,"* is the resplendent beauty of creation—the acme of existence; the image of God. Whoever mars this beauty by sin against human dignity is trampling on creation. And the duty to repair the damage brought about by social sins will be dependent on a Christology of liberation capable of claiming the authority of Christ in favor of Jesus the liberator, who has come to *redeem* the divine image of humans. The person of Jesus Christ, the man who was lifted up on the cross, therefore takes the center of any theological discourse about human history. How liberation theology understood this person of Christ is what we are going to look at in the next chapter.

2

The Centrality of Christology in Liberation Discourse

Hopes and Impediments

Christ as the Center of Liberation Theology

IT IS WELL KNOWN that liberation theology never had an easy ride with a catholic Magisterium that was wary about dealing with a new heresy. The concern of the Roman Pontiff was what he felt as need,—to oppose those who "claim to show Jesus as politically committed, as one who fought against Roman oppression and the authorities, and also as one involved in the class struggle. This idea of Christ as a political figure, a revolutionary, as the subversive man from Nazareth, does not tally with the Church's catechesis,"[1] the Pope declares. How central and significant the person of Christ is to all theological discourses cannot be overemphasized. For Latin Americans, he is a "Liberator." But to what extent does this perception of him as liberator deviate from or become affirmed by his identity as Savior or Redeemer? This question will become an issue of great controversy. In the controversy that ensued African theologians who admired the title of Ancestor were apparently ignored as if the formulation does not deserve any serious attention from the Church's teaching authority. The point of the controversy, however, is to determine

---

1. Novak, "Liberation Theology and the Pope," 173.

whether the Christian faith about Jesus Christ is not being compromised in giving theological legitimacy to the liberation struggle that has won numerous apostles across Latin America, Africa and Asia. In order to comprehend the import of this controversy and its value to a theology of fraternity, one needs to understand what Christology is all about.

Understanding Christology

Since the subject of Christology is as vast as theology itself, the treatment I will give to it here can only be propaedeutic, i.e., aimed at helping a layperson have an elementary grasp of the centrality and significance of the person and life of Jesus Christ in the understanding of human history upon which theology reflects. I use the notion of Christology in this book to mean the study, in traditional systematic theology, of the person and attributes of Christ, in particular the union in Him of divine and human natures. This study has since the mid-20th Century undergone a paradigm shift. No longer explicating the hypostatic union, it seeks to recapitulate the entire development of the Christological tradition in order to mediate Christ's redemptive significance in the contemporary cultural context.[2] It is beyond the scope of this book to go into a deeper investigation of the early debates about the co-subsistence of the two natures in the one divine person of Christ with its long history of controversies that gave birth to a number of heretical teachings and culminated in the Council of Chalcedon (451). A good number of authors who are experts in this topic offer ample detail of this most important and central theme of theology. Suffice it here to use Alois Grillmeier's explanation to highlight what is of relevance to the foregoing discourse. "In the course of its historical elaboration, Christology came to contain two parts which were not always very organically connected: Christology in the narrower sense (the doctrine of the person of Christ) and soteriology, which based its central theme—the satisfaction offered by Christ to God—upon the doctrine of the person of Christ as a divine subject of infinite value and dignity."[3]

The Christian creed testifies to this intrinsic connection between Christology and soteriology where it professes that Jesus Christ became a human being for our sake and for our salvation (*propter nos homines et propter nostram salutem*). This creedal statement of the Christian religion demonstrates that the key signature of Christology is soteriology. Hence

2. Walsh and Loewe, "Christology," 559.
3. Grillmeier, "Christology," 188.

Roger Olson would argue in his *The Story of Christian Theology*[4] that this story is precisely "the story of Christian reflection on salvation" and that this concern with salvation was especially evident in the formative and reformative stages of Christian doctrinal development so much so that the great debates over proper Christian belief about God, Jesus Christ, sin, and grace that consumed the attention of the early church fathers from approximately 300 to 500 were largely about guarding and protecting the gospel of salvation.[5]

Christology is in fact the center of this story. It encompasses the incarnation, the life of Jesus, which found its ultimate fulfillment in his cross, resurrection and ascension into heaven. And precisely because the salvation offered by Christ (i.e. his saving works), remain inseparable with his person, all christological statements have at the same time soteriological character and vice versa. To speak of Christology is to speak of Christ and what he did for us human beings, i.e., saving us. Liberation theology, however, has always shown discomfiture with any theological hermeneutic that will relegate salvation only to the realm of the post-temporal. Hence, what is important for liberation theology is that this saving should not be seen as specifically referring to the saving of our souls, but rather of our history (both temporal and eschatological). He liberates humanity from those shackles that make this world a vale of tears. Because of the two natures united in Jesus Christ, two distinct types of Christology became evident, namely, "Christology from above" and "Christology from below."

Christology from Below

One of the most prominent theologians of the past century to elucidate Christology was Karl Rahner. In trying to explain what he means by Christology from below Rahner says, "If a historical event such as the Christ-event is to mean the salvation of man in his entirety, it must possess an intrinsic structure, which claims man in his entirety."[6] This "intrinsic structure" is for Rahner the double but united structure of Christology, which are identified by him as *transcendental* and *categorical*. This implies that human's transcendental orientation towards the said historical redemptive event is only explicitly reflected on when humans meet with this event in history.[7]

---

4. Olson, *Story of Christian Theology*

5. Ibid., 13.

6. Rahner, "Jesus Christ," 197.

7. Ibid.

It follows that a transcendental Christology only becomes historically possible and necessary when humankind encounters the factual Christ-event in his or her own empirical, contextual, "categorical" experience. This categorical experience requires in the first place a Christology "from below," for humankind, of course, first meets the human being, Jesus before he or she can acknowledge him as Christ.[8] This inverted movement from below is declared legitimate by Walter Kasper thus: "In a situation in which the talk about God has become a big problem, one can in Christology no longer begin unmediated 'above,' from the Triune God, and then only bring into consideration the 'descent,' the incarnation, of the second divine person. It is rather recommendable to go the opposite way, namely, to start 'below' from the human experience, in order, according to the Christmas preface, to make radiant the invisible God in the visible Son."[9] Christology from below is therefore, concerned with talk about the concrete Jesus of Nazareth who is known *a posteriori*.

Christology from Above

Traditionally, Christology in its Old Testament biblical and primitive Christian roots emerges out of Christ's various titles. In contemporary exegesis, these titles—Messiah, Christ, Son of God, Servant of God, Kyrios, etc.—are not understood as statements of the earthly Jesus himself. On the contrary, they are the Church's post-resurrection proclamations of faith. Jesus did not preach his reign but rather the reign of God, which is the salvation of humans. The complete comprehension of the Christ-event requires a transcendental Christology—a Christology of *descent from above*, such as is already found in Pauline and Johannine theology.

In the New Testament, Jesus addressed God as Abba—Father. The radical novelty of his God-Talk comes out clear in this expression. God is therein presented as a God of humans. And in this "Abba-expression" is Jesus' own relationship with God elucidated. This Father-Son relationship has significance for our salvation. It is the basis of reconciliation of human beings with God and with one another. Many contemporary theologians see the foundation of all Christologies in this unprecedented Abba-relationship of Jesus. For Walter Kasper, for example, it is a relationship of mutual intimacy, of personal tie in love and devotion.[10] And in this mutual relationship

---

8. Ibid.

9. Kasper, *Christologische Schwerpunkte*, 18; translation is mine.

10. Ibid., 28.

of Jesus to his father, the revelation of who God is, become definitively given. This Christology of *descent* is known as Christology from above.

Liberation Christology: Hopes

Articulation of Liberation Christologies

In trying to relate Christology to contemporary historical and socio-political context liberation theology adopted two positions. In both positions, the picture of Jesus Christ as a liberator gets prominent attention. The one position, dealing with what is experienced, wants to articulate the field of sensibility in Christological terms. The other position, dealing with what is thought in contradistinction to what is experienced, articulates Christology in the area of analyses. The first position arises out of an ethical disgust, and the second out of a social analytic reasoning. Both, however, have something in common: they relate to the reality of misery of the poor and are identified as 1) sacramental and 2) social-analytic articulations.

Sacramental Articulation of Liberation Christology

Sacramental articulation is about the recognition of the presence of oppression and the consequent exigency of liberation. Reality is accordingly perceived in an intuitive and sagacious insight. The situation of poverty and oppression is seen to contradict God's plan of salvation. Poverty indicates the reality of a social sin that is not willed by God, and hence the necessity of recognizing and acknowledging the exigency of change. This acknowledgement is then translated into the prophetic language of denunciation on the one hand, and the encouragement of change on the other hand. Albeit this effort is most often unsuccessful, nevertheless its fundamental position remains clear: "...the social relationship must be changed and the oppressed groups must be empowered so that the emergent new structure will be less oppressive."[11] The situation of apartheid in South Africa represents very well a condition that elicits the sacramental articulation of liberation Christology. The question of which position Jesus will choose to take in such an oppressive socio-political environment hence becomes a decisive criterion for discernment.

Through sacramental articulation of liberation theology, things are appropriately considered in the light of Christological faith. Through the gestures, words and positions of Jesus, which call for conversion and change

---

11. Boff, *Jesus Christus, der Befreier*, 25; translation is mine.

of behavior, one sees that Jesus desired an integral liberation of humankind. Jesus' behavior towards people who were on the margins of Jewish society, his special concern for the poor, the conflict with those who want to perpetuate the religious and social status quo of his time, the political content of his proclamation of the kingdom of God as well as the motive which brought him to death etc., all these have a special relevance for and illuminates the picture of a liberation-oriented Jesus.

The concern here is a Christology of liberation, which is based on values and themes that are connected with change, and liberation. According to L. Boff, this type of Christology has a certain import: *it discloses the unavoidable intertwining of salvation in Jesus Christ with the historical liberation, overcomes an inner privatizing understanding of the Christian message, thus mandating it to meddle in politics.*[12]

Such a Christology goes hand in hand with a critical exegesis that devotes itself to a new interpretation of fundamental Christological dogmas and an elucidation of the liberative dimensions of the Christian faith. Traditional images of Christ are hence criticized as serving the colonial project and such criticisms are not without merits. Not only did Leonardo Boff criticize the Christology of resignation, in which providence is made responsible for unjust status-quo, he also denounced the Christology of a victorious warrior-like Christ thus making the case that liberation theology is not merely propagating violent activism as critics would want to assume, but rather seeks to rediscover the Christ who spoke and still speaks with a prophetic voice that is valid for all times.

However, the boundaries of the Christology of liberation are obvious and limited. Since its understanding of Christ emanates from a social-analytic observation of reality, it has little political effect. So it happens that its proponents could be theologically (i.e., theoretically) revolutionary, but in practice they remain either conservative or liberal, that is, still inclined to one ideological leaning or the other. One notices this, for instance, when one compares some inculturation theologians with some feminist theologians.

Social Analytic Articulation of Liberation Christology

This articulation of liberation Christology emerges out of the same spiritual experience of the poor. Its ethical disgust or aversion is not less. It analyses the reality, unveils the causes of the misery of the poor and sets a liberating praxis in motion. The concern is thus not to enhance the old power structure by merely seeking to make things better in a spirit of reformation,

---

12. Ibid.; my translation from German text.

but rather to bring a total change of relationship out of a real revolutionary will; the fundamental option aims unconditionally at liberation and breaking of dependence. In this sense, in order to achieve genuine liberation, it will not be deemed enough for Africans to identify slavery, racism, colonialism, imperial capitalism, and neocolonial dictatorship as causes of misery in the African continent. It is necessary to analyze in general those mechanisms that produce social injustice and combat them. Such mechanisms are adjudged in the light of faith as social and structural sins. It is sometimes the sins of the heart that refuses to behold the divinely fraternal imprint of otherness. And the Christology that emerges out of this theological effort is rightly called a Christology of liberation, and invariably of fraternity.

The Christology of liberation further builds upon two theoretical mediations: the social-analytic mediation refers to the changing reality, whereas the hermeneutic mediation is concerned with the theological *proprium*. In the hermeneutic mediation, the social-analytic text is read and understood in the light of Jesus Christ the Savior and the Word of revelation, but also in the recognition that the Word, who saves, saves by becoming flesh and making himself a brother to humankind. Through the hermeneutic mediation, the theological character of the theory and praxis of liberation is made secure. However, a major question confronts us about which social theory we must adopt in order to be able to articulate the Christology of liberation. In the post-colonial African context, where Africans are now exploiting and oppressing their own brothers and sisters "Ọ nụrụ ube nwanne agbala ọsọ" provides us with an adequate social theory.

In the choice of a social theory, some criteria play some roles that are not traceable particularly to objectivity and rationality but rather to the fundamental option of the researcher and his social location. Thus, L. Boff noted: "Every reflection about the human reality will be guided by the basic project or—to put it in other words—by a utopia, which a group creates for itself and in which they project their future. But such a utopia is not a pure ideology; rather it is based upon social and material preconditions."[13] Two models of projects, in other words two utopias, distinguish themselves here: 1) the desire of the ruling social class and, 2) the agenda of the oppressed class.

The utopia of the ruling class allows the structural cadre of the society to rest on it. The utopia of the oppressed class, on the contrary, wants a society of equality, in fact, of fraternity. The ruling class favors the functional method for social analysis. This method gives primacy to the idea of order and equilibrium and imagines the society as an organic whole whose parts

13. Ibid., 27.

complement one another. The existence of rich and poor is seen as a socially necessary and natural given. The oppressed group, on the contrary, rather makes use of the dialectic method. In this dialectic method, the idea of conflict and struggle takes the focal point. A potentially explosive situation thus reigns in the society. A liberal tradition, which considers society from above, exists side by side with a Marxist tradition that sees society from below. But beyond this dialectic of conflict is also the popular aspiration for reconciliation and harmony in the spirit of fraternal charity that takes into consideration the legitimate needs of all.

Faith respects the autonomy of reason but knows too well to distinguish and scrutinize which model of analysis that best corresponds to its demands. Hence, faith opts for such social-analytic scheme that best unveils the causal mechanisms of injustice—a scheme that should be able to provide means to eliminate the causal mechanisms of injustice and also favor most the idea of brotherliness, inclusiveness and civic and religious freedom.

Liberation Christology opts for the dialectic method in its analysis of the society. And this is always tied up with the revolutionary project of the oppressed. The word "liberation" expresses in itself a new option and a new agenda that is neither reform oriented nor progressive oriented but rather liberation oriented, and according to Boff, clearly connotes a clean break from the status quo. Liberation Christology is empowered by a new understanding of the historical Jesus and engages itself for the interest of the oppressed and marginalized. To be neutral means to give a tacit support to the privileged group that perpetuates structures of inequality and injustice. Hence, liberation is seen as a gospel imperative. Owing to this understanding of liberation as an imperative, theologians also felt the need to have a hierarchy of hermeneutical values in which certain elements have to be prioritized over others. These priorities are listed as:

i.   Priority of the Anthropological Element over the Ecclesial

ii. Priority of the Utopian Element over the Factual

iii. Priority of the Critical Element over the Dogmatic

iv. Priority of the Societal Element over the Personal

v.   Priority of the Orthopraxis over the Orthodoxy

Priority of the Anthropological Element over the Ecclesial

The central interest is shifted from the Church to the human being, who theology should uplift and humanize.[14] Because the models and struc-

---

14. Gibellini, *Handbuch der Theologie im 20. Jahrhundert*, 352.

ture of the Church was imported from Europe and reproduces European archetypes, faith in this context engendered little creativity. Hence, it has become exigent to review these models and structure. African liberation theology in comparison to its Latin American counterpart has yet a lot of job to do in this regard. What this shift entails for Africa, however, requires a little more explanation to which Bishop P. A. Kalilombe of Malawi has given us some clues. In his view, nineteenth-century Catholicism bore clear traces of a long post-Reformation experience. As we know, the traumatic events of the Protestant Reformation in the sixteenth century provoked a Catholic Counter Reformation. This was a period of struggles against the dissident churches in which the mother church strove to refute the heresies and errors of its protesting opponents. The theology of this period is consequently apologetic and polemical. The theology manuals of the period are usually a series of theses or topics of controversy, in which the need to fight back and attack prevents a serene, balanced, and objective exposition of the Christian message in its totality.[15]

Christian faith would have been able to express itself freely and quite naturally with its own characteristics within the social structures in which it found itself in Africa. Instead the post-Reformation rancor was transported from Europe to Africa and has succeeded in establishing a culture of "churchism" that is very unhealthy for community development. For instance, Anglicans and other Protestants were indoctrinated into the belief that Catholics are worshipping Mary and the saints, hence, practicing idolatry. Catholics, on the other hand, were indoctrinated into the belief that Protestants are heretics and are, therefore, headed on the road to perdition. Thus the mutual antagonism into which native Africans were converted still stultifies developmental efforts in many communities today. In my hometown of Azigbo in Nigeria, Protestants recently opposed vehemently an attempt to hand over to the Catholic bishop a Health Center project that was abandoned by the Federal Government. Although the bishop is interested in revamping the project and delivering the desired healthcare services to the community, and although it is less likely that sick people actually care about who owns the hospital in which they are treated, church bigots seem to prefer having the building dilapidate rather than see it administered by a church to which they do not belong. This is part of the sad but true reality of the missionary legacy, which will require inter-denominational cooperation between the churches to resolve. Such cooperation, however, can only hope to be nourished and sustained by an *enlightened* notion of fraternity and solidarity.

15. Kalilombe, "Presence of the Church in Africa." 24.

With emphasis on the anthropological rather than the ecclesial element of theology, liberation theologians seek to resolve such problems. Leonardo Boff argues that the common frame in which the Canon Law is dogmatically interpreted and dogma canonically applied hinders from the basis a healthy effort to create a new image of the church on the ground outside the inherited archetype of the traditional Greco-Roman worldview.[16] In view of the dwindling demography in Europe, however, it could be said that the future of the Church lies in the so-called Third World. Therefore, from a more anthropological point of view, elements emerge which dictate the need for a novel Christian reflection. The echoes of this precedence of the anthropological element also resound in the theology of Jean-Marc Ela, who insists that the basic project of Christianity in African society must be redefined. According to Ela, it is the Church and Christian theology that are expected to confront the forces of oppression that condemn men, women, and children to suffer atrocious living conditions.[17] But in order to accomplish this, the Church must learn to focus less on herself and more on the human being whose image is disfigured by suffering and whose dignity is in need of restoration. This is why the anthropological question takes precedence over the ecclesial.

Priority of the Utopian Element over the Factual

The decisive perspective of the African people is not the past but the future. Therefore, the utopian element in Africa is so important. African liberation theologians have emphasized this orientation to the future by rejecting such idioms like négritude, which they criticized for creating and advocating a celebratory return to an idyllic past of exotic customs that is only meant to masturbate the fantasies of westerners while ignoring the situation of exploitation and misery that is allowed to exist unabated in Africa. The utopia must not be misunderstood with illusion or escapism, for as philosophical and theological studies in the past years have shown[18] utopia is born principally out of hope. A hope which is responsible for the models that serve the perfection of our society—models which do not stagnate the social process nor ideologically absolutize themselves, but rather hold the process

16. Boff, *Jesus Christus, der Befreier*, 213; translation is mine. German text reads: "der allgemeine Rahmen, in dem das Kirchenrecht dogmatisch und die Dogmatik rechtlich interpretiert wurde, verhindert von Grund auf auch gesunde Versuche, hierzulande eine neue Gestalt von Kirche außerhalb der traditionellen, aus dem griechisch-römischen Weltverständnis ererbten Muster zu schaffen."

17. Ela, *African Cry*, 7.

18. Demaison, *Wege der christlichen Utopie*, 617–26.

open for a constant intensive change.[19] Faith proclaims a utopia of a wholly reconciled world and demonstrates also that such a world is already a reality in Christ. The Kingdom is anticipated in history and the new human being takes his or her shape in that history. The reconciliation that is promised and realized in Christ is the fulfillment of what the human being can accomplish by himself.[20] Theology only makes relevant the effort to build a more human and more brotherly world. It creates as well as anticipates that world that has been promised to us and which Jesus Christ has shown to be possible.

Priority of the Critical Element over the Dogmatic

Human beings and institutions have a tendency to stagnate when within a particular epoch they are apparently existentially established with relative success. Some mechanisms of self-defense and dogmatic thought-pattern emerge which fear and seek to suppress every kind of criticism that tend to argue that institutions should remain functional and open to change. But such criticisms are, however, very important for the society so that the rhythm of history do not go amiss. As a result, the critical element is especially important to theology, in view of the traditions and institutions of the church that had some meaningful functions in the past, but which have become anachronistic, such that they are now the center of hindrance to dialogue between faith and ideology, between church and society.[21] Feminist theologians, for instance, are calling for new forms of socialization that question present dogmatic stance. The criticisms of the prevalent dogmatic positions accordingly have the character of illuminating and making elaborate the nucleus of the Christian experience. This shift of emphasis is exigent so that the seed of Christian experience will take tangible shape under the conditions of our experience of history. In Africa, this involves also a revision of the clericalism that considers the decisions of the diocesan bishop or priests in their parishes unquestionable.

Priority of the Societal Element over the Personal

The major problem of the African society is that the number of people at the margins of the society makes up the majority of the population. The question cannot be settled merely on the level of personal conversion. There are social injustices for which no individual could be held responsible. Whether

19. Boff, *Jesus Christus, der Befreier*, 213.

20. Gibellini, *Handbuch der Theologie*, 352.

21. Boff, *Jesus Christus, der Befreier*, 214.

the Church wants it or not, she is entangled in a context that is beyond her, but in which she must play a vital role. And what must her function be? Must she be a clog in the wheel of social progress? Does she have to carve out a niche for her own little world and thus isolate herself from the public square? No, on the contrary, she must involve herself critically in the process of liberation in the African context.

In a society like Nigeria, for example, where lawmakers agreed to rob the state treasury simply because they have the power to vote their own salaries, who will challenge the corrupt status quo if not the Church? According to a report published by *The Economist* magazine on July 20, 2013, a Nigerian legislator receives an annual salary of about $189,000, equivalent of ₦30 million, which is 116 times the country's gross domestic product (GDP) per person. The figures (which did not include the quarterly bonuses that are still unknown) put the salaries collected by Nigerian senators and members of the House of Representatives way ahead of those received by fellow parliamentarians in the 29 countries whose data were compared by *The Economist*. In terms of volume of cash earnings, the Nigerian legislators exceed their counterparts in Britain who take $105,400 yearly, as well as those in the United States ($174,000), France ($85,900), South Africa ($104,000), Kenya ($74,500), Saudi Arabia ($64,000) and Brazil ($157,600). The $189,500 earned annually by each Nigerian legislator is estimated to be 52 percent higher than that of Kenyan legislators, who are the third highest paid lawmakers in Africa.[22]

There is something wrong with a church that will fail to give more than a verbal challenge to such impunity and gross irresponsibility on the part of political leaders in a country where there is more than 60.9 percent poverty. According to this percentage from *National Bureau of Statistics*, about 112.47 million people are living in poverty in the year 2010.[23] Given this situation: What value do the Church's pious exhortations have, if criminal politicians continue unchallenged in impoverishing the masses? Like Jesus Christ, the Church ought to pay special attention to the nameless victims of such unbridled cupidity and be the voice of the voiceless; she should underline the earthly and liberative dimension of Jesus' message; she should make Christ's promise of liberation in Luke's gospel (cf. Luke 4:18; Isaiah 61:1) actual in every generation, for "the future kingdom which grows between the wheat and the weeds is not just meant for a privileged few but for

---

22. Pindiga, "Nigerian Lawmakers Top Salaries Chart." See also J. S., I. B., and L. P. "Rewarding Work."

23. BBC Report of February 13, 2012, http://www.bbc.co.uk/news/world-africa-17015873.

all people."[24] The church in Africa should fight to break the yoke imposed on the poor by capitalist greed within and outside the continent. However, reasons will be shown later why we need, in addition to liberation, other effective and more adequate hermeneutic tools.

Priority of the Orthopraxis over the Orthodoxy

The weakness of the classical handbook Christology lies exactly in what it presumes to be its strength, namely, in the philosophical-theological systematization. The classical Christology has led neither to an Ethic nor to a pattern of behavior that is typically Christian. It has paid little attention to the fundamental theme of the synoptic gospels, which is discipleship and has hardly translated it into a concrete way of life. Orthodoxy, for instance, would imply that the correct thought about Christ has primacy over acting rightly in the light of Christ. So it happened that the Church often preached Christ as the liberator, but seldom liberates or supports liberation movements. Yet for Christ and the early Church, what mattered was not to summarize his message in systematic categories of an intellectual knowledge, but rather to create new behavior patterns for living and acting in the world. It is time for theological reflection in Africa to develop a special sensibility for this praxeological motive in Christ's message. But such theological sensibility should not be rest assured that identifying the need for liberation is enough; cultivating the spirit of fraternity is also necessary, so that the poor themselves will also be converted at heart and work together towards the utopia of a just and egalitarian society.

Liberation Christology: Impediments

There is no doubt that through the shifts in the priorities of liberation Christology, Jesus was rediscovered. Hitherto, I have shown the centrality of Christ in liberation theology and how his rediscovery in South America relates to the African context. Having appraised liberation Christology's prioritization in its engagements, the question now is: What is the significance of a theology of fraternity in this context and what is its relationship with liberation? What is the social relevance of this theology in Africa and in the world? In a nutshell, why do we need a theology of fraternity?

A new hermeneutic is made exigent by some vague analyses in the liberation discourses and by the doctrinal suspicion that greeted the aforementioned rediscovery of Jesus in the liberation discourse, especially

24. Boff, *Jesus Christus, der Befreier*, 214.

among conservatives, both in Africa and elsewhere. Some African theologians, for example, who opted for the hermeneutic of inculturation, were reluctant to associate themselves with liberation theology. Why? The hopes that were raised by the new christological hermeneutic soon turned into impediments as Latin American theologians struggled to clarify some vague issues concerned with the Christology of liberation. One of those issues is the question of answering to the accusations of doing Jesuology in the name of Christology.

Christology or Jesuology?

A spate of fundamental objections to the Christology of liberation began to emerge, especially in North America, as liberation theology became more systematized and popular. Speaking of "fundamental" objections, I borrow this nuance from James V. Schall,[25] who actually uses the word "fundamental" to refer to standard Catholic orthodoxy. That liberation theology has been at odds with the official teaching authority of the Church is well-known. In an article by Joseph Cardinal Ratzinger (Pope Benedict XVI) shortly before the Instruction *Libertatis Nuntius* in 1984 the German theologian, then Prefect of the Pontifical Congregation for the Propagation of Faith (*Propaganda Fidei*), notes that "an analysis of the phenomenon of liberation theology reveals that it constitutes a fundamental threat to the faith of the Church."[26] Ratzinger traces the origin of this threat to Rudolf Bultmann and observes that in Bultmann, the core of faith, Christology, was open to new interpretations because its previous affirmations had perished as being historically no longer tenable. This meant also that the Church's teaching office was discredited, since she had evidently clung to a scientifically untenable theory, and thus ceased to be regarded as an authority where knowledge of Jesus was concerned. In the future her statements could only be seen as futile attempts to defend a position which was scientifically obsolete.[27] But Bultmann's "historical Jesus," Ratzinger argues, is separated from the Christ of faith by a great gulf, for while Jesus is part of the presuppositions of the New Testament, he himself is enclosed in the world of Juda-

25. In an article titled "Ratzinger on the Modern Mind," Schall wrote that "Fundamentalism" is "taken to mean, from a relativist philosophy, the affirmation that there is a revelation of God in history through Christ, that is, taken to mean orthodoxy. This "fundamentalism" (that is, standard Catholic orthodoxy) is seen to be an attack on modernity and its essential philosophical roots in absolute tolerance and freedom, both taken to be without limits."

26. Ratzinger, "Liberation Theology," para. 2.

27. Ibid., para. 24.

ism. Accordingly, "The crucial result of this [i.e., Bultmann's] exegesis was to shatter the historical credibility of the Gospels: the Christ of the Church's tradition and the Jesus of history put forward by science evidently belong to two different worlds. Science, regarded as the final arbiter, had torn the figure of Jesus from its anchorage in tradition; on the one hand, consequently, tradition hangs in a vacuum, deprived of reality, while on the other hand, a new interpretation and significance must be sought for the figure of Jesus."[28]

Julio Lois formulated the objection in a nutshell saying: "In taking insufficient account of the Church's faith in Christ, expressed in the conciliar dogmatic formulas that recapitulate the fullness of the New Testament Christologies, liberation Christology is reduced to a 'Jesuology,' [in which] the central mystery of Jesus Christ as Son of God and universal Savior is evacuated."[29] This objection is lodged fundamentally against liberation Christology's approach "from below," i.e. against an "ascending" methodology that ignores the faith in Jesus as the incarnate Son of God. For the full "Christ" creed requires a "descending" approach or a Christology "from above." However, as already demonstrated, the proponents of liberation theology have unequivocally repudiated this objection and have distanced themselves from *liberal theology*.

Gustavo Gutiérrez warned against a simplistic interpretation of the favored interest of the Latin American theology on the historical Jesus. For the same reason, he considered it necessary to highlight the complexity of the relationship between the Jesus of history and the Christ of faith, between the glorified *Kyrios* and the carpenter's son from Nazareth.[30] Other liberation theologians across Africa and Asia share the same views with Gutiérrez, that the liberation theology's inquiry into the historical Jesus must not be understood in the sense of reductionism. The crux of the matter is whether Jesus becomes less Christ simply because he is seen to be a brother of humankind. For Kwame Bediako, for example, the critical question for the Christian is how to have the meanings of Christ become operative in human hearts. Hence, he identifies three aspects of what confronts us in the ministry of Jesus Christ as follows: "in Jesus Christ, the Holy Spirit reveals to us a divine paradigm which confronts all religions, challenging men and women in three specific areas—in our understanding of power and weakness, in our response to evil, and in our response to cultural and social enmity and exclusiveness."[31] Liberation theologians thus argue that the Christology of

28. Ibid., para. 23.
29. Lois, "Christology in the Theology of Liberation," 186–87.
30. Gutiérrez, "Option for the Poor," 239.
31. Bediako, *Jesus and the Gospel in Africa*, 42.

liberation stands clearly among the statements of the New Testament and the Councils about the divinity of Jesus. The Church has, however, never considered it her specific task to deepen this Christology nor make it a specific point of departure for her reflection. Noting that it is not Christianity that saves, but Christ, Bediako reiterates that "in Jesus, then, we have the threefold paradigm of divine vulnerability, the will to redemptive suffering and reconciling love, not as abstract notions, but as concrete events and deeds in human life, and achieved in ways which Christian faith reads as expressive of the divine nature itself."[32]

Similarly, Jon Sobrino contends that "the confession of the divinity of Christ (in all importance and indispensability of the knowledge about his divinity) is in the Christian sense only real, . . .when it is embedded in the simple and unconditional fellowship with Jesus, where one experiences from within that God has unconditionally come closer to us in Jesus; that Jesus is true God; and that the true God is made manifest in him."[33] Sobrino makes clear here that the Christology of liberation does not hesitate to acknowledge that the "descent" aspect of Christology is indispensable, because it positions the mystery of Christ formally as mystery.[34] Although the Christology of liberation understands itself as a Christology "from below" and favors the "ascending" methodology, it is well aware that the mystery of Christ is formulated in the orthodox "descending" route, be it in the statements of the Gospel, that "the Word became flesh" (Jon. 1:14), or in the dogmatic sentence of the hypostatic union, according to which the union of the natures in Christ takes place in the person of the Logos.[35] For, in order to understand Christ as mystery, one must understand him as God, although he becomes in that instance unfathomable.[36]

It remains true, however, that the descent of God cannot be comprehended—not even as gift—in its purely abstract formality, but rather in the perception of its concrete content, namely, Jesus.[37] Therefore, the Christology of liberation tries in systematic and pastoral way to reflect about Christ through Jesus, such that it is the human way of being—particularly the praxis—of the Nazarene, which fills with concrete content the sovereign titles and the dogmas that express the transcendence and divinity of Jesus.[38]

32. Ibid.

33. Sobrino, *Jesus in Latin America*, 40; translation is mine, from German text.

34. Ibid., 51.

35. Lois, *Christology in the Theology of Liberation*, 188.

36. Sobrino, *Jesus in Latin America*, 41.

37. Lois, *Christology in the Theology of Liberation*, 188.

38 Cf. Sobrino, *Jesus in Latin America*, 50–54

In this sense one might speak of a theological priority of the Christ of faith and a logical and methodological priority of the historical Jesus.[39]

However, with the Latin American christological title under fire, African theologians went in search of an alternative title that will suit the African context. Some of them with the inculturation leaning discovered Jesus in the "Ancestor," but this title never seemed to find any strong reception among African liberation theologians, like Ela. One of the reasons is that the ancestor role does not address sufficiently the situation of corruption and exploitation under which Africa is yoked.

The Crossroad with Marxism

As liberation theology struggles to survive the accusation of Jesuology, it came under further fierce attacks from North American theologians some of whom see liberation theologians as nothing more than a bunch of Marxist Christians who condemn the "imperialism" of multinational corporations and the "institutionalized violence" of capitalist society, using distinctly revolutionary rather than reformist language.[40] For Richard John Neuhaus, "the term liberation, with its socialist and frequently revolutionary content, invites the suspicion that theology is somehow being enlisted to legitimate a specific political option."[41] Edward Norman, an Anglican priest, sees liberation theology as "luxuriant in Marxist rhetoric" and despite heavy use of technical language to describe conscientization, is no more than ordinary political indoctrination whose objective is "the rise of Christianity with a proletarian character capable of being freed from the dominant bourgeois ideology."[42] Another evangelical theologian, Harold Brown, who thinks that the vision of liberation theology "to make an old message understandable, and thus both acceptable and effective" is a blurred vision, argues that "the liberationists . . . have put on the spectacles of an ideology that has indeed succeeded in changing the world, but not in understanding it, and moreover of an ideology that by virtue of its fundamentally atheistic orientation can never consider the Gospel of Christ as more than the ramblings of a deluded idealist."[43] In his turn, Ronald H. Nash notes that "The end liberation theo-

39. Lois, *Christology in the Theology of Liberation*, 188.

40. Norman, "Imperialism of Political Religion," 132.

41. Neuhaus, "Liberation Theology and the Cultural Captivity of the Gospel," 219.

42. Norman, "Imperialism of Political Religion," 131 and 135

43. Brown, "What is Liberation Theology?," 14. In the above excerpts of his article, Brown's hyperbole in characterizing the Marxist stance that religion is a form of idealism betrays this North American's disdain for liberation theology. In fact it may not be imputed to Karl Marx that he ever described the gospel of Christ as "the ramblings of

logians seek is to help people who are poor and oppressed. Their selection of socialism as their exclusive means for reaching their goal [however] is a mistake that is both tragic and ironic. It is tragic because they have rejected the one system that offers real economic hope for the masses they wish to assist. It is ironic because in promoting the violent means of exchange, they have taken a path that will not only deny *their people* bread but also deprive them of liberty. That such a movement should call itself liberation theology truly is ironic."[44]

The reference to *"their people"* betrays a cultural, ethnic, anthropological and moral distance which seems to suggest here that Nash does not see the poor in Latin America or elsewhere as his own people. Such antifraternal, often unconscious distancing is, in fact, the major problem that bedevils authentic witness to the gospel and the kingdom of God that respects no territorial boundaries. It engenders apathy and obscures an honest engagement with the issues of social injustice as it seeks spurious excuses to shake off one's own guilt. It also indicts Nash's reading of liberation theology as one that is at best shallow if not downright biased. Liberation theology surely has its handicaps, but if Nash seeks to castigate it on the basis of an argument on violence, what will he say about other forms of legitimate violence like the violence of the Second World War, which sought to liberate Europe from the despotic grips of Adolf Hitler and his Nazi cohorts? Or what would he think about the people's resistance to communism in Eastern Europe and to apartheid in South Africa? I do not intend to delve into a rejoinder to Nash's objections, but suffice it here to say that liberation theologians have always emphasized that its historical context must not be forgotten—a context that informs its reflections on structural injustice as a whole, be it in form of economic exploitation, political oppression, racial and gender discrimination.

From the foregoing, it has become clear that, in spite of its merits in awakening theology from *dogmatic* slumber, liberation theology's willingness to dialogue with Marxism continues to cast an unpleasant shadow on its tenets especially in the eyes of critics. Liberation theologians themselves make no pretense of a denial of Marxist relationship. They only contend in

a deluded idealist." Juan Luis Segundo makes this case for Marx against Paul Ricoeur when he pointed out that "Marx does not seem to have ever entertained the suspicion that ideology could have warped the thinking of the theologians and the interpreters of Scripture so that they ended up unwittingly interpreting it in a sense that served the interests of the ruling classes. Marx does not seem to have shown any interest in trying to find out whether a new interpretation favoring the class struggle of the proletariat might be possible or even necessary." See Segundo, *Liberation of Theology*, 17.

44. Nash, ed., *Liberation Theology*, 66; my emphasis.

answer to critics that Marxism is used by liberation theology purely as an *instrument* never to be venerated as it venerates the gospel, nor to be treated as a subject on its own but always *from and in relation to the poor.*[45] To put it in more specific terms, liberation theology freely borrows from Marxism certain "methodological pointers" that have proved fruitful in understanding the world of the oppressed, such as:

- The importance of economic factors;

- Attention to the class struggle;

- The mystifying power of ideologies, including religious ones.[46]

Hence, Boff admits that Karl Marx, like any other Marxist, can be a companion on the way, but can never be the guide, because "You have only one teacher, the Christ" (Matt 23:10).[47] But insisting that liberation theology is deficient both in its diagnosis and its prescription the North American critics succeeded in inflicting a good number of punctures that arguably deflated the logic of liberation theology and exposed its major weaknesses. They pointed out that it fails to explain the real causes of poverty and thus cannot hope to provide the cure of a disease whose nature it misunderstands. The problem consists in the fact that such terms as "oppressed" and "oppressor" and the opinions about what might be done to change their relationships are uninteresting abstractions until related to concrete and usually conflicting movements, struggles and political parties. The absence of conceptual clarity in the statement of its goal is thus matched by a deep obscurity about the means by which the goal is to be achieved. Neuhaus, for example, notes that Gutierrez sees Christian unity as requiring from the Church an unambiguously partisan commitment: creating division and pressing the class struggle in order to "build a socialist society, more just, free, and human, and not a society of superficial and false reconciliation and equality."[48] Against this idea Neuhaus contends that, "Of course a merely formal unity that seeks to contain conflicting elements can be profoundly dishonest. But there is nothing superficial or false about Paul's vision of the church, where in Christ Jesus 'There is neither Jew nor Greek, there is neither slave nor free, there is neither male nor female,' and, we might add, there is neither bourgeoisie nor proletariat (Galatians 3:28)."[49]

---

45. Boff, and Boff, *Introducing Liberation Theology*, 28.

46. Ibid.,

47. Ibid.

48. Neuhaus, "Liberation Theology and the Cultural Captivity of the Gospel," 234–35.

49. Ibid.

This is precisely where a theology of fraternity differs from and indeed supersedes a theology of liberation. For instance, whereas feminist theology protests against male dominance and subordination of women, it remains silent about oppression of women by women. And whereas black theology throws its weight against racial segregation and marginalization of blacks by whites, it also fails to address properly the oppression and exploitation of blacks by blacks. Consequently, what theology needs is a new language and hermeneutic that effectively addresses the problem of social injustice without having to take recourse to partisanship. And that inclusive language is fraternity, whose adequacy does not lie in deviating from the dialectics of liberation, but rather in identifying what is deficient in the diagnosis of liberation theology.

The liberation hermeneutic was further weakened fundamentally by the outcome of the judgment which the Sacred Congregation for the Doctrine of the Faith (SCDF) passed against it in the document *Libertatis Nuntius* of 1984. The document notes that "concepts uncritically borrowed from Marxist ideology and recourse to theses of a biblical hermeneutic marked by rationalism are at the basis of the new interpretation which is *corrupting whatever was authentic in the generous initial commitment on behalf of the poor.*"[50] The document also admits that the theologies of liberation deserve credit for restoring to a place of honor the great texts of the prophets and of the Gospel in defense of the poor, but they "go on to a disastrous confusion between the 'poor' of the Scripture and the 'proletariat' of Marx. In this way they pervert the Christian meaning of the poor, and they transform the fight for the rights of the poor into a class fight within the ideological perspective of the class struggle."[51] This alleged confusion is, however, eliminated through an African perspective that sees liberation in terms of fraternal solidarity. But this perspective will be made more comprehensible as we analyze in the next chapter the intrinsic ambivalence that besets the concept of poverty; the formal content of liberation as justice and as charity; and the Church's pastoral engagements with the issues of poverty.

---

50. *LN*, VI, 10; my emphasis.
51. *LN*, IX, 10.

3

The Church and the Poor

On the Magisterial Responses to the Problem of Poverty

The Church and the Poor

It will be fair to acknowledge that the Church's concern for the poor is not merely defined by her objection to liberation theology's social-analytical assumptions. For, if it were so, it would be unfortunately petty. Therefore, this chapter is intended to show how the Church has actually tried to develop social teaching that addresses the issue of injustice in human society. Among the encyclicals or apostolic exhortations that convey this teaching, I have selected six whose themes are particularly important to the discourse here,—i.e., to fraternal solidarity. Identifying justice and charity as the two essential elements of solidarity, I have categorized my reading of these documents in such a way as to classify them into two main themes, namely, "liberation as justice" and "liberation as service of charity."

As already mentioned in the preceding chapter, the notion of poverty is shrouded in an ambiguity that highlights the compelling logic of a shift in hermeneutic from liberation to fraternal solidarity—the hermeneutic of *Ọ nụrụ ube nwanne agbala ọsọ*. This shift is all the more illuminated when we confront ourselves with the question: Who are the poor?

Who Are the Poor?

In an attempt to elaborate on *Certain Aspects of the Theology of Liberation*, the Congregation for the Doctrine of the Faith tries to answer this question in its publication of the *Libertatis Conscientia*, March 22, 1986. In this second Instruction as in most of its social teaching, the Church addresses itself to the question of poverty and indeed shows a considerable measure of sensibility to the plight of the poor. The Congregation echoes the scriptural prophets by admitting that the situation of the poor is a situation of injustice contrary to the Covenant, and a grave sin which destroys communion with God.[1] It then goes further to prize communion with God as "the most precious treasure and the one in which man finds his true freedom," and the loss of this communion is seen as the most tragic misfortune. Hence, the fight against injustice finds its deepest meaning and its effectiveness in the desire to be freed from the slavery of sin.[2]

Ironically the ambiguity that consistently obscures the concept of poverty in theological discourses is not resolved. In fact, the question looms more glaringly: Who are the poor? Are they men and women who had lost communion with God by being enslaved to sin, as *Libertatis Conscientias* implies? Are they those who by following the divine precepts with humility and devotion have made themselves worthy, according to Jesus, of inheriting the Kingdom of heaven? (Matt 5:3). Or are they simply the weak members of society who are materially deprived and socially disadvantaged and in need of help? In fact, neither liberation theology nor the Magisterium could boast of a satisfactory answer to this ambiguity which the concept of poverty presents. It is an ambiguity that will certainly continue to dog the footsteps of theological debates on how the appropriate locus of theological emphasis and social options should be determined. Whether we agree to a unified concept of poverty or not, what we are reminded here is that the real issue is centered on the purpose of the gospel and the Church's role in making the gospel alive and active. According to the Nigerian theologian, Orobator, "Some African theologians believe that the credibility and relevance of the church in Africa hinge on its ability to address the issues of poverty, socioeconomic stagnation and political instability. The question of whether or not the church should provide solutions to economic problems or involve itself in politics does not adequately capture the essence of the point at issue. The issue at stake here concerns the mission of the church as the agent

1. *Libertatis Conscientia*, 46.
2. Ibid., 47.

of proclaiming the good news of the Kingdom."[3] This proclamation must, however, express itself in a theoretical framework that is valid and faithful to a correct interpretation of God's redemptive purpose in human history.

Once confronted with a question from John the Baptist about whether he is the expected Messiah or not, Jesus answered with a reference that the good news is being proclaimed to the poor (Matt 11:4–5; Luke 7:22). Thus he indicates that the poor are the principal subjects of the messianic mission. They are unequivocally the decisive actors in the gospel narrative. But who are the poor? The importance of this question cannot be overemphasized, nor can its content be easily captured by a simple definition. The double meaning of poverty in the scriptures makes the case for this obscurity. But the notion of solidarity as a fraternal duty, which is expressed in *O nụrụ ube nwanne agbala ọsọ*, provides a plausible resolution to this theological impasse. There are two main notions of being poor that are distinguishable in the Scriptures: (1) the socio-economic sense and, (2) the spiritual sense, which some scholars identify as the gospel sense.

The Poor in Socio-Economic Sense

The sense of poverty best captured by a nineteenth century novelist, Marie Corelli, is what we may regard here as poverty in its socio-economic sense:

> Do you know what it is to be poor? Not poor with the arrogant poverty complained of by certain people who have five or six thousand a year to live upon, and who yet swear they can hardly manage to make both ends meet, but really poor,—downright, cruelly, hideously poor, with a poverty that is graceless, sordid and miserable? Poverty that compels you to dress in your one suit of clothes till it is worn threadbare,—that denies you clean linen on account of the ruinous charges of washerwomen,—that robs you of your own self-respect and causes you to slink along the streets vaguely abashed, instead of walking erect among your fellow-men in independent ease, this is the sort of poverty I mean.[4]

This picturesque description in a famous novel more than a century ago still captures vividly the very essence of the poverty that plagues millions of men and women in the world today, especially in Africa. This poverty entails not only lack of money or valuable property, but also lack of dignity as a consequence of material and pecuniary indigence. Corelli describes this poverty

3. Orobator, *Church as Family*, 45.
4. Corelli, *Sorrows of Satan*, 1.

as "the grinding curse that keeps down noble aspiration under a load of ignoble care; . . . the moral cancer that eats into the heart of an otherwise well-intentioned human creature and makes him envious and malignant,"[5] and inclined to violence. Corelli's fiction, *The Sorrows of Satan*, says it all. For this nineteenth century novelist, this type of poverty is not only debilitating to its victims, it is also unjust. It is a harrowing experience that makes one irate at the sight of the idle and licentious comfort of the rich; an experience that turns the good blood of a man into gall such that his suffering spirit rises in fierce rebellion crying out: "Why in God's name, should this injustice be? Why should a worthless lounger have his pockets full of gold by mere chance and heritage, while the poor, toiling wearily from dawn till dusk can scarcely afford himself a satisfying meal?"[6]

This socio-economic poverty is real and prevalent in our contemporary world and it affects many adversely. It is a crucible whose sometimes excruciating yoke is not easily diminished by preaching *the gospel of consolation* alone. Social actions that are decisive in engendering equity are necessary in order to eliminate or alleviate such poverty in the society. What liberation theology maintains is that the vantage point of the poor is particularly, and especially, the vantage point of the crucified God and can act as a criterion for theological reflection, biblical exegesis, and the life of the Church. The poor are the means whereby the Church can learn to discern the truth, direction and content of its mission, and they can assure the Church of being the place where the LORD is to be found.[7] In the Scriptures this economic sense of poverty is never deemphasized; on the contrary, it is confirmed as a challenge that enriches a spiritual dimension to the concept of poverty. The former is an evil to be overcome, the latter is salvific.

The Poor in the Sense of the Gospel

> "Then fixing his eyes on his disciples he said: How blessed are you who are poor: the kingdom of God is yours." (Luke 6:20; see also Matt 5:3)

The immediate thought that comes to mind at reading this verse of Luke's gospel is: Could Jesus have been implying that economically less privileged persons have unconditional entry ticket to heaven? That is improbable, and yet it is exactly what this gospel verse suggests. A synoptic comparison with

5. Ibid.

6. Ibid.

7. Rowland, *Cambridge Companion to Liberation Theology*, 95

Matt 5:3, however, illumines the inherent ambivalence that besets the gospel sense of the poor. The gospel reveals in addition to socio-economic poverty a new dimension of poverty that is purely spiritual and yet cannot be divorced from the material. The New Jerusalem Bible hence comments on Matt 5:3 that "the word 'poor' is used with the moral connotations already found in Zephaniah . . .made explicit by 'in spirit,' which is lacking in Luke."[8] In this sense, poverty goes hand in hand with "spiritual childhood" required for entrance into the kingdom. But although the formula of Matt 5:3 stresses the spirit of poverty for the rich as for the poor, Jesus usually has in mind actual material poverty, especially for his disciples.[9] Quite a good number of passages also testify to the material connotation of Jesus' references to poverty in the NT. The parable of the Dives and Lazarus (Luke 16:19–31) makes a clear case for the gospels' sense of the "poor" as one of privation of material goods. However, since such privation does not necessarily translate into a virtuous life, it is the spirit of poverty, i.e. the humility and simplicity that comes from the fear of God and love of neighbor, which guarantees a share in the life of the kingdom. Accordingly, the gospel integrates an economic and a spiritual dimension in its concept of the "poor." In this way, it makes clear that persons who are materially blessed also have a share in the beatitudes of the kingdom to the extent that their *pathos* for the poor leads them to appreciating their position of advantage as a privilege and a gift that should be invested in an effort towards eradicating man-made poverty and renewing the face of the earth. In fact, Jesus' encounter with the rich aristocrat who wanted to know what he should do to inherit eternal life demonstrates that such pathos is indispensable for discipleship (Luke 18:18–23; Matt 19:16–22; Mark 10:17–22).[10] Therefore, to hear the cry of a

8. Cf. The New Jerusalem Bible, *Footnote d.* to Matt 5. See also footnote to Zeph 2:3. The verse reads, "Seek YHWH, all you humble of the earth, who obey his commands. Seek uprightness, seek humility: you may perhaps find shelter on the Day of YHWH's anger." With Zephaniah, "poverty" assumes a moral and eschatological significance. In short, the *"anawim"* (a Hebrew term to designate the poor) are the Israelites who submit to the will of God. In the Septuagint period, the word *"anaw"* (or *"ani"*) comes to mean becoming poor and humble for the sake of others, and the victim of oppression.

9. Ibid.

10. "Jesus, looking at him, loved him and said to him, 'You are lacking in one thing. Go, sell what you have, and give to (the) poor and you will have treasure in heaven; then come, follow me.' At that statement his face fell, and he went away sad, for he had many possessions. Jesus looked around and said to his disciples, 'How hard it is for those who have wealth to enter the kingdom of God!' The disciples were amazed at his words. So Jesus again said to them in reply, 'Children, how hard it is to enter the kingdom of God! It is easier for a camel to pass through the eye of a needle than for one who is rich to enter the kingdom of God.' They were exceedingly astonished and said among themselves, 'Who then can be saved?'"

brother or a sister in need (which is implied in *O nụrụ ube nwanne agbala ọsọ*), and yet refuse to hearken is tantamount to excluding oneself from the life of the kingdom. But a fundamental question that arises here is: What form must this pathos take? Is it the form of mere pious almsgiving, or is more required in terms of commitment to establishing structural justice in the world? Theology in every age must be equipped to deal adequately with this question. The spiritual dimension of poverty, which Matt 5:3 under-scores, helps us to understand why those who serve oppression undisput-edly cannot be counted among the elect, however much they may suffer in this service themselves. For the condemnation, which Jesus pronounces here, is not for possessing wealth, but for valuing possessions more than persons. Those who, even though they are materially poor themselves, yet grease the machineries of oppression are hence also excluded from the king-dom. The second sense of poverty is the interior disposition—the measur-ing yardstick—which constitutes the standard for distinguishing the human from the inhuman. In other words, to be poor in this sense is to be human and to have compassion.

This type of poverty is voluntary and has a redemptive value. It is an act of love and liberation. If the ultimate cause of human exploitation and alienation is selfishness, the deepest reason for voluntary poverty will then be altruism, lived out as love of neighbor, who is primarily seen as a brother or sister to be carried on one's back, if need be. Christian poverty, therefore, has meaning only as a commitment of fraternal solidarity with the poor, with those who suffer misery and injustice. The commitment is to witness to the evil which has resulted from sin and is a breach of communion. It is not a question of idealizing poverty, but rather of taking it on as it is,—an evil—to protest against it and to struggle to abolish it. Because of this fra-ternal solidarity, which manifests itself in specific action—a style of life, a break with one's social class—one can also help the poor and exploited to become aware of their exploitation and seek liberation from it. Christian poverty, and expression of love, is solidarity with the poor and is a protest against poverty. In fact fraternal solidarity is the concrete, contemporary meaning of the witness of poverty. It is poverty lived not for its own sake, but rather as an authentic imitation of Christ; it is a poverty which means taking on the sinful human condition to liberate humankind from sin and all its consequences. Finally, it is a poverty that makes the "ears of our heart" attentive to the cries of the needy and the marginalized, thus animating us with a spirit of charity that is willing to sacrifice time, talent, energy and resources to make the gospel fruitful in concrete terms. In solidarity the poor takes up a new identity: he or she is perceived in a new way, namely, as a brother or a sister.

From the foregoing it is clear that the beatitudes, seen as the promise of reward to the poor, evoke the idea of God's justice and charity as a true divine "brother's Keeper." Indeed in all the praxis of liberation or solidarity, justice and charity are inseparably bound together. Therefore, I will examine in the next section of this chapter how the commitment to justice and charity constitute an essential element of true discipleship in the engagement with liberation and solidarity. Brief reviews of relevant encyclicals and apostolic exhortations help us in gaining an insight into how the Social Teaching of the Church affirms the importance of liberation as justice and liberation as service of charity. The critique of the select documents aims at identifying what the official church has failed to emphasize and the implications thereof.

Liberation as Justice

Even with her insistence that the poor should not be confused with the proletariat, the Church could not dodge the fact that if she is to be defined by her conscious solidarity with the poor and oppressed, she cannot be herself in today's Africa without rediscovering herself among the little people who cry for justice and liberty. Hence, African liberation theologians insist that she should find insupportable everything that wounds women and men, everything that attacks their lives, their future, their freedom, and their dignity.[11] Also in 1968 at Medellín, Colombia, theologians conceded that injustice was indeed a scandalous condition that deserves aggressive attention: it injured human dignity and was necessarily contrary to the will of the Christian God. But if God is one, then He surely has no religious denomination. He is neither Jewish nor Muslim; neither Buddhist nor Hindi nor Christian. The theme of justice and liberation thus becomes very important even beyond Christian theological circle.

Shabbir Akhtar, a Muslim theologian, took up that theme in a thought-provoking criticism of Christianity, whereby he is actually inveighing against Anglicanism. According to Akhtar,

> Christianity is an established faith, a religion that has been domesticated within an essentially upper- and middle-class domain. This truncated religion is appreciated and even applauded by the powerful secular establishment precisely because Christians humbly acknowledge their limits and rarely ask awkward questions that might awaken memories of that poor, derided, outcast, crucified God come to earth at the sight

11. Ela, *African Cry*. 76.

of human hubris. This post-Enlightenment Christianity, willingly confined to the private sphere of piety, silently legitimizes the established order which, in turn, regularly manipulates it for its own secular ends.[12]

Although informed by a negative stereotype that is predominantly political, Akhtar's perception of Anglicanism is not entirely without merits, but ironically the same arguments could be used against his own religion, Islam. Akhtar's idea of vindicative justice, which he uses to justify violence, is not indispensable in achieving liberation goals. But admittedly, the aim of a decisive religion, or say prophetic gospel, is to ensure that love does not lapse into tyranny anywhere in life and that Caesar does not usurp what belongs to God.[13] Temporal justice in fact foreshadows eternal justice, and faith in the latter should not diminish the importance of the need to fight for the former with all the resources available to us human beings. And in order to exercise temporal justice liberation is necessary. Akhtar's Islamic perspective argues this in a remarkable way. In praise of Islam, Akhtar contends that

> Muslims reject the view that when the instruments of social justice are distributed, Caesar should get the things that matter while God and His spokesman get the leftovers . . . An authentic faith, seeking to perpetuate the heritage of the good, must trade on a fund of *fierce anger* at the sight of the callous, the graceless, the life-denying, the unjust, the sordid, the impure, the 'inhuman' in the fullest sense of that rich word. Such a temper of constructive yet militant wrath is vital to any ideology that seeks security, an audience, and the triumph of truth in a world of sophisticated impiety.[14]

Whether Islam as religion actually satisfies Akhtar's ideal of social justice is surely debatable, but that is not our concern here. It is good to learn that Islam has its own theology of liberation, so long as liberation is understood as unmitigated justice for all. An important question, however, is whether such a "fierce anger" against human hubris is not recognizable in the nature of the God who revealed himself in Jesus Christ. Can we as Christians not appreciate as a religious duty the necessity of a passion for social justice that is committed to fighting oppression and injustice in the world? In Akhtar's polemic against Anglicanism, for instance, we hear that

12. Ibid.,14

13. Ibid.,7

14. Akhtar, *Final Imperative*, 110–11; my emphasis.

"Establishment" compromises authentic religion and is an effective secular technique for controlling the moral passion of supernatural faith; a way of curtailing its role as a potentially powerful force that might check the excesses of secular hubris, power and avarice. And Christ, were he to return, would surely be more comfortable among the despised and impoverished British Muslims than the Anglicans, whose presence among the poor and deprived grows more tenuous by the day.[15] In fact, what is valid for marginalized British Muslims here is much more valid for the Coptic Christians in Egypt or the Orthodox Christians in Syria. In the same way that Anglicanism cannot be the establishment of the faith of Jesus and his disciples, but rather its manifest subversion, so is it also legitimate to question whether Islam as practiced today can be the establishment of the Will of Allah? Faith and a worshipping community are mutually inherent, for our individual profession of faith in God is anchored in the witness of a community. Akhtar's polemic is directed against Anglicanism, but it cannot be limited to Anglicanism alone. It is valid for all instances of subversion of faith including the Islamic Faith. But such subversion of faith is rooted in an excessive appeal to exclusive identities that loses sight of the universal dimension of fraternity as willed by God. This universal dimension, whose sacramentality subsists in the ecclesial community, indicates that faith is essentially a community faith and not the sum of individual faiths. This has been true since the resurrection of Christ, which did not simply produce individual faiths, but called into being a community and brought about a situation in which faith had communality as an essential dimension. This means that we carry one another in the faith, give our own faith and receive it, so that, formally, it is the community that believes in Christ.[16] Authentic faith also enables us to embrace other people outside our own faith community as brothers and sisters.

Now if the community will have an enduring relevance for the individual, it must make justice an indispensable podium in the service of faith, for a community or society cannot be truly human if it is not just. But as Benedict XVI teaches, justice must always be accompanied by the gratuity of fraternal love. Official Christianity has unfortunately tended, in many historical contexts, to abet cruelty and injustice. South Africa is an obvious example of a country in modern time where the Christian creed has been used, or rather prostituted, to legitimize oppression. In this regard Akhtar's contentions, even when they sound too fiery, call for a deeper reflection:

15. Ibid., 15.

16. Sobrino, *Jesus the Liberator*, 29.

If there are social dimensions to individual evil, then a right form of piety, in its confrontation with the evil of structures, must have the resources to deal with the social, not merely the personal, consequences of such evil. And this is particularly true given the fact that collective evil is very likely in practice to assume militant forms. To concede, as Christians do, that evil takes on a structural aspect, yet to deny the need for a corresponding form of reckoning that is alert precisely to this structural dimension is, in effect, to make for an unrealistic and immature model of piety.[17]

Impiety, he reckons, "has, does, and will always assume militant forms in its opposition to righteousness. That is the way of the world—and one very conclusively demonstrated, ironically, in the ministry of Jesus."[18] Wherever the apparatus of the state is used to subvert justice, it is the Church or any religious institution that becomes the hope of the hopeless. But in such instances, Akhtar reminds us, powerlessness can be a very demoralizing experience. "Apolitical religion," according to him, "can easily corrode the hearts of religious men, who feel obliged to stand back, merely wringing their hands when confronted with the spectacles of oppression. What . . . can [sic] have been the inner state of the Lutheran bishops who refused to struggle against Hitler's regime? Can one compromise so fully with evil, and still be capable of prayer? It is for the modern Christian to explain to the world how such a conjunction might be imaginable, let alone achieved."[19]

Truly one may preach on behalf of the good and just cause, yet the world rarely casts its vote for truth. It is rather unfortunate, but that is the evident reality of the human constituency. We are often like Pilate, who asks: "What is truth?"(cf. John 18:38), as if he were really interested to know, and then ends up crucifying the truth that stands before him and washed his hands in a travesty of innocence after having denied justice to the innocent. Is it the true hallmark of the man of God to feel constantly vulnerable and helpless in the face of the cruel powers of the world? Might we not reverently question such a verdict? These are the questions that both Muslim and Christian liberation theologians posit. They are admittedly also questions, which liberation theology as we know it cannot alone satisfactorily answer. An enlightened truth about the meaning of solidarity understood properly as a right perception of other people, and a theology that articulates this

17. Akhtar, *Final Imperative*, 38.

18. Ibid., 39–40.

19. Ibid., 62–63. What is said of Lutheran bishops here applies also to some Catholic bishops. However, it must be admitted that a good number of Christians including priests sacrificed their lives or took heroic risks in opposing the Nazi regime.

truth is required. For if we really perceive the oppressed, the marginalized and the weak, as brothers and sisters, our moral response to the harrowing conditions that yoke their life will witness radical change. It is such an enlightened perception of "the suffering other" that is antecedent to any objective and positive appreciation of liberative justice. And such a justice is not one that is rooted in the law, but rather in the Christian and humanistic conscience committed to reforming the structures of society. As Donal Dorr rightly noted,

> In order to bring about justice in society it is not enough to ensure that there is equality before the law. For instance, a poor person may have the right to take a court action against a wealthy but may not have enough money to hire the legal experts required to win the case. Or a worker may be forced by poverty to accept an unjust wage. The same kind of thing arises at the international level in trading relations between nations. Each country may have the right to sell goods on the open market. But this does not ensure just trading. The poorer nations are at a great disadvantage, for they are living 'from hand to mouth,' without the resources they would need to drive a hard bargain for their goods.[20]

What is required is a new attitude and form of interpersonal socialization that will then be instrumental to a corresponding change in structures of institution in order to effectively curb unbridled cupidity, religious bigotry, chauvinism, racism, ethnicism, and all the malignant "isms" that pollute harmonious coexistence. How the Catholic Church has fared in the past or how she will fare in the future concerning these social issues will depend on how and where she places emphasis in her Social Teaching. In reading through some of the social Encyclicals one sees ample support for a theology of fraternity as well as a failure to really see the theme of fraternity as being central in the global social context where theology operates. The first three encyclicals that I would like to review are selected because of their preoccupation with the theme of justice. They give us insight into what extent the social teaching of the Church have succeeded or failed in addressing the issues of solidarity in human society.

Rerum Novarum

This popular encyclical, *Rerum Novarum*, "On Capital and Labor" was issued on May 15, 1891 by Pope Leo XIII. Albeit an old document whose

---

20. Dorr, *Social Justice Agenda*, 27.

historical context is located in the nineteenth century industrial milieu, my choice of this important document for a review here is obvious. It is the first of its kind in articulating the Church's concern about the temporal welfare of peoples. *Rerum Novarum* launched the Church into the center of social issues in the society and thus represents the first litmus test of how attentive the Church is to the cry of suffering humanity. It was the Pope's opportunity to give the response of the Catholic Church to the social instability and labor conflict that heralded the rise of industrialization and ideological socialism in Europe. The Pope stated the obligation of the State to promote social justice through the protection of rights, and defended the right of the Church to speak out on social issues in order to teach correct social principles and ensure class harmony. He restated the Church's long-standing teaching regarding the crucial importance of the right to private property, but he also acknowledged, in one of the best-known passages of the encyclical, that the free operation of market forces must be tempered by moral considerations. And what are these moral considerations?

> Let it be granted then that worker and employer may enter freely into agreements and, in particular, concerning the amount of the wage; yet there is always underlying such agreements an element of natural justice, and one greater and more ancient than the free consent of contracting parties, namely, that the wage shall not be less than enough to support a frugal and upright wage-earner. If, compelled by necessity or moved by fear of a worse evil, a worker accept a harder condition, which although against his will he must accept because an employer or contractor imposes it, he certainly submits to force, against which justice cries out in protest.[21]

In the above sense, the brother's cry that is implied in *Ọ nụrụ ube nwanne agbala ọsọ*, includes situations of veiled injustice where the poor is shrewdly forced into accepting unpleasant compromises because of absence of any other favorable alternative. Such a clever manipulation of the poor would be against the spirit of fraternal solidarity. The encyclical *RN* is in this regard significant, for it represents the first major stride of the Church in defense of the poor as well as her first major intervention in social issues. Even though the document could be said to have been primarily motivated by the Church's anxiety over instability in the society as some critics claim,[22]

---

21. Leo XIII, *Rerum Novarum*, 63.

22. Dorr, *Option for the Poor*, 52. According to Dorr, "there was an almost neurotic fear of social disorder—so much so that nearly every other social value was in practice subordinated to the values of stability and harmony in the society."

RN, nevertheless, deserves credit for articulating some of the important principles of liberative justice, even if it is not concerned with liberation as such. It was the Church's first initiative toward what would later develop as a radical option for the poor. The encyclical criticizes socialism for what it sees as injuring the very ones whom it seeks to help and for throwing public peace into confusion.[23] It also defended vigorously the right to private ownership of property as inviolate, a right whose violation would only result in the repudiation of the State as commonwealth.

RN is remarkable for its vivid depiction of the plight of the nineteenth-century urban poor and for its condemnation of unrestricted capitalism. Among the remedies it prescribed were the formation of trade unions and the introduction of collective bargaining, particularly as an alternative to state intervention. *RN* recognizes that the poor have a special status in the consideration of social issues: the modern Catholic principle of the "preferential option for the poor" and the notion that God is on the side of the poor found their first muted expression in this document. But even in its stance in defense of the poor, it warns against the danger of claiming idealistic competence to wholly banish tribulations and suffering from human life. The Encyclical accuses ideological socialists of promising the poor in their misery a life free from all sorrow and vexation and filled with repose and perpetual pleasures, and condemns such promise as a perpetuation of fraud which ultimately leads to an imposition of greater evils.[24] It is perfectly right in this assumption, for we cannot eliminate suffering in the same way that we cannot eliminate hope.

RN also remonstrates against the notion that "one class of society is of itself hostile to the other, as if nature had set rich and poor against each other to fight fiercely in implacable war."[25] Nevertheless, its assertion of the complementarities of labor and capital, of rich and poor, begs the question about its understanding of the cause of perpetual strife in human society. Notwithstanding that the assertion of mutual complementarity is necessary and in itself true, it fails to see however, that the selfish attitudes that lie at the root of exploitation is rooted in the utilitarian and materialistic perception of one another—a perception that shuns to appreciate the common heritage of the human family and the dignity and equality of all members of that family. It fails to recognize that master/slave mentality should be destroyed entirely in order to make room for a brother/sister atmosphere in the society. In this sense, *RN* fails in adequately diagnosing the problem it

23. *RN*, 23.
24. *RN*, 27.
25. *RN*, 28.

sought to eliminate, for if the rich were to see in the exploited *poor* the faces of beloved sisters and brothers, who are dehumanized by capitalist greed, then human society may have acquired the type of conscience that is needed to advance human and Christian civilization.

But *RN* alone is not to blame for its myopic diagnoses; the influence of Marxist Socialism with its theory of dialectical scientific materialism, which led to an illusory classless society, is not to be overlooked. The problem with scientific materialism is that it sought to analyze society and social conflict only in terms of capital and labor. Such an analysis of society fails to give account of gender, racial, ethnic, and religious conflicts, which are sometimes much more volatile, much more widespread, much more dehumanizing and divisive than material class conflict in a homogenous society. Responding to the short-sighted socialist discourse, *RN* also laid emphasis basically on the right to private property and a fair wage. But it is, in fact, the arrogance and utilitarianism of the privileged and the envy of the less privileged that concert to blur the vision of fraternal unity of the human family and consequently jeopardize peace and common good. These vices are the insidious inclinations that erect walls of division in which material prosperity for some becomes a stumbling block rather than a blessing to societal harmony. The important revelation, which *RN* makes however, is that this stumbling block can be overcome by virtue. it asserts that "true dignity and excellence in men resides in moral living, that is, in virtue; virtue is the common inheritance of man, attainable equally by the humblest and the mightiest, by the rich and the poor; and the reward of eternal happiness will follow upon virtue and merit alone, regardless of the person in whom they may be found."[26]

According to Pope Leo XIII, the Church's contribution to the society lies in "the very fact that she calls men [and women] to and trains them in virtue."[27] One particular virtue could be named here as obviously indispensable in the task of ameliorating the human condition: the virtue of solidarity. It is this virtue that will become a major theme of most of later social encyclicals under subsequent Popes. Pope John Paul II defines it as a Christian virtue, which seeks to go beyond itself, to take on the specifically Christian dimensions of total gratuity, forgiveness and reconciliation. Through an awareness of the common fatherhood of God, of the brotherhood of all in Christ—"children in the Son"—and of the presence and life-giving action of

26. *RN*, 37.
27. *RN*, 42.

the Holy Spirit, this virtue brings to our vision of the world a new criterion for interpreting it.[28]

Having acknowledged the positive contributions of RN, it is pertinent to mention that its shortcoming lies in selling out an apparent image of the Church as an unconscious (or even hypocritical) ally of the powerful.[29] This perception is not without basis, for Pope Leo XIII "recognizes that it is those who are economically deprived who pose a threat to political stability. And he spells out the role of religion in helping to meet and overcome that threat by placating the poor. This is done most effectively by promising them rewards in heaven proportionate to the miseries they have endured patiently on earth."[30] Pope Leo, for example, unashamedly speaks of how the Church cheers and comforts the hearts of the poor by setting before them the example of Christ, or by reminding them that Jesus called them "blessed" and told them to hope for the reward of eternal happiness. The Pope adds that this is obviously the best way to lessen the undying struggle between rich and poor and uniting them in a new bond of friendship.[31]

The most unfortunate weakness of RN, thence, lies in its defense of political authority. It holds the view that the exercise of sovereign power derives always from God's moral authority. That means, irrespective of whether the structures of a sovereign state are better or its office holders more just than the previous regime, its legitimacy depends on the fact that it now holds effective power. To put it crudely, "God backs only the winners." God gives the right to demand allegiance and obedience only to those who successfully retain or gain actual control of the apparatus of government. The determining factor then is not justice but power.[32] Worse still, if citizens cannot obtain justice within the existing system they may not take further step of trying to topple it by means declared illegal by the regime itself. Injustice must then be endured, for to challenge the system, even in defense of justice, is to challenge the authority of God.[33] Similar arguments have been evoked also in criticizing liberation theologians. Donal Dorr makes an important and plausible observation about the historical background of the encyclical:

28. John Paul II, *Solicitudo Rei Socialis*, 40.

29. See Dorr, *Option for the Poor*, 35. According to Dorr, critics believe that the Catholic Church and its associations served the function, whether deliberately or not, of making workers less likely to take militant action in pursuit of better pay and conditions.

30. Ibid.,39.

31. Cf. *RN*, 37.

32. See Dorr, *Option for the Poor*, 46.

33. Ibid.,47.

There was an almost neurotic fear of social disorder—so much so that nearly every other social value was in practice subordinated to the values of stability and harmony in society.

One effect of this conservative stance was that many of those who worked for radical change in society perceived the Church as part of the established order; so they tended to be anti-Christian, or at least anti-Church. The effect of the sharp polarization was that each side lived up to the worst expectations of the other. The revolutionaries fulfilled the fears of Church leaders that their aims were anti-Christian. And the Churchmen lived up to the Marxist accusation that they were allies of the dominant class, using religion to inhibit radical social change.[34]

Certainly Pope Leo XIII seems to be oblivious of the inherent contradiction of his own position. He felt obliged to defend the existing political order while condemning the existing economic order despite his acknowledgement of the fact that the two were so closely interlinked; that the rich, who he admits have gained power (*RN* 35), could use the machinery of the State to promote their interests at the expense of the poor. It is difficult for critics not to see this imbalance as a result of ideological prejudice. Hence, liberation theology would later favor a new hermeneutic in theological discourses. And according to this new hermeneutic, God is partial (standing on the side of the poor), and to pretend to be impartial is to renounce God's side in the struggle for social justice. A shift became imperative in which subsequent social teaching, especially since Pope John XXIII, no longer saw the need to emphasize private property rights, but rather justice. *Populorum Progressio* represents remarkably such a new shift in Catholic Social Teaching.

Populorum Progressio

Populorum Progressio (PP) distinguishes itself as an encyclical that makes a thorough and laudable diagnosis of the problems of the human society. In one of its lines *PP* categorically declares that the world is sick, and its illness consists less in the unproductive monopolization of resources by a small number of men than in the *lack of brotherhood* among individuals and peoples.[35] This important observation marked out this encyclical as an indispensable vade mecum for the theology of fraternity. Obviously, the problem with the world is not the fact of having rich people in the society living side

---

34. Ibid., 52–53.

35. Paul VI, *Populorum Progressio*, 66. Hereafter cited as *PP.*

by side very poor people, but rather the rich man's lack of awareness that the poor man is his brother. The encyclical prays for the day to dawn when international relations will be marked by mutual respect and friendship, interdependence in collaboration, and when the betterment of all will be seen as the responsibility of each individual.[36] That new dawn has for long remained elusive as a result of human hubris and has thus challenged some theologians to set a new and radical emphasis, no longer on development but on liberation. No one can doubt the urgency and moral imperative of the radical transformation demanded by such a new emphasis whose goal is to improve the living conditions of millions of people, mostly Africans, who are languishing in abject poverty. Hence, Paul VI in this encyclical, *Progress of Peoples*, urges: "We must make haste: too many people are suffering, and the distance is growing that separates the progress of some and the stagnation, not to say the regression, of others."[37] This growing distance between rich and poor betrays an internal disposition that is diametrically opposed to the culture of our Christian ancestors of the Jerusalem community in Acts 4:32–35.[38] This is not to advocate a return to the Christian culture of the first century, but to underscore that we must understand that the success of the Church and of human civilization is rooted in such positive mutual perception and appreciation of one another as sisters and brothers, which made it possible for them to be united in solidarity by carrying one another.

The encyclical *Populorum Progressio* frankly and aptly observes that industrialists, merchants, leaders or representatives of larger enterprises are not lacking in social sensitivity in their own country, yet they unfortunately return to the inhuman principles of individualism when they operate in less developed countries.[39] Why? To answer this question is apparently the task of a theology of fraternity. It is a question that calls all of us to re-examine how we perceive and relate with one another in general; a question that will continue to provide the material resources for a theology of solidarity and fraternity in an era of globalization.

In its first paragraph, *PP* makes explicit those to whom the Church's developmental efforts are dedicated: the concern is of "those peoples who are striving to escape from hunger, misery, endemic diseases and ignorance; of those who are looking for a wider share in the benefits of civilization and a more active improvement of their human qualities; of those who are

36. *PP*, 65.

37. *PP*, 29.

38. St. Luke the Evangelist tells us in Acts 4:32–35 that the members of the early Christian community were united, heart and soul. None was ever in want, for people shared what they had so that each person's needs could be satisfied.

39. *PP*, 70.

aiming purposefully at their complete fulfillment."[40] And as long as the goal of complete fulfillment still remains unachieved, developmental dynamics in the modern world stand to be constantly revised theologically. To abandon this utopia is to betray the gospel or make it barren; it is to kill the spirit of hope for humanity. Hence, the Church gives as reason for her ardent concern a renewed consciousness of the demands of the Gospel and the urgency of solidarity in action.[41] The restoration of solidarity will not only be a sacred duty for the Church, but also one of the most essential tasks of aggiornamento, of which the Church is a powerful advocate. It is a task that consists in hearing and responding urgently to the cry of suffering humanity, not only through humanitarian crisis relief, but also more importantly through global filial friendship. The Encyclical, *PP* remarkably takes up this humanitarian task and calls for a loving response of charity to the *brother's cry for help*—a cry of anguish at which the Church shudders.[42] Hence, the document asserts:

> There can be no progress towards the complete development of man without the simultaneous development of all humanity in the spirit of solidarity . . . Man must meet man, nation meet nation, *as brothers and sisters* [my emphasis], as children of God. In this mutual understanding and friendship, in this sacred communion, we must also begin to work together to build the common future of the human race.[43]

Thus *PP* emphasized the ethical and cultural character of the problems connected with development, as well as the legitimacy and necessity of the Church's intervention in this field.[44] And in a brief and very cautiously worded statement it even acknowledged that in certain extreme circumstances a revolutionary uprising might be permissible.[45] This is a view, which some conservative Catholics have hoped to fault with a rather ambiguous theory of violence.[46] Albeit the document was careful to avoid details on this

40. *PP*, 1.

41. *PP*, 1.

42. *PP*, 3

43. *PP*, 43.

44. See John Paul II, *Solicitudo Rei Socialis*, 8. Hereafter cited as *SRS*

45. *PP*, 31.

46. George Weigel of the Ethics and Public Policy Center in Washington, DC, while appraising the latest Encyclical, *Caritas in Veritate*, criticizes *Populorum Progressio* and suggests that "Paul VI himself had recognized that the Encyclical had misfired in certain respects, being misread in some quarters as a tacit papal endorsement of violent revolution in the name of social justice." He makes a bogus claim that *Centesimus Annus* implicitly recognized the defects and that Pope Paul tried to correct this mistake in

type of intervention, one could read between its lines a tacit endorsement of the opinion that a pure individual heart alone is no bulwark against an unjust order. According to such opinion, to refuse to move from the realm of preaching to that of activism when necessity calls for it is seen as a subtle form of compromise. For militant evil can only be dislodged by the forces of good in an equally militant posture.[47] But in order to be able to shun such militancy (*which is what the Church desires*), the Encyclical proffered as solution a humanism that is complete and ethical, in contradistinction to an isolated or inhuman humanism. It cautioned against the latter as a humanism that is closed in on itself, and not open to the values of the Spirit and to God, and accordingly capable of achieving only apparent success.[48]

If true humanism is to be achieved, better-off nations are obliged on a threefold aspect:

1. the duty of human solidarity—the aid that the rich nations must give to developing countries;

2. the duty of social justice—the rectification of inequitable trade relations between powerful nations and weak nations;

3. the duty of universal charity—the effort to bring about a world that is more human towards all men and women, where all will be able to give and receive, without one group making progress at the expense of the other.[49]

---

his 1971 apostolic letter, *Octogesima Adveniens*. Instead of lauding the Pontiff for such bold sincerity, Weigel sees it as an unintended misfiring (Weigel, "*Caritas in Veritate* in Gold and Red"). It is worth noting that the same Weigel, who is so wary of papal endorsement of violent revolution, has remained a zealous defender of the Iraq War with all sorts of vehement arguments in favor of legitimate and necessary violence in the service of "World Order." Cf. Weigel, "Just War and Iraq Wars," 14–15. See also "What Catholics Forgot," where Weigel eulogizes Pope John Paul II for playing a significant role in effecting the collapse of the Soviet Union, igniting revolution in Poland and in the Philippines, and helping democratic transitions in El Salvador, Nicaragua, Chile, and Argentina. Weigel speaks as if all these came about without the heroic sacrifices of those committed to the liberation struggle. However, I think that Weigel's opinion represents a cross-section of bourgeois theologians whose opinions seem to mask an ideological prejudice that seek to hijack catholic teaching and twist it to serve partisan idiosyncrasies. Their inconsistent and selective logic betrays an insincerity that could be exasperating.

47. This view is that of a Muslim theologian, Shabbir Akhtar, *The Divine Imperative*, 85. But it is an opinion that is obviously shared by some catholic theologians, especially liberation theologians.

48. Pope Paul VI, *PP*, 42.

49. *PP*, 44.

"Peace," the encyclical notes, "cannot be limited to a mere absence of war, the result of an ever precarious balance of forces. No, peace is something that is built up day after day, in the pursuit of an order intended by God, which implies a more perfect form of justice among men."[50] The work of development will draw nations together in the attainment of goals pursued with a common effort, if all, from governments and their representatives to the last expert, are inspired by brotherly love and moved by the sincere desire to build a civilization founded on world solidarity.[51] *PP* is convinced that the struggle against destitution, the task of eliminating hunger or reducing poverty, is not enough. What is required is building a world where every man or woman, no matter what his or her race, religion or nationality, can live a fully human life, freed from servitude imposed on him or her by other men and women or by natural forces over which he or she has not sufficient control; a world where freedom is not an empty word and where the poor man Lazarus can sit down at the same table with the rich man.[52] The responsibility to create such a world is a gospel imperative. This type of justice envisaged in *Populorum Progressio* finds an inculturated echo in the Igbo saying, "*Ọ nụrụ ube nwanne agbala ọsọ.*"

Solicitudo Rei Socialis

Twenty years later Pope John Paul II notes with disappointment that the problems of society, which the Encyclical *Populorum Progressio* set out to address, still remain unresolved. Neither through the fault of the needy men, women and children, nor "of inevitability dependent on natural conditions or circumstances," there still exist serious problems of unequal distribution of the means of subsistence originally meant for everybody, and an unequal distribution of the benefits deriving from them.[53] The hopes for development, once alive, suddenly appeared far from being realized.[54] Faced with a waning optimism about overcoming the ever widening gap between rich and poor, between the different *worlds*,[55] the Pontiff acknowledges that

50. *PP*, 76.

51. *PP*, 73.

52. *PP*, 47.

53. John Paul II, *SRS*, 9.

54. *SRS*. 12.

55. *SRS*, 14. Pope John Paul II observes that the nomenclature that speaks of different worlds within our *one world* is an unhealthy symptom of a divided humanity. Such expressions as "Fourth World," he notes, is used not just occasionally for the so-called *less advanced* countries, but also and especially for the bands of great or extreme poverty in countries of medium and high income. But all in all, this invention of a

the unity of the human race is seriously compromised—a fact before whose moral content the Church cannot afford to remain indifferent. Hence, he says,

> However much society worldwide shows signs of fragmentation, expressed in the conventional names First, Second, Third and even Fourth World, their *interdependence* remains close. When this interdependence is separated from its ethical requirements, it has disastrous consequences for the weakest. Indeed, as a result of a sort of internal dynamic and under the impulse of mechanisms which can only be called perverse, this interdependence triggers negative effects even in the rich countries.[56]

Accordingly, the Pope saw a need to denounce the existence of those economic, financial and social mechanisms which, although they are manipulated by people, often function almost automatically, thus accentuating the situation of wealth for some and poverty for the rest. These mechanisms, which are maneuvered directly or indirectly by the more developed countries, by their very functioning favor the interest of the people manipulating them.[57] A typical example is the case in the USA in 2010, where C.E.O.s, apparently unabashed by their greed and fiscal irresponsibility which brought about the collapse of global economy, are nonetheless cashing in enormous amount in bonuses from taxpayers' money in the midst of an economic recession. The poor were losing their jobs in millions and the rich, unruffled, were sharing out the money provided by the state to help cushion the financial distress for the benefit of poor people. Who would not be outraged with a system or structure that makes such a scandal thinkable let alone possible? It is, in fact, symptomatic of "a real desertion of a moral obligation" about which the Encyclical speaks. It is a betrayal of humanity's legitimate expectations in the task of alleviating human misery—a betrayal that is a harbinger of unforeseeable consequences.[58]

However, *SRS* observes with optimism that "in a world divided and beset by every type of conflict, the conviction is growing of a radical interdependence and consequently of the need for a solidarity which will take up interdependence and transfer it to the moral plane."[59] If there is anything a theology of solidarity is expected to achieve, it is precisely this. The start-

---

new hierarchy of worlds is a shameful index of an undesirable stratification that serves neither mutual respect nor human development.

56. *SRS*, 17.

57. *SRS*, 16.

58. *SRS*, 23.

59. *SRS*. 26.

ing point, however, is a deep and revolutionary attitude that recognizes that we all share a common destiny and a common aspiration, which demands a renunciation of selfishness. It is part of the divine plan that the human community will rise, through personal and collective efforts, to overcome those obstacles that obscure our way to God. And one of the most crucial of those obstacles is a vision of self and the other that has lost its theistic orientation because it is rooted in an exclusive identity that is oppressive as much as it is jaundiced. Hence, *SRS* adroitly points out that "the obstacles to integral development are not only economic but rest on more profound attitudes which human beings can make into absolute values."[60] Therefore, theology today, far from investing too much in an abstract intellectual sport on the nature of God and history, must point out the direction of change for human attitudes.

Liberation as Service of Charity

As already mentioned above, the two inseparable components of liberation and solidarity are justice and charity, that is, charity understood as an act of love for another human being. The encyclicals treated above provide us handful information on how the Social Teaching of the Church has understood and dealt with the issues of social justice in the society. In this section of this chapter, I will study further two encyclicals from Pope Benedict XVI in addition to the post-synodal apostolic exhortation *Ecclesia in Africa*. The following documents' engagement with the theme of charity informs the interest in them as relevant to the theology of fraternity. According to Pope Benedict XVI, the essential elements of Christian and ecclesial charity consist in the simple response to immediate needs and specific situations: feeding the hungry, clothing the naked, caring for and healing the sick, visiting those in prison, etc.[61] These services constitute not only examples of humanism, but also the ultimate imperative of the kingdom of God: "So far as you did it to one of the least of these my brethren, you did it to me," says Jesus (Matt 25:40). The vision of humankind that is made explicit in these corporal works of mercy is one that sees and treats others as brethren of Jesus Christ, the God who takes human form. It is on this note that *Deus Caritas Est* enunciates how charity liberates by complementing justice. Hence, the encyclical rightly states that even in the most just society, love—*caritas*—will always prove necessary.

---

60. *SRS*. 38.
61. Benedict XVI, *Deus Caritas Est*, 31. Hereafter cited as *DCE*.

> There will always be suffering which cries out for consolation and help. There will always be loneliness. There will always be situations of material need where help in the form of concrete love of neighbor is indispensable. The State which would provide everything, absorbing everything into itself, would ultimately become a mere bureaucracy incapable of guaranteeing the very thing which the suffering person—every person—needs: namely, loving personal concern.[62]

Thus the Church views liberation also in terms of service of charity. However, charity is to be understood here not merely as a sharing of one's possession but rather of one's self, through a deep personal sharing in the needs and sufferings of others. John Paul II clarifies that solidarity is not a feeling of vague compassion or shallow distress at the misfortunes of so many people, both near and far. On the contrary, it is a firm and persevering determination to commit oneself to the common good; that is to say, to the good of all and of each individual, because we are all really responsible for all.[63] How the church should articulate the nature of this mutual responsibility is an important subject-matter of the theology of fraternity. And in an African context that is central here, *Ecclesia in Africa* is an important theological resource that deserves special attention.

Ecclesia in Africa

"Charity begins at home" is a popular saying that cannot be made trite even by clichéd usage. And home is undoubtedly that place where individuals normally find solace in the profound awareness and appreciation of their mutual interdependence. It will be improper to talk in context about charity as an essential aspect of solidarity without bringing the discussion home, to Africa. How does the present Africa meet up with the above definition of home? This is a question that has been partially dealt with in chapter one. *Ecclesia in Africa (EIA)*, which is the fruit of the Synod of Bishops for Africa, made significant observations that are not previously unknown, but which remain relevant and always in need of being reiterated. The Synod Fathers regrettably noted that, within the borders left by the colonial powers, one often meets obstacles to co-existence of ethnic groups with different traditions, languages, and even religions. Inter-tribal oppositions, arising from mutual hostility, at times endanger not only peace, but also the pursuit of the common good, and create difficulties for the life of the Churches and

62. *DCE*, 28.
63. John Paul II, *SRS*, 39.

the acceptance of Pastors from other ethnic groups.[64] Healing these divisions poses a great challenge to the Church in Africa. Acknowledging this challenge, the document asks: "How could one fail to take into account the anguished history of a land where many nations are still in the grip of famine, war, racial and tribal tensions, political instability and the violation of human rights?"[65] As the Synod grappled in its deliberations with the issue of how Christians could bring to bear upon the social fabric an influence of change not only on the ways of thinking but also on the structures of society, the Synod Fathers came up with an ecclesiology that taps from the anthropological, theological and sociological resources of the African life.

> Not only did the Synod speak of inculturation, but it also made use of it, taking the *Church* as *God's Family* as its guiding idea for the evangelization of Africa. The Synod Fathers acknowledged it as an expression of the Church's nature particularly appropriate for Africa. For this image emphasizes care for others, solidarity, warmth in human relationships, acceptance, dialogue and trust. The new evangelization will thus aim at *building up the Church as Family*, avoiding all ethnocentrism and excessive particularism, trying instead to encourage reconciliation and true communion between different ethnic groups, favoring solidarity and the sharing of personnel and resources among the particular Churches, without undue ethnic considerations.[66]

The Synod expressed the hope that theologians in Africa will work out the theology of the Church as Family with all the riches contained in this concept, showing its complementarity with other images of the Church.[67] But as much as this image of the Church as family has been mouthed, to what extent its connotation goes beyond empty platitudes to touch the depth of theological consciousness of Christians who adopt and endorse the image leaves much to be desired. Agatha Radoli aptly notes that

> It is shocking to Christians that church buildings were turned into sites of carnage during the 1994 Rwandan genocide. They keep on asking themselves questions like: How could Catholics desecrate Christ's Presence in the Blessed Sacrament by slaughtering their *brothers and sisters* in the churches? What drove

64. John Paul II, *Post-Synodal Exhortation, Ecclesia in Africa*, 49. Hereafter cited as *EIA*

65. *EIA*, 51.

66. *EIA*, 63.

67. *EIA*, 63.

them to such a degree of savagery that *they could not even hear
the cries of innocent children* as they died in agony?[68]

The most adequate and pertinent question here would be: Do those
Catholics really realize that the innocent victims they slaughtered were their
"brothers and sisters"?[69] If they did not, as would be supposed, how could
theology help to heal such a dangerous spiritual blindness? And if they
knew, what moral justification, if any, could be proffered for slaughtering
one's brothers and sisters, or stand as spectator to watch it happen? These are
the kind of relevant questions that ought to shape the outline of a theology
that seeks to go beyond liberation hermeneutics. Hence, in the light of *Ọ
nụrụ ube nwanne agbala ọsọ*, what transpired in Rwanda is an abomination
which undermined the ecclesiology of the African synod. In recent times,
there have also been cases where catholic faithful vehemently rejected the
installation of diocesan bishops simply on the ground that the elected can-
didate is not from their ethnic group. What do such xenophobic attitudes
portend for the church's evangelical mission? They only empty Christian
evangelization in Africa of authentic meaning and rob its transformative
power for building community. For the significance of the ecclesiology of
the "Church as family" is that it speaks of the depth of the concept of family
in African culture and worldview, and enables Africans to understand the
dynamic interrelationship between Church and family. No better term than
family expresses the beauty and richness of the Church in Africa. One of the
Synod's post-plenary reports notes:

> African family is a living cell from which models of the Church
> and experiences lived in Africa is found. The family is a place of
> reproduction, of transmission and of protection of life, a place of
> learning and of interiorizing cultural values, a place of sharing,
> of support and of fraternal welcome, a place where people live
> together. The family is the fundamental base of humanity and
> of society. It is the place where human problems are realistically
> solved—problems of orphans, of the aged and of the lonely.[70]

This is why the recrudescence of ethnicism within the church's sanctu-
ary remains a vital challenge that must not be ignored. The Synod Fathers,
appropriating the image of the family, pledged a renewal of commitment to

---

68. Radoli, Preface to Aguilar, *Rwandan Genocide*, vi; my emphasis.

69. It is true that the victims of the Rwandan genocide were first of all disparaged as
"cockroaches" in a nation-wide hate propaganda in order to make it easier to slaughter
them in hundreds of thousands without qualms of conscience.

70. *Relatio Post Disceptationem*, 5. Cited by Omuta, *From Vatican II to African
Synod*, 96.

the Church's prophetic role to be the voice of the voiceless[71] and an agent of reconciliation. In a continent burdened by man-made suffering, this is understandably the essential task of liberation in the service of charity, but it is a task that can be achieved by first and foremost identifying the root of the problems that plague human society as a family. *EIA's* unfortunate pitfall is that it glossed over this task. For instance, what is the meaning of charity and solidarity in the context of a Church that sees itself as a *Family of God*? What type of attitude or spirituality should characterize the people of God in such a family? These are important questions to which *EIA* failed to provide adequate answers. In search of the answers that corroborate a theology of fraternity we turn then to the pontificate of Benedict XVI.

Deus Caritas Est

This encyclical begins with an affirmation of the biblical identification of love with God, which is read in the First Letter of John as expressing the heart of the Christian faith, i.e., the Christian image of God and the resulting image of mankind and its destiny.[72] Pope Benedict XVI explains that his choice of this theme was necessitated by a world in which the name of God is sometimes associated with vengeance or even a duty of hatred and violence.[73] With the rise of global terrorism, which is motivated more by hatred than by religious puritanism, the Pope's pastoral consideration to present Love to the world in its most radical form could not have come at a better time. The Pope's idea of contemplation of the pierced side of Christ (cf. John 19:37), in which the Christian discovers the path along which his life and love must move, evokes the image of the *crucified people*, which is at the center of liberation theology's contemplation of the incarnate Logos. Building upon Pauline theology of the Eucharist, the Pope reminds us that "union with Christ is also union with all those to whom he gives himself. (. . .) Faith, worship and *ethos* are interwoven as a single reality which takes shape in our encounter with God's *agape*."[74] But what is this God's agape in concrete terms?

The biblical parables that were cited by the Pope to corroborate his theological argument are very informative and important here. In the parable of Lazarus and dives, for example (cf. Luke 16: 19–31), the rich man begs from his place of torment that his brothers be informed about what

71. Cf. *EIA*, 70.

72. Benedict XVI, *DCE*, 1.

73. *DCE*, 1.

74. *DCE*, 14.

happens to those who ignore the poor man's needs. Jesus takes up this cry for help as a warning to redirect his hearers to the right path—the path of righteousness characterized by the consciousness of the bond that makes all, rich and poor, children of Abraham and ultimately brothers and sisters in God's family. Again the parable of the Good Samaritan (cf. Luke 10: 25–37), which the Pope cites,

> offers two particularly important clarifications. Until that time, the concept of 'neighbor' was understood as referring essentially to one's countrymen and to foreigners who had settled in the land of Israel; in other words, to closely-knit community of a single country or people. This limit is now abolished. Anyone who needs me, and whom I can help, is my neighbor. The concept of 'neighbor' is now universalized, yet it remains concrete. Despite being extended to all mankind, it is not reduced to a generic, abstract and undemanding expression of love, but calls for my own practical commitment here and now.[75]

This parable helps us in understanding the ecclesiology of *Nwanne dị na mba* which will be treated later in chapter 4. Meanwhile, one sees from the above mentioned parables that the most revolutionary aspect of Jesus' teaching is that he helps us rediscover ourselves in a new form of boundary-breaking socialization. In other words, he offers us a perspective that helps us look beyond *the individual* in order to see *the human being*. The object of our hatred or disdain is the *individual* who may be lazy, ugly, wretched, unlettered, and ill-mannered; he may be the brother or sister of a terrorist, or whatever makes him or her objectionable to us; but *the human being* is always the *imago Dei*. The more sacrificial it is to love *the human being*, the nearer that love brings us to the kingdom of God and makes us truly our "brother's keeper." Such a love is the nursery bed for cultivating the virtues of humility, tolerance and solidarity. The demands of this love are justified by the eschatological dimension of human history, which tends toward a transcendental fullness of contingent experiences. Accordingly, by evoking the parable of the Good Samaritan, the Pope points to a new yardstick for human relationship—a yardstick that is grounded in a new hermeneutic that recognizes the value of a positive perception of other persons as the spiritual basis for every action of justice or mercy. In the light of such a congenial perception, the helpless victim of unjust violence will be immediately recognized in my judgment as a neighbor in need—a brother or sister—whose groans (*ube nwanne*) I cannot ignore without being counted as inhuman.

75. *DCE*, 15.

Deus Caritas Est (*DCE*) also does not hesitate to condemn versions of a philosophy of progress whose most radical form is Marxism. Such ideologies claim that in a situation of unjust power anyone who engages in charitable initiatives is actually serving the unjust system, making it appear at least to some extent tolerable. This in turn slows down a potential revolution and blocks the struggle for a better world.[76] The Church vehemently rejects such an analysis of the society and insists that one does not make the world more human by refusing to act humanely here and now. But one cannot deny that the bedrock of humane initiative or action is the apprehension of the unitive purpose of human history and of its undivided ontological origin in which all human beings are inextricably bound together as members of one "meta-physical" cosmic family.

Therefore, what this encyclical failed to highlight in its treatment of love as charity, is the essential aspect of love as *Philia*. Much attention was paid in the encyclical to *Eros* and *Agape*. Love as *Philia* ought to have been given a better treatment than it received. Owing to the significance of *Philia* as the bond of the family, its marginal treatment in *DCE* should be regarded as a great omission. Despite acknowledging an "added depth of meaning" given to the term in St. John's Gospel to express the relationship between Jesus and his disciples (*DCE*, 3), a sufficient appraisal of *Philia* appear to be lacking in the Encyclical. But what makes *Philia* so important is that it is primarily encountered in the family between brothers and sisters, parents and children, or in extended form in friendship. If the origin of love is God, then it is God's *Philia*, made flesh in the incarnate Logos, which is the decisive bond of the Divine-Human relationship. God's *Philia* makes us God's children and members of a family through the Son, who He "*filiated*" (begot) in eternity. Agape should be understood as the inundation of love, which divine grace effects in human *philia* engendering it to reach beyond the temporal (consanguinity) to the ontological (humanity). In order that charity maintains its splendor, it is important that it be exercised not as if to a wretched, helpless poor whose appearance evokes my pity, but rather to a needy brother or sister whose situation questions and challenges my humanity and spirituality. On this point I agree once again with Jean-Marc Ela who says that

> The mission quest must not be motivated by condescension and pity. Ah, the poor blacks! The Africans were evangelized in the charity tradition of colonial Christianity. This tradition persists in disguised forms. The myth of aid to the third world, in certain milieus, built on the habits of many generations, is of a piece

---

76. *DCE*, 31. This refers to a tenet of Marxism which the Church always deplores.

with the notions of mission countries and young churches. In the context of dependency and unequal exchange in which we live today, the transformation of alienating social relationships and the obligation of justice have become part and parcel of mission itself.[77]

Similar observation was made by Stan Chu Ilo in his book, *The Church and Development in Africa* (2011), about all forms of humanitarian activities and new initiatives for African development that proceed from a single narrative of Africa as a poor continent—a narrative without an immersion in the diverse and rich stories of the continent, which go beyond poverty and suffering.[78] For developmental initiatives to work, they must be designed in such a way that recognizes the beneficiaries less as objects of pity and more as brothers and sisters. Therefore, one of the major shortcomings of *DCE* is that it allowed *Philia* (that taken-for-granted manifestation of love that is neither demanding nor self-centered) to recede to the background, while *Eros* and *Agape* are juxtaposed as the predominant expressions of love. Mary's spirituality, which was eulogized, such as assisting her cousin Elizabeth in the final phase of her pregnancy, or supplicating for the spouses at Cana, which form part of the concluding reflection of the Encyclical, should be seen, among other things, as an impelling testimony of how the human *philia* transforms itself into *Agape*. Her *Magnificat* anticipates and celebrates likewise God's *Philia* that has taken flesh in her womb in order to liberate the downtrodden and restore to them their lost dignity.

In summary, however, *DCE* still deserves great respect among the Church's encyclicals for its relevant contributions in shedding light on how apathy and negative perception of other persons could constitute an impediment to the commitment to liberating the poor. In this sense, *DCE* strengthened the theological base of fraternity. It became a further proof of the Church's commitment to the practice of charity. The encyclical at least reminds us that the truly pious Igbo Christian will be the one who recognizes in the saying "*Ọ nụrụ ube nwanne agbala ọsọ*" an indigenous re-telling of the parable of the Good Samaritan. This theme of charity which was not exhausted by *Deus Caritas Est* will be taken up again by Pope Benedict XVI in the encyclical *Caritas in Veritate*.

77. Ela, *African Cry*, 26.

78. Ilo, *Church and Development in Africa*. 4.

Caritas in Veritate

With the publication of *Caritas in Veritate* (*CIV*), pundits were speculating whether Pope Benedict XVI could be said to be on the "right" or the "left" side of the ideological divide. I think that such speculations totally miss the point. The encyclical notes the globalization that has taken place since *Populorum Progressio* was issued over 40 years ago. And alas, it laments, *"as society becomes ever more globalized, it makes us neighbors but does not make us brothers."*[79] This observation is the crux of the problem of social injustice. Pope Benedict XVI acknowledges that globalization is a complex phenomenon which might represent great opportunities, but at the same time might lead to new forms of exploitation, if it is not guided by charity in truth. But what is this truth which the Holy Father presents as an essential vessel of charity? What is this truth, if not the truth of a theistic anthropology that seeks to understand the mystery of the human person and his or her needs according to his or her relationship to God, the creator, and to other human beings? "Hunger," which is a principal threat to the basic physiological needs, *CIV* observes, "is not so much dependent on lack of material things as on shortage of social resources, the most important of which are institutional."[80] Identifying the cause of underdevelopment as the lack of brotherhood among individuals and peoples, therefore, the encyclical acknowledges a need for the deep thought and reflection of wise men and women in search of a new humanism which will enable modern man to find himself anew by embracing the high values of love and friendship.[81] By love and friendship here is surely not meant the ephemeral romantics that have characterized many modern relationships today, but rather a deeper appreciation of our interdependence. True development of peoples, the encyclical continues elsewhere, *"depends, above all, on the recognition that the human race is a single family* working together in true communion, not simply a group of subjects who happen to live side by side."[82] The goal of such development, which is rescuing peoples from hunger, deprivation, endemic diseases and illiteracy, cannot be achieved without building true communion in global fraternity. As such, this encyclical doesn't really strengthen liberals or conservatives, nor does it exhibit any kind of "ism" other than Catholicism. In fact, the bedrock of the ideas that informs *Charity in Truth* is simply the New Testament.

79. Benedict XVI, *CIV*, 19; my emphasis.
80. *CIV*, 27.
81. *CIV*, 27; see also *PP*, 20.
82. Benedict XVI, *CIV*, 53; my emphasis.

Benedict XVI believes that if people understood God's love for every single human person, if they appreciate his divine plan for us, then believers would recognize their duty to unite their efforts with those of all men and women of good will, with the followers of every religion and with non-believers, so that the social dynamics of this world may effectively correspond to the divine plan, that is, living as a family under the Creator's watchful eye.[83] Such fraternal collaboration that is inspired and sustained by divine charity will ensure that man's earthly activity contributes to the building of the universal city of God, which is the goal of the history of the human family.[84] Such is the noble aspiration which *CIV* envisions, in view of the insistent appeal being made by the cry of the hungry to those blessed with abundance. A cry, which is at the same time a vocation, a call addressed by free subjects to other free subjects in favor of an assumption of shared responsibility.[85] The hope that this mutual responsibility is possible, and the realization that it is urgent in our time, has created a podium for theology to reaffirm its social relevance today in a language that is intelligible to its grassroots' constituency. The truth about God and man which theology articulates has to be made to resonate with the Igbo constituency as well as other constituencies of the people of God.

The great credit of *CIV* lies in the encyclical's ability to make vivid and plausible (even if sometimes fleeting) diagnoses of the problems that belabor human development today. For example, Benedict XVI sees the necessity of correcting the malfunctions that cause new divisions between peoples and within peoples, and also of ensuring that the redistribution of wealth does not come about through the redistribution or increase of poverty.[86] Hence, acknowledging that globalization is a concept that must be grasped in the diversity and unity of all its different dimensions, Pope Benedict XVI maintains that if we hope to be able to appropriate the underlying anthropological and ethical spirit that drives globalization towards the humanizing goal of solidarity, we must have to steer the globalization of humanity in relational terms, in terms of communion and sharing of goods. Such, accordingly, is the theological dimension of globalization.[87] Now to be able to read such theological dimensions of globalization in popular idioms of African peoples is of important value to autochthonous pedagogy. Accordingly, such pithy sayings like "*Ọ nụrụ ube nwanne agbala ọsọ,*" dis-

---

83. *CIV,* 57.
84. *CIV,* 7.
85. *CIV,* 17
86. *CIV,* 42.
87. *CIV,* 42.

close the fountains from which theology draws local nutrients in securing cultural springboards or steppingstones for the Church's theological and evangelical mission among local peoples. The humanistic value imbedded in African culture and apprehensible in such dictums constitute articulate traditional and theological compass with which African people can chart their way through the Gospel message in today's world. The remarkable note of consonance which *CIV* strikes with *Ọ nụrụ ube nwanne agbala ọsọ* secures for this encyclical a special place in the discourse on African theology of fraternity. Benedict XVI recognizes that to tackle the task of global development, "what is needed is an effective shift in mentality which can lead to the adoption of new life-styles in which the quest for truth, beauty, goodness and communion with others for the sake of common growth are the factors which determine consumer choices, savings and investments in our world."[88]

This shift in mentality requires such magnanimity that was demonstrated by a little boy who, carrying his sibling sister on his back, boldly declares that the burden is not heavy for him because she is his sister.[89] It is a mentality of gratuity. *Caritas in Veritate,* towing the path of *Populorum Progressio,* sees such magnanimity as inherent in the famous principle of subsidiarity, a principle which respects human dignity and fosters freedom and participation through assumption of responsibility; and which, according to Pope Benedict XVI, must remain closely linked to the principle of solidarity. The Pope could not ignore the need to reemphasize the importance of these two inseparable principles: subsidiarity and solidarity, as he cautions that, "while the poor of the world continue knocking on the doors of the rich, the world of affluence runs the risk of no longer hearing those knocks, on account of a conscience that can no longer distinguish what is human."[90] In the face of such eventuality of becoming apathetic, a theology of fraternity in the African context exhorts as it seeks to influence the social attitude that ought to underlie all efforts at global human development. In order to salvage humanistic values in a continent so battered by selfishness, exploitation, and bigotry, African idioms are pointers to a rich cultural heritage from which public service as well as ethnic and interreligious relations are supposed to draw inspiration. According to the Bishop of Kumasi Ghana, Peter K. Sarpong, "the magnanimity with which Africans display racial tolerance after all they have endured at the hands of Europeans is nothing

88. *CIV,* 51.
89. See Introduction above.
90. *CIV,* 75.

short of heroic.[91] Such magnanimity should not be seen to be lacking among Africans in their relationships with one another. For there is nothing laudable in being magnanimous with Europeans when Africans have not yet learnt to deal kindly with their own brothers and sisters at home. Indeed the true heroes and heroines of the Kingdom of God are persons who are not lacking in the spiritual childhood that is necessary for carrying one another without feeling burdened by the yoke. The future of Africa's development and wellbeing will always depend on the vision of a progressive awareness of the fraternal bond that unites her sons and daughters with a common dream of collectively overcoming internal divisions and poverty.

Acknowledging the failure of human institutions, especially in Africa, to guarantee the fulfillment of humanity's right to development, *CIV* invests anew the hope of integral human development in "a free assumption of responsibility in solidarity on the part of everyone."[92] Such integral development requires a transcendent vision of the person, for only through an encounter with God are we able to see in the other something more than just another creature. Only through a theistic anthropology are we able to recognize the divine image in the other and thus truly come to discover him or her and to mature in a love that becomes concern and care for the other.[93] Without such a theistic anthropology global development risks the loss of an essential human and social orientation; it risks being deaf or apathetic to the cry of *nwanne m*—my brother/sister.

Finally, as thoughtful and topical as this Encyclical has been, one can only hope that it will be vindicated by time as having really impacted on the society whose malaise it set out to diagnose. However, owing to its excessive preoccupation with the global financial crisis and market economics, it seems to have glossed over important points related to a theology of solidarity. Some critics have observed that the encyclical has been too encompassing in its treatment that it runs the risk of being seeing as vague, without particular emphasis. And as a result it may suffer the same fate as other previous social encyclicals, that is, being consigned to the remote libraries of theological institutes. To avoid this unpleasant fate, the message of *CIV*, like those of other social encyclicals, needs to be accompanied and complemented by a somewhat unrelenting "jingles" of a theology that is committed to liberation and solidarity.

Now looking back in this chapter we see how the ambivalence that besets the notion of being poor in biblical theology necessitated a shift of

---

91. Peter K. Sarpong, Foreword to Ehusani, *Afro-Christian Vision*, x.

92. Cf. *CIV*, 11.

93. *CIV*, 11.

emphasis in theological discourse—a shift that does not betray or undermine the Church's fundamental option for the poor. The movement of this shift is from the theme of liberation to that of fraternal solidarity—a theme that is neither lacking in the Social Teaching of the Church nor in the liberation discourses. In view of the importance of this shift we have reviewed the relevant magisterial documents that offer valuable insights that support a theology of fraternity. In this process it has become also clear that *Ọ nụrụ ube nwanne agbala ọsọ* synthesizes the perspectives of liberation as justice and liberation as service of charity in a new perspective that transcends both the liberation and scholastic hermeneutic. The hermeneutic of fraternal solidarity emerging from this shift will now be used to analyze the peculiar Igbo cultural and historical context in the next part of this book.

PART II

Igbo Experience of Need for
Liberation in the African Context

4

Africa
The Crucibles

Social and Historical Context of Igbo Liberation Theology

THE CHOICE OF TERM "Igbo liberation theology" here is not meant to negate the fact that we are actually concerned with the African context in general. However, because of the vastness of the African context and the fact that I am using an Igbo idiom as hermeneutic tool here, it is important to use the adjective "Igbo," thereby leaning on a specific context while bringing to light all those common historical experiences of the African people which constitute the raw materials for theology in the African context. As South African theologian, Willa Boesak, rightly states: "To write a critical contextual theology requires a serious encounter with history."[1] It requires a critical confrontation with the people's history and their way of being human. Such sensitivity to history has many advantages: first, it allows us to understand why certain forms of theologizing (e.g. Liberation or Inculturation) received priority over others and what historically identifiable factors shaped the exercise or choice of theological themes in Africa. The history of modern African politics is what shapes and will continue to shape the tone of theological discourse in the black continent. And that history is characterized by many crucibles where power has been vaunted over a manacled brotherhood. If, accord-

1. Boesak, *God's Wrathful Children*, 52.

ing to Edward Antonio, "politics and power are ceaselessly played out in historical time—if human existence is always bounded by time and produced in and through time, then genuine political sensitivity can only take the form of sensitivity to the work of time."[2] It is such sensitivity that gave birth to inculturation theology, which has become the mainstream brand of African theology, and which represents the specifically religious or theological reassertion of African memory. It is both a quest for liberation as well as authentic identity—an identity that has been so much smeared and ridiculed in the course of Africa's political encounter with the European other. Strictly speaking, liberation theology for some obvious reasons is widely regarded as a Latin American phenomenon. However, it is true that the Igbo (African) historiography has been punctuated by the people's struggle against injustice, domination, oppression and hatred; against constraints to achieving freedom and self-determination, against the forces that conspire to vitiate the efforts at establishing a society that will be a fertile ground for human development. Theologians, politicians, pastors, writers and music artists[3] have variously put these aspirations in perspectives, articulating as it were, the people's indigenous knowledge and philosophy; religious and cultural worldview; and their will to achieve integral development.

Knowledge of the historical experiences of Igbo people holds the key to appreciating the distinctive character of their perspective to the liberation struggle, and their unique adaptation to dogmatic principles in the teachings of the Church. For instance, there was nothing as disconcerting to Igbo Christians as the suspicion and mutual antagonism that characterized the missionary preaching and activities—a rivalry that was a by-product of the polemics that bedeviled Christian mission for centuries since the protestant schism. Today this division is still a shameful heritage that continues to stultify efforts at community development and pitch Catholics against Protestants in an apparent cold war that defies comprehension. I have mentioned above how a catholic bishop was refused the request to take over and manage a health center project that was abandoned by the federal government, based on the premise that the said project belongs to the community and cannot be left at the hands of one church alone. Describing the division which the encounter with Europeans brought to African traditional

---

2. Antonio, *Inculturation and Postcolonial Discourse*, 7.

3. The pithy saying "*O nụrụ ube nwanne agbala ọsọ*" was brought to popular limelight by the music artist Bright Chimezie and his Zigima Sound with the song "Ube Nwanne," which can be downloaded online from You Tube: http://www.youtube.com/watch?v=qO4ZR1xjvzI

communities, Chinua Achebe writes in *Things Fall Apart*, the Whiteman "has put a knife on the things that held us together and we have fallen apart."[4] But prior to the divisions brought about by the legacy of schismatic polemics which was transported by the missionaries, the African childhood was severely tested in its first crucible of recorded history—the Trans-Atlantic slave trade. In dealing with this phenomenon, the aim here is not to do as if African theology is still mired in the single narrative of victimhood and thereby merely stuck in the past. No, it is simply to show how the past contributes in shaping the present, for as an Igbo proverb puts it, "if one does not know where and when the rain started beating him, how can he/she know when it stopped?" The diagnosis of the problems associated with liberation or development and poverty alleviation in Africa must be able to identify the causes of the situations of oppression and exploitation.

Elucidating wherein the African cry (*ube nwanne*) consists historically and how that cry provides the subject-matter of a theology of fraternity in the Igbo context is part of what is required when we speak of *Ọ nụrụ ube nwanne agbala ọsọ*. Simply put, what is the African cry? Therefore, in this chapter we remember and re-evaluate theologically, the experiences of slavery, colonialism, racism, civil wars and bad governance which make Africa a type of modern gibbet where God is continually crucified or held to public scorn. These life-denying phenomena that have affected human development in Africa are seen here as attributable to anti-human attitudes that refuse to recognize the bond of fraternity that enables us to carry each other—a bond that unites the entire human family (rich and poor, great and small, male and female, believers and unbelievers) as brothers and sisters. The personal responsibility which all humans bear on a much broader level for these social evils cannot be overemphasized. Beginning with the memory of the Trans-Atlantic Slave Trade, its damage on the African psyche, and the foundation it laid for subsequent oppressions and exploitations of Africans, one is led to admit the anti-fraternal thrust that made such dehumanization possible.

Experience of Slave Trade

In pre-colonial time, Igboland was characterized by a dense population and small states. This meant that it suffered at the hands of slavers because there were no large states to protect the people.[5] The facts of this situation are well summarized by historian J. F. Ade Ajayi:

4. Achebe, chap. 20 of *Things Fall Apart*, 152.

5. Ade Ajayi, *General History of Africa*, 6:298.

Different Igbo groups engaged in wars to capture slaves which they sold to the delta states and the Efik of Calabar who were the middlemen . . . Despite the fact that the slave trade was abolished in 1807 by the British and that it lingered on the coast till about 1850, it continued in Igboland throughout the [19th] century where it constituted an important factor for social change. The slave trade in Igboland was disruptive. First, the manner in which slaves were obtained largely through kidnapping, raiding and wars tended to destroy social and political structures. Second, it also disrupted normal agricultural activities. Moreover, what the Igbo obtained in return for slaves was not equal to the total loss sustained as a result of the slave trade.[6]

The insecurity that characterized this period was such that among the agricultural Igbo, parents going to farm normally hid their children in the ceilings (*uko*) of their homes.[7] As James Walvin aptly puts it,

The word "slavery" sounds neutral—a word that simply describes an institution—but it masks a complex social and human reality. What the Western world came to rely on were Africans and their descendants, enslaved in unprecedented numbers, and consigned to a lifetime's bondage which they bequeathed to their offspring born in the Americas . . . It was a unique form of bondage which, from an early date, was highly racialised. By 1750, to be black in the Americas (and often in Europe) was to be enslaved. Never before had the institution of slavery been so shaped and defined by colour, or, more properly, ethnicity. Many consequences of this racialised system have survived down to the present day.[8]

The Trans-Atlantic Slavery was in essence a brutal system which was conceived in violence, maintained by draconian punishments, and all for the betterment of the Western world. However, the grim human realities at the heart of slavery practically went unnoticed because it was rationalized on racial otherness that considers it abhorrent to think of any proximate relationship between the racial divide. To suggest any idea of fraternity between whites and blacks will be considered an insult, if not a blasphemy. And as long as slavery delivers profitable trade and production, its critics were silenced. Between 1662 and 1807 British ships carried 3.25 million Africans across the Atlantic. Survival of the crew during the slave transport

---

6. Ibid., 298–99.

7. See Uzukwu, *Listening Church*, 23.

8. Walvin, *The Trader, the Owner, the Slave*, xvi.

depended so much on vigilance and violence that chains, manacles and gun were ever present. When the crew dropped their guard, the results were disastrous. Slave revolts saw black and white butchering each other with callous savagery. The sailors feared the slaves, and the slaves hated the sailors. This produced a volatile and inflammable brew which simmered on every single slave ship.[9]

In spite of the desired economic benefits of the human cargoes, the relationship between slaves and slave traders was marked by the most brutal disdain and strong antipathy. Racial otherness effectively eclipsed the human essence and made it difficult for slavers to feel any sense of scruple for what they were doing. It was not until the grace of God touched John Newton—a slave trader who turned abolitionist—that he realized the reprehensible lethargy with which he hitherto treated the sufferings of African slaves on transit on board British slave ships. Writing for his abolitionist readership, Newton narrates: "I have seen them [slaves] agonizing for hours, I believe for days together, under the torture of the thumbscrews; a dreadful engine, which if the screw be turned by an unrelenting hand, can give intolerable anguish."[10] Not all were as repentant as John Newton though. A German slave merchant, Sömmering, arrogantly asserted, "The people are more insensible than others towards pain and natural evils, as well as towards injuries and unjust treatment. In short, there is none so well adapted to be slave of others."[11] Newton's repentance, however, has a very important lesson to teach. In the first place, it was a light in the darkness considering its significance to the abolition that brought the inhuman trade to an end. Attributing it to the grace of God, it is remarkable to see what difference it makes when an oppressor awakes to a supernatural vision of man that enables him to see himself and his victim with the eyes of God who created both. Such an enlightenment which one may call a conversion to fraternity will also be the heart of the solution to new forms of slavery today. The good news is that such a conversion from antipathy to fraternity is always possible.

The psychological damage which Trans-Atlantic Slave Trade dealt to the African psyche dictates the need for a theology whose primary objective will be the unity of the human race in a bond of fraternity. For it created a racial underclass in the world, people who were left in the broken lower levels of global development, seemingly powerless to change their condition

9. Ibid., 35.

10. Ibid., 51.

11. Davidson, *African Slave Trade*, 156. See also Hammond and Jablow, *Africa That Never Was*.

and powerless to make people of other races appreciate them for who they are. Throughout a period of four centuries Europeans viewed Africans as naturally subhuman, as descendants of apes, and as lacking in any culture and civilization. There was simply no basis nor desire for brotherliness, and this absence of fraternity exacerbated the violence of Trans-Atlantic slavery and sustained the antipathy that survived even after the abolition of slavery.

It should also be remembered that the famous phrase, "all men are created equal," drafted by Thomas Jefferson in the American Declaration of Independence was written and endorsed in an America of the eighteenth century which did not consider the enslaved blacks among the human species. Western thought and attitude to slavery at the period were sustained by a spurious theory known as the theory of providential design, which purports that the enslavement of Africans in America, and the subsequent colonization of the African continent were an act of God's providence. God had ordained slavery as the mechanism for raising a new African elect into Christianity. And once blacks had been civilized in America, it was reasoned, God caused slavery to be ended and Africa to be opened so that African Americans could "bring it to Christ." This theological justification for slavery and colonialism appealed to many Europeans as plausible.[12]

However, scholars abound who believe that the Trans-Atlantic slave trade paved the way for the poverty of the African continent. It disrupted Africa's political, economic and social life for over three hundred years and effectively put an end to any meaningful integration of the diverse African ethnic groups.[13] Furthermore, the dehumanizing nature of this trade has no comparison in history: before auctioning the slaves, prospective buyers inspected their wares, prodding the slaves' stomachs, inspecting their teeth and eyes, pinching their muscles and gauging the working capacity of each slave.[14] Afterwards the new owners of the slaves marked their initials on the

---

12. See a paraphrase in Ehusani, *Afro-Christian Vision,* 82; see also Williams, *Black Americans and the Evangelization of Africa (1877–1900),* 6–7. The theory of providential design was actually expounded by a white missionary in an address to the students of Atlanta University in 1888. This missionary said he foresaw that African Americans, with the help of God, will be able to overcome "the ignorance, the animalism, and the barbarism of the African tribes." Alongside these theological justifications for slavery, there were philosophical justifications too. Hegel for example gave rational expression and legitimacy to every conceivable European myth about Africa, some of which I wish to pay attention to later. In fact the theory of providential design could be explained as another way of demonstrating acquiescence to human vagaries on account of an assumption that God ordains evil so that good may come out of it. But what it reveals in reality is a human society that is willing to justify any systemic evil.

13. See Ilo, *Face of Africa,* 59.

14. Stride and Ifeka, *Peoples and Empires of West Africa,* 213.

slaves' faces with a brazen iron as a seal of proprietorship. Worse still, the slaves lose their identity, for nobody really cared whether they had a name before they were captured. As Christopher Bowes, a surgeon who kept a medical log on one of the slave ships, recounted: "Throughout this listing of human misery, we never once encounter an African name. We know the slaves, and remember them, by their numbers."[15] There was a pervasive feeling of extreme distress, despair and melancholy among these African slaves as they were torn from their roots and loaded on board the slave ships ready to sail into the unknown. An Igbo boy, Olaudah Equiano or Gustavus Vassa (1745–1797), kidnapped at the age of eleven and sold into slavery, perhaps gives the most authentic and touching account of the evils of the slave trade in his autobiography of 1794. In one passage in which he seems to be sermonizing, Equiano relates:

> . . .without scruple, are relations and friends separated, most of them never to see each other again. I remember . . . several brothers, who, in the sale, were sold in different lots; and it was very moving on this occasion to see and hear their cries at parting. O, ye nominal Christians! Might not an African ask you, learned you this from your God, who says unto you, 'Do unto all men as you would men should do unto you?' Is it not enough that we are torn from our country and friends to toil for your luxury and lust of gain? Must every tender feeling be likewise sacrificed to your avarice? Are the dearest friends and relations, now rendered more dear by their separation from their kindred, still to be parted from each other, and thus prevented from cheering the gloom of slavery with the small comfort of being together and mingling their sufferings and sorrows? Why are parents to lose their children, brothers their sisters, or husbands their wives? Surely this is a new refinement in cruelty, which, while it has no advantage to atone for it, thus aggravates distress and adds fresh horrors even to the wretchedness of slavery.[16]

To corroborate this wretchedness, there were myriads of irrefutable evidence about the sadistic brutality which underpinned the slave system. And yet how such evil was condoned for years by great religions like Christianity and Islam remains a big question. A cloud of silence seemed to have descended upon men and women of faith in Europe and America. The saints, heroes and heroines of faith maintained a sacred silence in what one would consider the worst institutional evil that affronted the authentic

---

15. Walvin, *The Trader, the Owner, the Slave*, 181.
16. Equiano, *Interesting Narrative*, 30.

worship of God and the service of humanity since the time of Christ. Why was there hardly any Christian theological stand or condemnation of this evil by churches in Europe?

The only plausible explanation for the dubious silence of the Church and pious men and women in Europe and America at that time is that Africans were never perceived as brothers and sisters, who share with them a common humanity, equality, and dignity. With apparent exception of the Quakers it seemed that pious Christians, who profess belief in a Creator-God who is Father of the human race, were unable to grasp the implications of God's universal paternity and the obligations it imposes on all who call themselves God's children. Prejudice was too strong as to have obscured the truth and excluded blacks from the human race. It was allegedly the industrial revolution with the emergent innovations in mechanized agriculture and industries, which made the use of massive slave labor dispensable and thereby made the abolition of slavery expedient. The Christian response to slavery up until the 18th century in the United States was at first largely focused on making slavery "more humane." It was only in the nineteenth century, many years after the Abolition of Slavery Act, first in 1807 and then in 1833, that Pope Gregory XVI with the Papal Bull of 1839, *In Supremo Apostolatus,* eventually condemned slavery as "inhumane" and "contrary to the laws of justice and humanity."[17] But it was not until February 1992 during his visit to the notorious slave island of Goree in Senegal that Pope John Paul II became the first European to publicly apologize to Africans in the name of Christianity and humanity for the crime of slave trade. On that memorable visit the Pope said: *"The slave trade is a tragedy of a civilization that called itself Christian. And deep causes of this human drama, of this tragedy, can be found in all of us, in our human nature, in sin. I have come here to pay homage to all the unknown victims of this crime, whose names and number can never be known."*[18]

Africans will always appreciate the Pope's sensibility in acknowledging that the slave trade was a crime against humanity, but we may not stop asking why this crime happened in the first place. In fact, it is theologically pertinent to ask why, so as to accentuate the importance of critical discernment in ensuring that the service of justice and fraternal solidarity remains an indispensable choice, especially for a religion whose votaries are known in history to have compromised justice and morality with impunity in the bid to gratify an avaricious appetite and brutish power. This has brought the Church such embarrassment as being indicted for justifying great social

17. Assaf, "Nun Speaks of African-American Catholics."

18. See Bujo, *African Theology in Its Social Context,* 9.

evil, or of having to apologize for inaction in the face of such evil, as Pope John Paul II was forced to apologize at the island of Goree in Senegal. The position of the Church and of many pious men and women in Europe and America during the slavery years thence calls for vigilance today in scrutinizing the extent to which the Church may be influenced covertly or overtly by ideological prejudice in her proclamations. The indictment of liberation theology by conservative North American theologians is comparable to the condemnation of abolitionist activists in the past and should be evaluated in that light. A visit in 2007 to the abolition monument at Harper's Ferry in West Virginia USA dedicated to the memory of John Brown—a man of extraordinary zeal who led an aborted armed campaign with his sons and a handful of men to free slaves in the USA in 1858, says it all. Overpowered by the Federal troops, John Brown was captured, tried of treasonable felony against the state of West Virginia, and hanged. However, his violent campaign later received tremendous attention in US historiography as a catalyst that provoked the moral conflict, which led to the American civil war months after his execution. Today, history has vindicated him, as he is remembered and honored as a US national hero. His story remains a lesson that enlightens us about the ironic and mysterious ways in which history opens our eyes to see the injustice of the evil structures we once regarded as sacrosanct and which we fought to entrench and perpetuate. The posthumous decoration of John Brown as a United States' hero thus reveals how our jaundiced perception of one another could change dramatically with time when it is illuminated by the light of the transcendental truth of our primordial fraternity.

But more importantly, John Brown's heroic intervention on behalf of West Virginia's black slaves and his subsequent execution discloses the depth of the moral question which slavery threw at humanity—a question so important as to generate a bloody conflict. Walking up to the gallows Brown held a bible in the hand vociferously indicting his executioners as the real criminals who are on the wrong side of history. He died for the belief that to refuse to engage in violent struggle when one recognizes the need for it is effectively to compromise with militant evil, to sell short the service of God, to deny the greatness of God—and to allow the over-refinements of intelligent hypocrisy to vindicate the resulting lapse from ideal.[19] Such a stance is, in fact, as compromising as encouraging violence when it is thought morally preferable to eschew it.

The history of the enslavement of Africans cannot be undone, but it can always serve as a valuable theological compass with which to navigate

19. Akhtar, *Final Imperative*, 36.

in our contemporary analyses of the situations of oppression and the causes of man's inhumanity to man. Theology should not fail to ask the question: Since in Christ all have become one and "there is no longer Jew or Greek, slave or free, male or female" (Galatians 3:28), why was it possible for the western Christian slave masters to mete out so much cruelty to their African victims in the name of slavery? The answer is that as long as they are still not regarded as sisters and brothers, Galatians 3:28 will remain an illusory hope. St. Paul and Timothy emphasized the fraternal consciousness as a necessary condition for eliminating slavery when they urged Philemon to take back Onesimus (cf. Philemon 16). Jon Sobrino is correct to observe that the oppressed call into question the assumptions about the character of human relationships, both local and international, in a suffering and unjust world.[20] What liberation theology is clamoring is that the vantage point of the poor is particularly, and especially, the vantage point of the crucified God and acts as a criterion for theological reflection, biblical exegesis, and the life of the Church. Slavery is an ever present phenomenon that takes ever changing forms, and the poor, most of whom today live in Africa, are the means whereby the Church can learn to discern the truth, direction and content of its mission, and they can assure the Church of being the place where the LORD is to be found. Therefore, known as the continent of poverty, Africa with her history of enslavement, past and present, continues to furnish the Church with a rich repository of theological materials for reflection as well as potential dynamics for positive social change for the benefit of all humankind. The most important redemptive value of the experience of the Trans-Atlantic slave trade and the struggle to abolish it, therefore, lies in making us see how the rediscovery of universal brotherhood and the unity of the human race actualizes the hope of the kingdom—a hope from which all sacrifices—human or divine, temporal or eternal, bloody or unbloody— take their ultimate meaning.

---

20. See Sobrino, *True Church and the Church of the Poor*, 222.

Figure 5: Slave Sister

Figure 6: Slave Brother

Figure 7: Slave Taskmaster
(I found these images at the National Monument in Harper's Ferry, West Virginia, built to commemorate the cruelty of the era of slavery in American history.)

Experience of Anthropological Poverty

Earliest studies about African philosophy, history, arts, religion or society were done in the late nineteenth and early twentieth centuries by European and American ethnologists, anthropologists, sociologists and missionaries who were motivated more by the desire to justify existing racist and colonial structures than by a true spirit of scholarship. With their *Eurocentric* posture of superiority, they sought to study those "primitive," "pagan," "heathen," "savage" or "barbaric" tribes of Africa. There was a tremendous lack of sensibility for the folks whose culture they intended to study. They described Africans as "humanity's burnt out husks" or "nature's outcast children," and the land as "governed by insensible fetish." To them, as indeed to the Western mind of the time, Africa was "such a physically and spiritually dark world that nothing good could reside in, or come out of it."[21] Anthropological poverty is the name given to the debilitating shackle which their prejudice laid on the African psyche. It is a phenomenon that is poignantly described by Cameroonian theologian, Engelbert Mveng, as the

21. Ehusani, *Afro-Christian Vision*, 77

fundamental predicament tormenting Africans.[22] In the "African Report" presented at EATWOT's Second General Assembly at Oaxtepec, Mexico, in 1986, this reality was expressed as a theological challenge to all who seek to interpret the gospel of Jesus Christ within the African social context.[23] The Report notes,

> The social underdevelopment of Africa represents a fundamental aspect of the anthropological pauperization of the African person. If we define pauperization as the fact of becoming or making poor, namely being deprived of all that we have acquired, all that we are and all that we can do, we shall recognize that Africa is subjugated to structures which result in complete pauperization: political, economic, and social. When it is not a matter of being deprived of all that we own, but rather of all that we are—our human identity, our social roots, our history, our culture, our dignity, our rights, our hopes, and our plans—then pauperization becomes anthropological. It then affects religious and cultural life at its very roots.[24]

The truth is that a coalition of forces, historical, economic and political, has resulted in the material destitution of Africans. Anthropological pauperization is one of the instruments of domination used to crush the African spirit on the altar of European racial superiority. This reality is better understood in the words of Mveng:

> When persons are deprived not only of material, spiritual, moral, intellectual, cultural, or sociological order, but of everything that makes up the foundation of their being-in-the-world and the specificity of their "ipseity" as individual, society, and history—when persons are bereft of their identity, their dignity, their freedom, their thought, their history, their language, their faith universe, and their basic creativity, deprived of all their rights, their hopes, their ambitions (that is, when they are robbed of their own ways of living and existing)—they sink into a kind of poverty which no longer concerns only exterior or interior goods or possessions but strikes at the very being, essence, and dignity of the human person. It is this poverty that we call anthropological poverty. This is an *indigence of being*, the legacy of centuries of slavery and colonization.[25]

22. Mveng, "Impoverishment and Liberation," 156.
23. See Martey, *African Theology*, 38.
24. EATWOT, "African Report." See Abraham, *Third World Theologies*, 35.
25. Mveng, "Impoverishment and Liberation," 156.

This impoverishment, which was exacerbated by the prolonged cruel trans-Atlantic slave trade, laid the foundation for racism in Europe's culture and history, especially in her relationship with Africa. It is unfortunate that this fatal anthropological blow to the "African Being" found its pristine plot in the European Enlightenment epoch, and its veterans are the intellectuals who are almost worshipped as gods. It is, in fact, a repudiation of the spirit of Enlightenment, and its deplorable vestiges are still perceptible in the wide chasm it has been able to create between the Black race and the Caucasian till date. One prominent "arrow-head" of this anthropological death-blow is George Wilhelm Friedrich Hegel, whose views on Africa are indeed pathetic. It is ironical how this German philosopher, who conceived reality as the self-unfolding of the Absolute, does not consider the "African Being" as having or deserving a place in this self-unfolding or *Phenomenology* of the *Absolute Spirit*. In his introduction to *The Philosophy of History*,[26] Hegel undertakes for unfounded reasons a very malicious libel against Africa that does not only insult the philosophical intellect, but also casts a dark shadow on Hegel himself.

Hegel's dubious and malicious intent was betrayed from the onset by his purposeful geographical dismembering of Africa, in order to steal and secure for Europe the glories of the Egyptian civilization. Africa for him "must be divided into three parts: one is that which lies south of the desert of Sahara—*Africa proper*—the upland almost entirely unknown to us, with narrow coast-tracts along the sea; the second is that to the north of the desert, European Africa (if we may so call it), a coastland; the third is the river region of the Nile, the only valley-land of Africa, and which is in connection with Asia."[27] Accordingly, having excised Egypt from Africa, to suit his own version of history, Hegel zeroed in on what he refers to as "Africa proper" and singled it out for an extremely malicious libel, the outlines of which have continued to define the epistemic narrative about Africa in the consciousness and institutions of Hegel's descendants. According to Hegel, "Africa proper, as far as History goes back, has remained-for all purposes of connection with the rest of the world, shut up; it is the gold-land compressed within itself—the land of childhood, which lying beyond the day of self-conscious history, is enveloped in the dark mantle of Night."[28]

Although Hegel had earlier written that Africa proper—the Upland is almost entirely unknown to him and his students, yet that did not restrain him from proclaiming that this "Africa proper" "is enveloped in the dark

---

26. Hegel, *Philosophy of History*.

27. Ibid., 196.

28. Ibid.

mantle of Night." It never occurred to him that this "dark mantle of Night" might be the mantle of his own ignorance about Africa. Yet writing under the dark shadow of this mantle, Hegel pretends to have some information about these Africans proper, and so he writes:

> The peculiarly African character is difficult to comprehend, for the very reason that in reference to it, we must quite give up the principle which naturally accompanies all *our* ideas—the category of Universality. In Negro life the characteristic point is the fact that consciousness has not yet attained to the realization of any substantial objective existence—as for example, God, or law—in which the interest of man's volition is involved and in which he realizes his own being.[29]

Worthy of note is that Hegel's lectures were given more than three decades after Olaudah Equiano had published his autobiography in 1794. Hence, it is clear that given the agenda that Hegel had, there was no way he could have come to a different conclusion about the African character whose "being" (*dasein*) he deliberately wanted to treat with scorn. According to Olufemi Taiwo, consistent with the practice that dominates discourse about Africa in Euro-America, Hegel was oblivious of the irony that he had puffed his peculiarity into a universality and that giving up the principle, *universality*, which naturally accompanies all European ideas may indeed be required if the African world is to be treated with the requisite respect for its integrity and heteronomy.[30] But treating Africa with respect for its integrity and heteronomy does not translate into the kinds of *Eurocentric*[31] deductions that Hegel desired to make about the African situation of his time. In fact, respect for Africa would be absurd since the Negro, for him, exhibits the natural man in his completely wild and untamed state, and Europeans must lay aside all thought of reverence and morality; all that they call feeling, if they would rightly comprehend the Negro, for "*there is nothing harmonious with humanity* to be found in this type of character."[32] Such haughty narratives have exerted tremendous pernicious influence on

29. Ibid.

30. Taiwo, "Exorcising Hegel's Ghost," 3–16.

31. "Eurocentric" refers to the psychological and philosophical framework that projects European-White-Caucasian people, their history, culture, philosophy, values etc., as the center of the universe on which all else depends and around which all else revolves. Piero Gheddo calls this frame of mind a mania, and says Europeans and Euro-Americans will begin to understand something about the "third world" when they are freed from their ethnocentrism. See Gheddo, *Why Is he Third World Poor?*, 41. Cited by Ehusani, "Afro-Christian Vision," 112.

32. Hegel, *Philosophy of History*, 196–97; emphasis mine.

the African self-understanding, psyche and socio-cultural development. By refusing to acknowledge, not to say the least, tolerate any form of semblance between African and European humanity, Hegel authored a narrative in which the idea of brotherhood/sisterhood between the two races will be considered untenable and unacceptable.

To corroborate his libel Hegel invokes the authority of biased missionary accounts and hearsay. And building his thesis on such fallacies, he saw nothing in Africa except "magic," "sorcery," "cannibalism," "worship of the dead," "absence of transcendence and political constitution," in fact, a negation of all that is good and noble. According to him, "the Negroes . . .indulge that perfect contempt for humanity, which in its bearing on justice and morality is the fundamental characteristic of the race. They have no knowledge of the immortality of the soul. . .. The undervaluing of humanity among them reaches an incredible degree of intensity."[33] One can only imagine how Hegel's students were roaring with laughter or musing with incredulity as he dismissed the 'Negro' as "an object of no value," and "capable of no development or culture."[34] Concluding his haughty lecture on African history this beacon of European Enlightenment declares with a note of finality to his gullible students:

> At this point we leave Africa, not to mention it again. For it is no historical part of the world; it has no movement or development to exhibit. Historical movements in it—that is, in its northern part—belong to the Asiatic or European world. Carthage displayed there an important transitionary phase of civilization; but as a Phoenician colony, it belongs to Asia. Egypt will be considered in reference to the passage of the human mind from its eastern to its western phase, but it does not belong to the African spirit. What we properly understand by Africa, is the unhistorical, undeveloped spirit, still involved in the conditions of mere nature, and which had to be presented here only as on the threshold of the world's history.[35]

As a renowned professor of history, it is to be presumed that Hegel would have been privy of archeological, historical and other relevant information about Africa. His dilettantish glosses on the information available to him are embarrassing, since the racial identity of the ancient Egyptians must surely be available to him from the eyewitness account of Herodotus of Halicarnassus (born ca. 490–480 and died 425 B.C.) who in the fifth century

33. Ibid.
34. Ibid, 198–99.
35. Ibid., 199.

B.C. recorded that, ". . .the natives are black because of the hot climate."[36] And to demonstrate that the Greek oracle at Dodona is of Egyptian origin Herodotus explains: "As to the bird being black, they [the Dodonaeans] merely signify by this that the woman was an Egyptian."[37] Then he asserted that "it was the Egyptians too who originated, and taught the Greeks to use, ceremonial meetings, processions, and liturgies: a fact which can be inferred from the obvious antiquity of such ceremonies in Egypt, compared to Greece, where they have been only recently introduced.[38] Also speaking about the Colchians who he believes to be of Egyptian descent, Herodotus says: "My own idea on the subject was based first on the fact that they have *black skins and woolly hair* (. . .), and secondly, and more especially, on the fact that the Colchians, the Egyptians, and the Ethiopians are the only races which from ancient times have practiced *circumcision*."[39] Thanks to Anta Diop, the falsification of history in which Hegel and his peers were indoctrinated has been convincingly debunked by offering extensive logic that Blacks have originated the first civilization which flowered on earth, a civilization to which humanity owes most of its progress. It is important to note, according to Diop, that even one of Hegel's contemporaries, Count Constantin de Volney (1757–1820), after being imbued with all the prejudices of his milieu, had gone to Egypt between 1783 and 1785, while Negro slavery flourished and reported as follows:

> . . . all have a bloated face, puffed up eyes, flat nose, thick lips; in a word, the true face of the mulatto. I was tempted to attribute it to the climate, but when I visited the Sphinx, its appearance gave me the key to the riddle. On seeing that head, typically Negro in all its features, I remembered the remarkable passage where Herodotus says: 'As for me, I judge the Colchians to be a colony of the Egyptians because, like them, they are black with woolly hair. . .' In other words, the ancient Egyptians were true Negroes of the same type as all native-born Africans. That being so, we see how their blood, mixed for several centuries with that of the Romans and Greeks, must have lost the intensity of its original color, while retaining nonetheless the imprint of its original mold. We can even state as a general principle that the face is a

---

36. Herodotus, *Histories*, 137. See also Diop, *African Origin of Civilization*, 1.

37. Herodotus, *Histories* 152.

38. Ibid.

39. Ibid, 167; my emphasis. Circumcision is known to have been practiced by most African tribes of Hegel's time.

kind of monument able, in many cases, to attest or shed light on historical evidence on the origins of the peoples.[40]

Diop's explanation to the Negro myth of Hegel's contemporaries gives an invaluable insight into the anthropological pauperization that has become one of the Blackman's burdens:

> Inflated by their recent technical superiority, the Europeans looked down on the Black world and condescended to touch nothing but its riches. Ignorance of the Black's ancient history, differences of mores and customs, ethnic prejudices between two races that believed themselves to be facing each other for the first time, combined with the economic necessity to exploit—so many factors predisposed the mind of the European to distort the moral personality of the Black and his intellectual aptitudes.
>
> Henceforth 'Negro' became a synonym for primitive being, 'inferior,' endowed with a pre-logical mentality. As the human being is always eager to justify his conduct, they went even further. The desire to legitimize colonization and the slave trade—in other words, the social condition of the Negro in the modern world—engendered an entire literature to describe the so-called inferior traits of the Black. The mind of several generations of Europeans would thus be gradually indoctrinated, Western opinion would crystallize and instinctively accept the equation: Negro = inferior humanity. To crown this cynicism, colonization would be depicted as a duty of humanity.[41]

Indeed such pauperization of the African being and the negative characterization of black humanity contributed in setting the sad tone in relationship which defined European encounter with Africa. It led to the existence of covert and overt xenophobic attitudes and the crafting of programs, which aim at setting certain racial groups in the world apart for the meanest kinds of job opportunities. The xenophobic impact is felt most radically in the immigration policies of western countries. Ian Law made a remarkable revelation to this regard.

> The Treaty of European Union signed at Maastricht will forbid any member state from running its own visa policy after June 1996 when a common policy will come into operation. This will force the United Kingdom to scrap preferential arrangements which allow citizens of most Commonwealth countries the right to visit relatives in Britain. The European Commission's

---

40. Cited by Diop, *African Origin of Civilization*, 27.
41. Diop, *African Origin of Civilization*, 24f.

proposed list of countries, whose nationals will need a visa to enter, has been dubbed a 'blacklist' by officials because most of the people to whom restrictions will apply are from African and Caribbean countries. Not a single white Commonwealth country is included, with Canada and New Zealand being specifically exempt from restrictions. The government is likely therefore to 'snub' the black Commonwealth and to gain European support for cutting the ties of Empire.[42]

Law further informs us that "the secretly agreed measures to improve police identification and expulsion of illegal immigrants are challenged and emphasis is placed on legislating against employers who give jobs to such migrants."[43] Accordingly, the prospect of the European Community establishing racist immigration law that is broadly effective, "balanced" by anti-discrimination measures which are not, may be what the future holds.[44] And that future is indeed already present. There are, however, many white people who are endowed with fraternal sensibility toward black people and who are making efforts in challenging and combating racial discrimination. In all honesty, most anti-racism initiatives come from white people. Nevertheless, it must be maintained that as a tool of imperialism, racism obscures human wellbeing by devising a system of obscurantism through the media, the arts, culture, beliefs, school systems, values, and even philosophies, like Hegel's. The adverse effect is an African psyche forced to be puerile, resigned, and whimpering as he accepts the verdict of his own inferiority with a kind of victim-syndrome that will require much effort to overcome, simply because there is often actual victimization.

Having stolen the glories of the Egyptian civilization, Hegel's decision to ignore what he calls "Africa proper" and *"not to mention it again"* seem to have resonated among his docile students. Even though it is no longer tenable today to brazenly affirm the garden variety of racist epithets of Hegel's peers, in their docile students' attitudes towards African intellectual productions, a more benign but no less pernicious variety of racism continues to define the relationship between the West and Africa. The attitude of passing over the continent in silence and mentioning it only in relation to humanitarian disaster, or of adopting a double standard in dealing with its socio-political and economic problems, has become a sad unfortunate reality in international relation with Africa. Invariably, the fact that Hegel and his ilk authored the frame in which subsequent generations perceive Africa is

---

42. Law, "Immigration and the Politics of Ethnic Diversity," 240.

43. Ibid., 242.

44. Ibid.

confirmed by his final declaration concerning Africa's place in the discourse of world history. Africa must be forced to squat on the "threshold of world's history," all in an effort to destroy the memory of a Negro Egypt. There is no doubt that Hegel was schooled under the influence of such dishonest scholars like Champollion-Figeac, Chérubini, Fontanes, Gaston Maspero, etc., who were merely interested in crafting mostly disingenuous arguments, equivocations and wild assumptions in an attempt to demonstrate against all contrary evidence that the ancient Egyptian civilization was not a Negro civilization. According to Diop, these specialists were "convinced that everything valuable in life can come only from their race and that, if we look carefully, we are sure to be able to prove it. An explanation is not complete until it attains that objective."[45] It matters little whether the demonstration is supported by facts; it is self-sufficient, if its valid criterion merges with its aim. I cannot go into further details of Diop's debunking of the arguments used by these men to sustain the myth of Negro inferiority, but suffice it to mention the dubious argument of its pioneer, Champollion-Figeac. After expressing regret that Volney's account has become popular, Champollion advances as a decisive argument to refute the thesis of that scholar and all his predecessors, that black skin and woolly hair "do not suffice to characterize the Negro race," only to contradict himself 36 lines later by saying that "frizzy, woolly hair is the true characteristic of the Negro race."[46] Such is the nature of the dubious scholarship in which Hegel and his ilk were schooled; it was an agenda whose intent was simply to demonstrate ways in which the African person has fallen short of the glory of humankind.

What does this narrative hold for a theology of fraternity? Why is it important to retell these stories? Consider how noble and edifying it would have been, and what giant strides global human development would have recorded, if Europe had decided to carry Africa as a little boy carries his sister; if there has been a genuine interest to teach rather than to exploit and dehumanize. Both continents would have benefitted tremendously from such a fraternal encounter. The sad and tragic inter-racial relation could have been avoided if such relation is built and nurtured on the basis of fraternal consciousness that is an indispensable pillar of true and genuine humanity. Hence, it is important that theology recognizes that, narratives are sometimes stolen in order to impose a dictatorship of racial prejudice that desires only to feed itself on negative stereotypes. Deeply influenced by centuries of condescending, denigrating literatures and anthropological studies about African peoples, studies whose authenticity are now seriously

---

45. Diop, *African Origin of Civilization*, 65.

46. Ibid, 50–53.

questioned or debunked, the Western world should challenge itself to chart a new course marked by a more brotherly relation with their African brothers and sisters. This challenge has to be supported by a new theological hermeneutic and an authentic revision of history whose aim is to heal the wounds of the past through *charity in truth*. Western Media's presentation of Africa today with its many negative images, even when inspired by pure motives of solidarity, are often far from repairing the damages of Africa's anthropological pauperization, since it adds to projecting, rather falsely, a situation of hopelessness. A BBC reporter sent shock waves around the world on the floods in Mozambique in 2000 when he said: "Africa is cursed: if people do not destroy each other, nature will destroy them."[47] This was of course before the floods hit England.

The attitude of inventing mythic curses to explain away humanitarian disasters is not new. It has been invoked by some conservatives in the US after the devastation of New Orleans by hurricane Katrina and after the Haitian earthquake.[48] At the First Vatican Council, an Italian missionary, Daniel Camboni, allegedly prayed the Council Fathers to lift the curse on the children of Ham, a curse through which the Almighty had been punishing the black race with a cruelty unknown in history.[49] Such a request betrays a mind-set that accepts a ready-made world in which the status imposed on the colonized peoples is justified by a popular theology that interprets the condition of the black race as a punishment from God. This is symptomatic of a mentality that seeks to repress a guilty conscience or distract attention from questioning the root of injustice and human misery. By evoking the curse of Ham (Gen 9:18–27) and the curse of Eve (Gen 3:16), such a mentality seeks to justify Negro slavery and subordination of women respectively. Even the Jewish holocaust was sometimes associated with a biblical curse (cf. Matt 27:24–25). What these mythic curses have in common is that they

47. This broadcast was made on March 2, 2000.

48. See Neuhaus, "New Orleans That Was," 10–12. See also http://www.time.com/time/specials/packages/article/0,28804,1953778_1953776_1953804,00.html. In his January 13, 2010 appearance on *700 Club*, the TV evangelist Pat Robertson shocked the world at the wake of the tragic earthquake in Haiti by alluding that Haitians made a pact with the devil to free them from the French, and are probably reaping the fruits of the "deal."

49. Cf. Uzukwu, *Listening Church*, 22. In 1873 the Congregation of Indulgences published a prayer for the conversion of Ham's offspring in Central Africa, approved with a 300-days indulgence by Pope Pius IX. Part of the prayer read: "Let us pray for the most miserable Ethiopian peoples in Central Africa, who form a tenth of humanity, so that God Almighty may take away from their hearts the curse of Ham and give them the blessings of Jesus Christ, our God and LORD." Ilo, *Face of Africa*, 51–52; and Ela, *African Cry*, 30, also mention this curse.

are actually narrative weapons in the hands of the oppressor who is deluded by the idea of his or her racial, chauvinistic, or religious superiority. I do not wish to digress into an examination of the rationality of the "curse-mentality," but suffice it to say that humanity can never thrive on the ruins of the anthropological pauperization of the brother by brother.

According to Emanuel Martey, "The struggle against this anthropological pauperization of the African person is what gives Africa its theological agenda. It is indeed the pivot on which all relevant African theological interpretations and methodological considerations must rotate. Contextually, any attempt at giving theological interpretation to this agenda must wrestle with the two interpenetrating dimensions of African reality, and any God-talk in sub-Saharan Africa must be done in the light of these unyielding dimensions of African theological reality."[50] The two realities which Martey is referring to are the politico-socioeconomic and the anthropologico-religiocultural realities. And I am convinced that Ọ nụrụ ube nwanne agbala ọsọ clearly presents us with an adequate all-inclusive theological perspective that responds to these realities. For as deplorable as Europe's theft of African civilization might be, it is merely prototypic of many anti-fraternal encounters that could be found in all cases of *unredeemed* social relationships across continents and cultures. This is why a radical and positive change in the mutual perceptions and appreciations of one another as equal human beings remains the social and theological desideratum for the achievement of the goals of integral human liberation and development. In recent time, European scholars have come to acknowledge that European social anthropologists have often failed to understand African traditional religious thought for some reasons. Firstly, many of them have been unfamiliar with the theoretical thinking of their own culture and are thus deprived of a vital key to understanding. Secondly, even those familiar with theoretical thinking in their own culture have failed to recognize its African equivalents, simply because they have been blinded by a difference of idiom.[51] But as the spirit of brotherhood grows across racial borders this misunderstanding is being gradually dispelled.

The search to find an all-inclusive idiom has made a theology of fraternity a plausible alternative, or better said, complement to liberation theology. Contrary to Hegel's assumption, African conceptions of God are, in fact, as profound as Western conceptions of God in their implications, even if the indigenous mode of articulation may differ. How and why nineteenth and early twentieth century European writers arrived at a different conclusion

50. Martey, *African Theology*, 38.
51. Horton, *Patterns of Thought*, 179.

remains a question which a theology of fraternity should grapple with. John Mbiti demonstrates that the God-consciousness of Africans can be seen in every instrument of culture: language, art, proverbs, songs, names and so on. And he quotes an Ashanti proverb which says that "no one shows a child the Supreme Being."[52] A stranger only needs an objective, humble, and open mind in order to apprehend them. In his apologetic theological poem, *I Am an African*, Gabriel Setiloane argues how ancient the ideas of transcendence are in Africa:

> They call me African;
> African indeed am I;
> Rugged son of the soil of Africa,
> Black as my father, and his before him;
> As my mother and sisters and brother, living and gone from this world
> They ask me what I believe . . . my faith.
> Some even think I have none
> But live like the beasts of the field. . . .
> 'What of God, the Creator
> Revealed to mankind through the Jews of old
> The YAHWEH: I AM
> Who has been and ever shall be?
> Do you acknowledge him?'
> My fathers and theirs, many generations before knew him.
> They bowed the knee to him
> By many names they knew him,
> And yet 'tis he the One and only God-
> They called him:
> UVELINGQAKI: The first One
> Who came ere ever anything appeared;
> UNKULUNKULUL the BIG ONE,
> So big indeed that no space could ever contain him;
> MODIMO: Because his abode is far up in the sky.
> They also knew him as MODIRI
> For he has made all;
> And LESA: The spirit without which the breath of man cannot be.
> But, my fathers, from the mouths of their fathers, say
> This God of old shone
> With a brightness so bright

52. Mbiti, *African Religions and Philosophy*, 96.

It blinded them . . . Therefore . . .
He hid himself. UVELINGQAKI,
That none should reach his presence,
Lest they die, (for pity flowed in his heart),
Only the fathers who are dead come into his presence.
Like little gods bearing up the prayers and supplications
Of their children to the Great Great God . . .[53]

Other scholars before me have already shown how traditional African names of persons reveal a hidden but profound element of transcendence. Such names affirm the reality of God through His beneficent actions to man. The first generation of African scholars did their best in clarifying this against western misconceptions. The problem is that one finds at the root of the denigration of the African being and in all instances of oppression, marginalization and exploitation, the oppressors conscious or unconscious attempt to distance himself or herself from the "mischaracterized other" in order to justify the breach of fraternity. This withdrawal is in form of a mental fixation that is exacerbated by vices (e.g. selfishness, pride, greed, hatred, etc.) and can only be eradicated, i.e., displaced by virtues (of love and fraternal solidarity).

The jaundiced and conceited narrative that sought to rob Africa of humanity is as a result of such vices, and of having to speak from the vantage point of arrogant power. Such an arrogance which the Igbo call "nkalị" is one of the characteristics of "a single story" against whose dangers in literature the Igbo novelist, Chimamanda Adichie, warns.[54] The major characteristic of "a single story" is that it is told by the powerful to justify a self-defined sense of superiority and to uphold the inferiority of the perceived subordinate. Ample examples of single story typology are found in most colonial and missionary narratives. The danger they pose is that such stories reproduce negative stereotypes of their victims as they are told and retold. And the major problem with single stories is not that they are untrue (for they actually take refuge in half-truths), but that they are incomplete. They are often mischievously exaggerated, as they present a biased perspective of the whole story—a perspective which deliberately touts the negative and obscures the truth. And behind this partial and twisted truth lies a hidden element— *power, megalomania*, and a hidden agenda—*discrimination*. Nkalị is thus the unjust phenomenon that emerges wherever power is abused to gain personal or group advantage. And since power is always

---

53. Setiloane, "I Am an African," 128–31.
54. Adichie, "The Danger of a Single Story."

transitory and never pitches its tent with one master, a potential vicious circle of strife is what is to be expected from the propensity to entrench single-story narratives to advance the politics of racial, religious, gender, or class superiority vis-à-vis subordination. Evident in the partiality of the single story phenomenon, *nkalị,* which is a negative manifestation of power, is the antithesis of what *Ọ nụrụ ube nwanne agbala ọsọ* stands for, and it is to be reckoned with wherever the fact of fraternal proximity is repressed in the consciousness of exclusive identity.

Most laureled spirits of Europe's Enlightenment (John Locke, Immanuel Kant, etc.), were unfortunately trapped in the historical moment of Europe's cultural immaturity which was defined by the repression of the universal fraternal consciousness. Caught in the mire of a single story bias, they gave their illusion of grandeur a hermetic value in the quest to gratify their sense of anthropological superiority. The African, confronted with the veracity of his or her racial otherness and of the weakness of his technical progress, begins gradually to believe that since he or she cannot be like the Whiteman, he or she cannot achieve what the Whites have achieved. This is when anthropological pauperization sets in to deal its damage to the African psyche. Responding to Joseph Conrad's fiction, *Heart of Darkness,* Chinua Achebe educates us about the desire "in Western psychology to set Africa up as a foil to Europe, as a place of negations at once remote and vaguely familiar, in comparison with which Europe's own state of spiritual grace will be manifest."[55] *"Heart of Darkness"* (used as a metaphor for Sub-Saharan Africa), projects the image of Africa as "the other world," the antithesis of Europe and therefore of civilization, a place where man's vaunted intelligence and refinement are finally mocked by triumphant bestiality.[56] For Conrad is concerned not so much with Africa as with the deterioration of one European mind.[57] Achebe contends that Conrad (and the same could be said of Hegel and others) did not originate the image of Africa which we find in his book. It was and is the dominant image of Africa in the Western imagination and Conrad merely brought the peculiar gifts of his own mind to bear on it.[58] Suffering deep anxieties about the precariousness of its civilization, the West seems to have a need for constant reassurance by comparison with Africa. Achebe thus succinctly summarizes this Western fear that is portrayed in the *Heart of Darkness:*

55. Achebe, *Hopes and Impediments,* 3.
56. Ibid.
57. Ibid, 12.
58. Ibid, 17.

> Africa is to Europe as the picture is to Dorian Gray—a carrier on
> to whom the master unloads his physical and moral deformities
> so that he may go forward, erect and immaculate. Consequently,
> Africa is something to be avoided just as the picture has to be
> hidden away to safeguard the man's jeopardous integrity. Keep
> away from Africa, or else! Mr. Kurtz of *Heart of Darkness* should
> have heeded that warning and the prowling horror in his heart
> would have kept its place, chained to its lair. But he foolishly
> exposed himself to the wild irresistible allure of the jungle and
> lo! the darkness found him out.[59]

Certainly aware of the dangers of such unhealthy (*Hegelian* or *Conradian*) conceit, Pope Benedict XVI cautions that "technologically advanced societies must not confuse their own technological development with a presumed cultural superiority, but must rather rediscover within themselves the oft-forgotten virtues which made it possible for them to flourish throughout their history."[60] This exhortation should find an echo in all the diverse niche of human interactions across the globe. The times when pseudo-anthropological claims are made in order to deny the humanity of Africans are past. However, attitudinal complexes still bedevil relationships across the racial divide. And a retrospective glance at the history of humanity compels us to admit not only the possibility but also the necessity of eliminating those barriers that stand in the way of mutual respect and the acknowledgement of our ontological equality and fraternal bond. Such barriers ignore the undeniable richness of the diversity that characterizes the human family—a richness now tainted by a preponderance of parochialism. Healing such parochialism and prejudices by consistent efforts at harmony-oriented education that is nurtured and sustained by theological scholarship is the challenge of a new shift in theological hermeneutic today. And the task of overcoming those obstacles to healthy human interactions is one which a theology of fraternity must cease as an opportunity to redeem Africa from the anthropological pauperization under which the continent has been yoked since its contact with Western civilization. It is also a task that will change the underlying impulse of all dimensions of human relationships within and outside Africa, thus raising the entire humanity (privileged and underprivileged) to a new level of maturity and friendship whose cornerstone is the consciousness and appreciation of being one Family of God. Part of the healing is already noticeable in so many projects where black

---

59. Ibid, 17–18.
60. Benedict XVI, *CIV*, 59.

Africans and white people are able to collaborate as equals and as brothers and sisters.

Experience of Colonialism

> I have listened to your words but can find no reason why I should obey you—I would rather die first. I have no relations with you and cannot bring it to my mind that you have given me so much as a pesa (fraction of a rupee) or the quarter of a pesa or a needle for a thread. I look for some reason why I should obey you and find not the smallest. If it should be friendship that you desire, then I am ready for it, today and always; but to be your subject . . . I do not fall at your feet, for you are God's creature just as I am . . . I am sultan here in my land. You are sultan there in yours. Yet listen, I do not say to you that you should obey me; for I know that you are a free man . . . As for me, I will not come to you, and if you are strong enough, then come and fetch me.[61]

The above is an excerpt from a dispatch sent by Macemba, the Chief of Yao people in present day Malawi, in 1890 to a German imperialist, Herman Von Wissman, which demonstrates the position of most African leaders and people at the beginning of the colonial rule in the latter half of the 19th Century. It contradicts the many wrong assumptions of people like Hegel that were based on myths about "savage Africans" who neither had a cohesive society nor political constitution[62] prior to colonialism. Colonialism is generally understood as the ideological and political phenomenon, which is documented in African historiography as emerging from the European *"scramble and partition of Africa."* Note that it was an ideology of intimidation and exploitation designed to serve Western cupidity, but which was cleverly masked as pretense to *civilize* Africa. African discourse, as it is known today, is a response to Africa's negative encounter with its European other, and colonialism takes the center stage of that encounter. According to Edward P. Antonio,

> The establishment of Christianity in Africa was often shaped, conditioned and mediated through colonial rationality and in turn colonial rationality was recurrently shaped, deployed and propagated through Christian mission. This historically contingent relationship . . . has been perceived in Africa as largely negative for it instituted and actualized regimes of cultural, political

61. Quoted by Ilo, *Face of Africa*, 62.
62. See Hegel, *Philosophy of History*, 198.

and historical power which produced the social structures within which missionaries, colonialists and natives encountered each other and whose effects were the alienated relations which constituted the substance of that encounter.[63]

In the first place, no African was present at the Berlin Conference of 1884/5 where the boundaries of the various colonies were decided and the political future of Africa sealed without any consideration for her traditional monarchies, chiefdoms and ethnic societies. It was an all-white affair. In some cases, African societies were rent apart: the Bakongo were partitioned between the French Congo, Belgian Congo and Portuguese Angola; Somaliland was carved up between Britain, Italy and France. In all, the new boundaries cut through some 190 culture groups.[64] In Nigeria, the result of the amalgamation of the Southern and Northern part in 1914 by Lord Fredrick Lugard who admitted that the two regions *are like water and oil and therefore can never mix*, has been a long harvest of conflicts and bloodbaths that have claimed uncountable number of victims in Nigeria till date.

The disruption brought about by colonialism succeeded in draining African societies of their very essence. Colonialism trampled on African culture, undermined African institutions, confiscated its lands, smashed its religions, destroyed its magnificent artistic creations and wiped out extraordinary possibilities.[65] And in doing this, most Western colonialists were convinced that if all that Africa represented were to be obliterated from the face of the earth "the world would lose no great truth, no profitable art, no exemplary form of life . . . no memorable deduction from anything but the earth's black catalogue of crimes."[66] It is no surprise then that none of the European theologians, not even Karl Barth, despite his stance against the naked brutality and violence of Nazi Germany, addressed the issue of colonial violence and military oppression against African peoples.[67] This invariably highlights, according to Martey, the irrelevancy of North Atlantic theology to the African situation. In fact, both Christianity and colonialism were socially, culturally and historically disruptive. Both the mission to civilize which was part of the basic framework and driving principle of colonialism and the desire to convert "natives" to Christianity, the fundamental *telos* of missionary activity, sought to displace and reorganize African spaces in the name of new orders of social and cultural existence derived from and

63. Antonio, *Inculturation and Postcolonial Discourse,* 10.

64. Meredith, *Fate of Africa,* 1.

65. Martey, *African Theology,* 8.

66. Foote, *Africa and the American Flag,* 54. Quoted in Ilo, *Face of Africa,* 51.

67. Martey, *African Theology,* 8.

essentially modeled upon Europe as the inherent (and thus only) paradigm of authentic human sociality.[68]

On the socio-economic terrain Western colonial powers, as we have already seen above, never regarded Africans as equals and never entered into any mutual economic relations with them. The story of "pacification of the Lower Niger" is a striking example. The emergence of free trade, which replaced the slave trade at the time, was primarily because of change in demands by Europeans for new forms of merchandise. The Europeans needed cash crop products (cotton, palm oil, rubber, etc.) gold, lodes and skins, timber, and ivory, which they took from Africa in exchange for cheap goods like gin, gunpowder, textiles, and toilet soap.[69] A deep-seated racial contempt that expressed itself in both the nature of the interaction and the structure of oppression and suppression adopted in colonial politics distinguished African colonial experience from colonialism in places like Australia, United States of America and New Zealand. It is a racial contempt, for which even the noblest of Western minds were not immune. For instance, Abraham Lincoln, who was widely revered as the symbol of Christian compassion and democratic sensibilities; an icon of America's democratic and liberal ideals, and who was one of the leading figures of the anti-slavery Movement in the United States and the rest of the free world, is quoted to have said in a speech in Charleston, Illinois on September 18, 1858:

> I do not understand that because I do not want a Negro woman for a slave I must necessarily want her for a wife (*cheers and laughter*) . . . I will to the very last stand by the law of this state, which forbids the marrying of white people with Negroes . . . I will say then that I am not, nor ever have been, in favor of bringing about in any way the social and political equality of the white and black races (*applause*)—that I am not, nor ever have been in favor of making voters or jurors of Negroes; nor of qualifying them to hold office, nor to intermarry with white people."[70]

Whether motivated by political expediency or personal conviction, Lincoln's speech reflects the underlying attitude that structured the relationship between whites and blacks throughout the period of colonial history. And even most missionaries and prominent church men and women were not immune to this attitude. One Rev. Muller, making reference to the perceived backwardness of the Africans before colonialism, was quoted as

---

68. Antonio, *Inculturation and Postcolonial Discourse,* 11.

69. Sogolo, *Foundations of African Philosophy,* 266.

70. Quoted in Mazrui, *Cultural Forces in World Politics,* 122.

saying, "Humanity must not, cannot allow the incompetence, negligence, and laziness of the uncivilized peoples to leave idle indefinitely the wealth which God has confided to them, charging them to make it serve the good of all."[71] Today the question may be asked: Whose good has colonialism actually served? Arguing for an economic policy, which he designated as "*dual mandate*," the colonial Governor General of Nigeria, Lord Lugard, said: "Let it be admitted at the outset that European brains, capital and energy have not been and never will be, expended in developing the resources of Africa from motive of pure philanthropy."[72] No wonder there was no effort made to teach technological skills in colonial schools.

The fruits of the encounter are seen in the anthropological and economic pauperization, to which the African continent was subjected and which she continues to suffer today as a result of the colonial stillbirth. The colonial lords simply took control of all the mineral resources of the African continent for the good of the "mother country." Nigeria's coal, Ghana's gold, Kenya's copper, and Sierra Leone's diamonds all went to the "mother country" for nothing. Worse still, colonial schools became the "citadels for the indoctrination of Africans on the inferiority of their cultures, and the need for them to enter into the higher and exclusive portals of Western civilization."[73] One cannot help being amazed at how Count Zinzendorf, a Moravian spiritual leader, rationalized away the evil of slavery by arguing thus: "God punished the first Negroes by making them slaves, and your conversion will make you free, not from control of your masters, but simply from your wicked habits and thoughts, and all that make you dissatisfied with your lot."[74] The school served as bases for the loss of African identity. It neither produced authentic Africans nor authentic Europeans, but a class of alienated Africans. The following excerpt from Nelson Mandela's autobiography illumines this fact:

> On the first day of school, my teacher, Miss Mdingane, gave each of us an English name and said that from thenceforth that was the name we would answer to in school. This was the custom among Africans in those days and was undoubtedly due to the British bias of our education. The education I received was a British education, in which British ideas, British culture, British institutions, were automatically assumed to be superior. There was no such thing as African culture.

71. Cesear, *Discourse on Colonialism*, 39.
72. Lugard, *Dual Mandate*. 917.
73. Ilo, *Face of Africa*, 75.
74. Quoted in Nebechukwu, "Third World Theology," 20.

Africans of my generation—and even today—generally have both an English and an African name. Whites were either unable or unwilling to pronounce an African name, and considered it uncivilized to have one. That day, Miss Mdingane told me that my new name was Nelson. Why she bestowed this particular name upon me I have no idea.[75]

Contrary to European names, however, traditional African names of persons, as I already mentioned, have deep religious significance and reveal a profound sense of the ontological origin of man such that their very names are a constant reminder of and cipher-scripts for the transcendence. As African names were snubbed and rejected in colonial schools, so were African arts, values and languages. Hence, Chu Ilo laments:

> There was no genuine effort in the colonial schools to churn out literate and educated elites for fear of competition or an incipient drive for political emancipation, which education usually engenders. The understanding of education as mere clerical competence, which was introduced in the colonial schools continued even in post-colonial Africa. The kind of education in Africa during the colonial era and today is one that will never introduce Africa into the technological age nor will it help Africans discover their artistic, scientific, technological and creative genius. It will not unravel the beauty of the African continent and her people. In this sense, colonial rule was very destructive of the cultural identity of the Africans. It left Africans with, 'A Culture without economic autonomy or strength; a culture without political power; a culture with no flowering of the arts or the intellect. . .of incomplete synthesis. A culture without inner unity.'"[76]

To appropriate Chinua Achebe's metaphor, colonialism is the proverbial knife that was thrust into the center of Igbo or African socio-cultural cohesion and caused it to fall apart.[77] According to Jean-Marc Ela in his *Af-*

75. Mandela, *Long Walk to Freedom*, 13–14.

76. Ilo, *Face of Africa*, 76.

77. *Things Fall Apart* is a classic African novel that provides an inside view of traditional religion and the way in which it was disrupted by a pervasive Christianity that blessed the sword of olden colonialism. According to Kwame Anthony Appiah, "Not only does Achebe draw a compelling picture of life in one part of Igboland before the arrival of Christianity and colonialism, he manages to convey to all of us, Igbo or not, both the tragedy of the loss of that world and the possibilities created by the new situation" (Appiah, Introduction to Achebe, *Things Fall Apart*). One of those possibilities is that Christianity achieved bringing the *Osu* and the freeborn under one roof—a hitherto undreamed-of possibility. Achebe describes it thus: "These outcasts, or *osu,*

rican Cry, no reflection on African history can afford to ignore the relationship between Christianity and colonization. In fact colonialism exploited evangelization as an epistemic tool to propagate the cultural and political supremacy of the West.

> The God of the missionary preaching [regrettably] was one whose power signifies not liberation but economic oppression, cultural and political alienation, and a racist contempt for the native. The indictment of Western imperialism rests on a reinterpretation of the message of the Bible from within the colonial situation and calls for a search for a God-for-the-emancipation-of-the-black who has spokespersons among the Africans themselves. The black prophets seek not to return to the God of the ancestors, but to make the message of the gospel heard in an African context.[78]

This unmistakable cry of protest is understandable and should win our attention in the post-colonial context of African theology. The havoc wreaked by colonialism is so insidious that Anta Diop has compared it to "an obstinate weed which, at the sign of a drought, pushes its roots deeper into the soil in search of nutrients."[79] In other words, colonialism has not ceased to impede development in Africa. The state structure it created was crafted to ensure an atmosphere of perpetual conflict that will continue to serve the interest of exploitation. The achievement of political independence and the establishment of sovereignties in Africa in the second half of the twentieth century gave the people only an illusion of being free from "the Whiteman." But in truth the real oppressor or enemy is not just "the Whiteman," but his legacy. The real enemy is the malignant proclivity to abuse one's advantage over others and refuse to treat them, according to the "golden rule," as one would himself or herself love to be treated. In fact, it is such tendency (which unfortunately dominated colonial politics), which has remained till today the bane of a true civilization of love and the challenge of a theology that is committed to justice, solidarity and *aggiornamento*. It is the above mentioned malaise that, in fact, corrupted the Whiteman's encounter with black history and culture. Accordingly, the reinterpretation of the message of

---

seeing that the new religion welcomed twins and such abominations, thought that it was possible that they would be received. And so one Sunday two of them went into the church. There was an immediate stir; but so great was the work the new religion had done among the converts that they did not immediately leave the church when the outcasts came in. Those who found themselves nearest to them merely moved to another seat. It was a miracle" (*Things Fall Apart*, 136).

78. Ela, *African Cry*, 48.

79. Diop, *Towards the African Renaissance*, 70.

the Bible, which Ela proposes, should no longer be done only "from within the colonial situation" nor from the perspective of "a search for a God-for-the-emancipation-of-the-black," but from a much broader perspective that is all-inclusive and integral, namely, the perspective of universal fraternity and solidarity. Stationed on this new inclusive foothold, human relationship should no longer be governed by economic expediency and egotistical utilitarianism but by a deeper appreciation of humanity's mutual sharing in one undivided spiritual and existential patrimony that prefigures the life of the kingdom of God.

The Biafran Revolution (1967–1970)

If I consider Biafran story important in this discourse, it is not because the story is peculiar in itself or has any moral precedence over the numerous stories of conflicts in Africa. On the contrary, its election here is as representative of all the blood baths across the continent that cannot be fully covered by any narrative. Biafra is only one of the indices that remind us that we have not yet landed where we should be in terms of authentic liberation and community building in Africa.

As soon as colonialism gave way to pseudo-independence and neo-colonialism it became clear that African states were destined to implode into scenes of consuming conflicts of alarming scales. Such conflicts, even when they were predictable as inevitable consequences of the legacy of the colonial structure, go a long way to prove that the hitherto discussed anti-fraternal relations can no longer be attributed to racial prejudice in which the Whiteman is the presumed villain. Whether regarded as a tragic off-spring of the colonial structure, or simply as the human will to murderous exclusion, it will surely be considered a lacuna in a theological discourse of the Igbo context not to remember this significant event that has impacted Igbo history more than anything else.

The Biafran or Nigerian civil war of 1967–1970 was the most violent phase in a complex series of convulsions that shook the young Nigerian nation in the wake of decolonization. Chinua Achebe calls it "a cataclysmic experience that changed the history of Africa."[80] Facilitated, or better said, exacerbated by British arms supplies from the Harold Wilson Labor government and the Soviet bloc, the conflict centered on the hate-filled suppression of the break-away Republic of Biafra by the Federal Military Government of Nigeria. That Nigeria was, from the outset, a pragmatic and ambivalent construction is hardly a matter of debate, since the current geopolitical divi-

80. Achebe, *There Was a Country*. 2.

sions of West Africa were negotiated between Western European powers in the 1890s, and the emergence of Nigeria itself as a national idea can be traced to the *London Times* in 1897.[81] Therefore, as a conflict whose plot is to be located within the context of neo-colonial politics, there are valid reasons to consider the Biafran saga as very relevant to theological discourse in Africa. Firstly, the war (described by the then Biafran leader as an anti-colonial Revolution[82]) was another traumatic experience for the Igbo people on their march to liberation and self-determination. It was an experience whose historical lessons and ethical values can never be overemphasized. According to Frederick Forsyth, the conflict remains, for those intimately involved in the fighting and the suffering, a scar that will never fade.[83] It is indeed a lesson that evokes the memory of the true face of evil when men and women, leaders of the world, for no good reason other than self-interest or apathy, deliberately acquiesce to the injustice of denying freedom to a people who earnestly yearn and have the right for it.

The Biafran Revolution, widely acknowledged as a tragedy of untold magnitude, could have been prevented if the world was willing to hearken to the cry of legitimate aspirations of the oppressed. The Biafra story (similar to all war stories) is a tragic story of extreme harsh and traumatic experiences of fleeing enemy bombs and shells, of humanitarian disaster in refugee camps. A sorrowful story of lost childhood, as makeshift provisions replaced familiar conveniences and new friendships quickly dissolved into devastating departures to foreign climes in search of safety; a story of babies' premature capitulation to deadly protein-deficient kwashiorkor. It is a story of the incredulity of seeing a one time family friend suddenly thirst to spill the blood of his pal on the "altar of ethnic loyalty." It is a story of hate, brutal massacre, starvation and decimation of an innocent folk whose sole sin was that it seeks political autonomy. But it is also a story of the unsung heroes and heroines whose sacrifices and stoicism are awesome; who treasured the values of sharing, compassion and solidarity in harsh circumstances of war when selfishness appears to be every victim's god. There are a good number of such heroes, both indigenes and expatriates, whose examples demonstrate what it means to be a true brother or sister to one another. Recalling his own experience of that war, Father Byrne, an Irish missionary, admits that "In normal times, most people are proud of their hospitality but, in times like these, when the next supply of food is uncertain, hospitality requires a certain foolhardiness or heroism—or faith. Perhaps it takes a

---

81. Cf. Morrison, "Imagined Biafras."

82. See Ojukwu, "Ahiara Declaration."

83. Forsyth, Foreword to Byrne, *Airlift to Biafra*, 7.

mixture of all three."[84] One hundred and twenty-two Biafran and thirty-five North American and European JCA [Joint Church Aid] workers, including seventeen pilots, sacrificed their lives during the relief program organized to help starving children.[85] Biafra is a story that draws one into the epicenter of strong family emotions as mothers fought and surrendered to the higher call to service to fatherland. Like the story of Cain and Abel, it is also a story of fratricide—a war that sadly pitted brother against brother—African brothers, who once lived peacefully together. This story, of course, does not begin with the first firing of artillery shells; no, it began with the ominous darkness that enveloped the hearts of men and women, rousing, as it were, their wildest instincts to fratricidal frenzy. It began with the will to ethnic exclusion where the rhetoric of national integration is ironically conveyed by the sounds of mortar and machine-gun fire. Whenever and wherever a similar tragedy is repeated on the face of earth, one could always pin the responsibility on a jaundiced perception incapable of appreciating the common heritage of the belligerent parties. If such malignant predisposition to exclude were overcome, humanity will be better equipped morally to expend its energies and resources in building community and perfecting mankind's creative genius rather than wasting them in wars and ethnic or religious conflicts.

This is why the Biafra story should be retold by theology in Africa. Many versions of that story have provided ample evidence of a plot to decimate or exterminate an ethnic group by the Nigerian government, and how powerful western governments became onlookers while the cruelest weapon of mass destruction was applied in a war of attrition, where the starvation of men, women and children was endorsed as a legitimate military strategy. This plot to starve Biafrans to death was rationalized by a good number of arguments by leaders of the Nigerian government:

1. Chief Obafemi Awolowo, finance commissioner and vice chairman of the Federal Executive Council in the Nigerian government stated, "All is fair in war, and starvation is one of the weapons of war. I do not see why we should feed our enemies fat in order for them to fight us harder." (*Financial Times*, London, June 26, 1969; *Daily Telegraph*, London, June 27, 1969).

2. Chief Anthony Enahoro, federal commissioner for labor and information stated, "There are various ways of fighting a war. You might starve your enemy into submission, or you might kill him on the battlefield" (*Daily Mirror*, London, June 13, 1968).

84. Byrne, *Airlift to Biafra*, 59.
85. Ibid., 150.

3. Yakubu Gowon, the head of state of Nigeria, in an interview with Tom Burns stated, "Food is the means to resistance: It is ammunition in this sense and the mercy flights into rebel territory are looked upon as tantamount to gun running." (*Tablet*, London, December 7, 1968; *Spectator* December 27, 1968).

4. Brigadier Hassan Usman Katsina, Chief of Staff of the Nigerian Army stated, "Personally I would not feed somebody I am fighting" (*Times*, London, June 28, 1969).

5. Brigadier Benjamin Adekunle, commander of the 3rd marine commando stated, "In the sector which is under my command—and that covers the entire southern front, from Lagos to the frontier of Cameroon—I want to see no Red Cross, no World Council of Churches, no Pope, no missionary, and no U.N. delegation . . . . . You have a keen intellect my friend. That's exactly what I mean . . . .. Until the entire population capitulates, I want to prevent even one Ibo having one piece of food to eat." (*Stern Magazine*, August 18, 1968).[86]

6. Col. Shittu Alao, commander of the Nigeria Air Force stated, "As far as we are concerned, we are hitting at everything flying into Biafra, Red Cross or not." (*Washington Post*, June 7, 1969).

All are brilliant logics of war, one could say, but they are regrettably the sadistic logics of an anti-human will toward murderous exclusion. It is a logic whose advocates cannot but be considered as villains of the human social project. And even though this starvation policy of the Nigerian military government was being executed after the historic Geneva Convention and all of these statements were documented by the British Media, yet it neither induced Harold Wilson's government and its allies to break its support for Nigeria nor move them to recognize Biafra's inalienable right to sovereignty. In fact, "following the blockade imposed by the Nigerian government, 'Biafra' became synonymous with the tear-tugging imagery of starving babies with blown-out bellies, skulls with no subcutaneous fat harboring pale, sunken eyes in sockets that betrayed their suffering."[87] It is an image that will haunt the soul of any righteous man or woman when he or she closes the eyes to pray.

86. An interview granted by Brigadier Benjamin Adenkule of the Nigerian Army to German Reporter, Randolph Baumann, of STERN Magazine on August 18, 1968 in Port Harcourt was published by www.kwenu.com. Because of its capacity to engender hatred, I have decided not to reproduce that interview in this book. Ironically, Adekunle was never prosecuted for any war crimes. On the contrary, he was promoted to Brigadier General in 1972 before he retired from the army in 1974.

87. Achebe, *There Was a Country*, 199.

Today's headlines are still inundated with such images and the cruel-
ties and horror which they evoke always delineate a fact which theological
reflections must take seriously. Ethnic and religious hatred and conflicts are
still rife, and they are often planned by powerful and wealthy individuals.
Is it not ironic that humanity will rally together in solidarity to victims of
natural disasters and yet powerful leaders will contrive to create a lot of
man-made disasters by prizing selfish interests above common good and
the need to relate to one another as true brothers and sisters? In a painful lamentation of this disaster, Father Byrne writes: "Thinking of the root
cause of this bitter war—the rich oil resources of Biafra—made me fume
with anger. This war might never have happened if those resources were
not there. No one need have died."[88] And in a public lecture organized in
Vienna in which he also deplored the war, Monsignor Carlo Bayer, the then
Secretary General of *Caritas Internationalis* put it succinctly while responding to questions from students about the humanitarian role of the Church
in the conflict:

> The war would never have happened if there were no rich oil
> wells in the Port Harcourt area. More than a million people
> died. I'm convinced those people were sacrificed on the altar
> of oil . . . That's the easy part of the answer . . .The more dif-
> ficult part to explain . . ., was the role of the colonial and former
> colonial powers. Everybody knows that colonialism is finished
> in Africa, but there are many countries who still want to buy
> their raw materials at the old colonial prices, or less, from their
> former colonies. These powers are also keen to defend their past
> behavior by trying to show that Africans are not mature enough
> to manage their own affairs.[89]

In order to conceal the capitalist greed behind its questionable position with regard to the war, the British government had to invent a spurious
argument claiming that to concede sovereignty to the Biafrans will lead to
the balkanization of Africa. And to prevent such a "terrible" occurrence
hundreds of thousands of children must die. "Balkanization" thus became
another attempt to cease the narrative and transform it into a "single story"
of the powerful. It is for this reason that recalling the Biafran Revolution
remains an essential subject-matter of theology in the Igbo context in order to appraise the memory of a people that refused to have their story be
told by others. Biafra was a struggle against exclusion even as it was for
self-determination. And theology should remember and honor the struggle

88. Byrne, *Airlift to Biafra*, 13.

89. Cited by Byrne, *Airlift to Biafra*, 169.

of such a people so that history will not trivialize the lessons of fraternal solidarity or the lack thereof embedded in the tragic stories of intractable ethnic conflicts that plague African democracies today.

The memory of Biafra is a memory of the strangulation of the age-long republicanism of the Igbo which is attested to by social anthropologists, or historians like A. E. Afigbo. Writing about the Igbo society Afigbo informs us: "Being basically segmentary, central government within each autonomous unit is a federation of equivalent segments, each of which retains a large measure of power and authority and regards as binding, decisions only to which it has given assent."[90] The Biafran revolution was a legitimate struggle of a people to reclaim this political authority that is based on the belief that leadership should always be accountable to the people—Oha. Believing that all persons are created equal, even before America was colonized, the people sought to defend their belief in collective leadership and communal governance. Afigbo's study shows that the original, i.e., pre-colonial, constitution of the communities of Biafra (i.e. the Eastern Provinces of Nigeria) was founded on gerontocracy.[91]

> Contrary to the impression which the myth of high forest tends to convey, the communities in this region [Igboland] were far from being disparate units. There were many integrative links—common and centrally located markets, the long-range traders . . . And what is more, many of the social institutions of the Ibo and their neighbors served as agencies for cultural integration among otherwise politically disintegrated groups.[92]

The extraordinary blending of individualism and collectivism formed the backbone of the Biafrans' die-hard resilience during this most tragic moment of their history. Achebe also recalls that, beyond the understandable trepidation associated with a looming war, one found a new spirit among the people, a spirit one did not know existed, a determination. The spirit was that of a people ready to put in their best and fight for their freedom.[93] In rising to reclaim and defend a prized autonomy the Biafran people became an example of a people to be grilled on yet another crucible of African history, for being, as Father Byrne would put it, "a people who had been keenly enthusiastic about progress and development."[94] Being receptive to fruitful change, individualistic and highly competitive; unhindered by a wary

90. See Afigbo, *Warrant Chiefs*, 15.

91. Ibid, 22. Gerontocracy means government by a council of elders.

92. Ibid.

93. Achebe, *There Was a Country*, 171.

94. Byrne, *Airlift to Biafra*. 40.

religion and unhampered by traditional hierarchies—fearing no god or man—the Igbo were custom-made to grasp the opportunities, such as they were, of the white man's dispensations. And they did so with both hands.[95] This ambition unfortunately fetched them envy, resentment and persecution. Now it is Africans who are killing themselves, they do not have the Whiteman again to blame for it. The truth, however, is that ethnic exclusion is no less pernicious than racial exclusion as a sin against fraternity.

From the Biafran side though, it was not a war that was fought for its own sake. No, it was the struggle of a God-fearing people, to break the yoke of anthropological pauperization, which the neo-colonial structure was designed to entrench. Trusting their God, the Supreme Being, *"Ama Ama Amasị Amasị"*—the Unknowable and Unfathomable ONE; *"Chi na Eke"*— the God who creates; *"Chi Ukwu"*—the Great God, who created them as free people before the advent of the major religions of today, the people took to arms to defend themselves. As a people that call themselves *"Ụmụ Chukwu*—the children of the great God;"[96] a people who in great numbers willingly embraced Christianity with awesome joy and dedication, not because of, but rather in spite of the Whiteman's arrogance, their struggle is no less different from that of the biblical Israelites. Being a people that believe in their individual *Chi* (destiny or *Genius*) and collective *Chi* (Supreme Being); a people that believe that both the weak and the strong have inalienable right to live in peace (*"egbe belụ, ugo belụ, nke sị ibe ya ebela, nku kwaa ya"—let the falcon perch and the eagle perch, any that refuses the other the right to perch, may its pinions break*),[97] the death of Biafra stood for a tragic loss. It was a loss both of a moral and enterprising genius, which was sacrificed on the altar of ethnic exclusion. Due to ethnic hatred and circumstances which made it difficult for Biafrans at the time to find in the colonial construction that was Nigeria a fatherland that they will call a safe home, it was a struggle provoked by the need for survival. Millions of them were punished with deliberate starvation through a policy of economic blockade, in an effort to bend their will or wipe them off the face of the earth, and the uncaring world leaders turned a blind eye and a deaf ear to this tragedy of immense proportion. Such is the fate and the story of a people who Ignacio Ellacuría refers to as "the crucified people."

Christian Theology will always be indebted to such people in its efforts at finding answers to the numerous questions about human existence in

95. Achebe, *There Was a Country*, 74.

96. See Ikenga-Metuh, *God and Man in African Religion*.

97. This is an Igbo proverb that is often used in Igbo traditional prayers for breaking the kolanut—a significant Igbo ritual of hospitality and brotherliness.

the world, and of man's transcendental vocation to fraternal communion. Hence, it is important to reassert to historical memory that the Biafran revolution was a loud and desperate *cry* for freedom. That cry was deliberately ignored, in fact exacerbated, by the titans of capitalism and communism in a world whose conscience and perception of truth and justice has been badly warped by selfish materialistic interests. In his version of the story Father Byrne also recounted how the colonial Portuguese government in the island of Sao Tomé, whose strategic position was something to reckon for aid-lifting into Biafra, unashamedly and without any sensibility wanted to take advantage of the tragic situation of Biafran children to its selfish benefits.[98] In a way reminiscent of *Theologie nach Auschwitz*, the historical memory of Biafra reaffirms the importance of theological engagement with the intractable conflicts that threaten the meaning of fraternity in a world where human relationships are destroyed by greed and murderous exclusion. Such an engagement will need to be sustained by a theological hermeneutic that accentuates positive, mutual, interpersonal perceptions of all human beings and deplores the sin of hatred. *Theology after Biafra*, just like *Theologie nach Auschwitz*, offers an important theodicy lessons in this regard. The anguished cry of the Biafran child dying of kwashiorkor offers a context in which the passion of Christ could be contemplated. The Nigerian Church in its *Lineamenta for the First National Pastoral Congress* in fact acknowledges the evangelical significance of the challenge of the Biafran war when it admitted that

> The civil crisis, which raged between 1966 and 1970, was not only trying for the nation as a whole but also for the Church in particular. During the crisis Nigerians lived the worst in ethnic divisions, prejudices and loyalties . . . Hundreds of thousands of innocent lives were lost in the carnage. Property was lost, confiscated or destroyed. Deep-seated suspicion was installed as principle of inter-ethnic relations. This situation calls for a courageous and decisive action by the Church.[99]

The irony of the above statement and call for "a courageous and decisive action" is that it came thirty years after the end of the war. But thankfully, it came with the sincerity of acknowledging that the Biafra crisis "weakened the witness of a Church that was unprepared by less than one hundred years history to handle such upheaval with courage."[100] There was clear division of the Church along ethnic lines. Missionaries took sides depending on where

98. Achebe, *There Was a Country*, 112.

99. Catholic Secretariat of Nigeria, *Church in Nigeria: Family of God on Mission*, 16.

100. Ibid.

they happened to be working. The end of the war saw the expulsion of about 300 Irish missionaries from Nigeria. The massive expulsion of missionaries in Eastern Nigeria and the silence of the Catholic Church during that exercise reveal a lack of the prophetic voice in the Nigerian Church and a poor understanding of the meaning of one family of God.[101] Since Biafra was vanquished with military arms, ethnic and religious violence has rocked Nigerian society in a way that leaves much to be desired. And as a post-colonial crisis, Wole Soyinka, who was incarcerated for his opposition to that civil war, defines the crisis in terms of the legacy of the Berlin Conference:

> What God (white man) has put together, let no black man put asunder. The complications of neo-colonial politics of interference compel one to accept such a damnable catechism for now, as a pragmatic necessity. Later perhaps, the black nations will themselves sit down together, and, by agreement, set compass and square rule to paper and reformulate the life-expending, stultifying, constrictive imposition of this divine authority. What is clear, miserably clear is that a war is being fought without a simultaneous program of reform and redefinition of social purpose. A war of solidity; for solidity is describing a war which can only consolidate the very values that gave rise to the war in the first place, for nowhere and at no time have those values been examined. Nowhere has there appeared a program designed to ensure the eradication of the fundamental iniquities which gave rise to the initial conflicts.[102]

Can and should Christian theology today contribute in eradicating the misperceptions and intractable conflicts from which the Biafran war was only an undesirable and catastrophic offspring? Can it help to forge a new and strong spirit of solidarity and brotherliness in the human family across ethnic allegiances in Africa? If modern society hopes to rise above and overcome the causes of the divisions that stultify integral human development, then it must be prepared to find answers to these questions, but most importantly, they must be answers that lie within the epistemic ambience of autochthonous wisdom. It is the argument of this book that such answers are to be found in a theology of fraternity through the vehicle of native idioms. The pithy saying, *Ọ nụrụ ube nwanne agbala ọsọ*, originating from the wisdom of a people who have endured the crucibles of persecution, offers us a theological tool for eschewing vengeance and promoting fraternal love.

---

101. Ibid.

102. Soyinka, *The Man Died*, 181.

But more importantly, the saying helps us to see the Biafran tragedy as a cry of brothers and sisters against injustice.

Captivated by the meticulous nature with which Biafrans conducted the affairs of their short-lived state, Richard West, a British journalist lamented in an article: "Biafra is more than a human tragedy. Its defeat, I believe, would mark the end of African independence. Biafra was the first place I had been to in Africa where the Africans themselves were truly in charge."[103] This statement should of course be seen as an appraisal of the African spirit of resilience and resourcefulness. Unfortunately through the instrumentality of the British and Soviet arms-supply there is no doubt that the Nigerian independence, at least, was effectively confiscated in the Biafran tragedy. But the tragedy that was Biafra is indeed the tragedy of a lost humanity too jaundiced to recognize and appreciate the bond of fraternity that holds us together and constitutes the enabling roller in the march of civilization. In this sense, Biafra could be understood as a symbol which can have any other name: Darfur, Liberia, Rwanda, Zaire, Uganda, Central African Republic, etc. Hence, there is a sense in which it is legitimate to say, as some do, that *In Biafra Africa died.*[104]

Experience of Bad Governance

Development depends on good governance. That is the ingredient which has been missing in far too many places, for far too long. That's the change that can unlock Africa's potential. And that is a responsibility that can only be met by Africans.

—U.S. President Barrack Obama to African leaders in Accra, Ghana, 11th July 2009

The moral justifiability and acceptability of any form of political government depends on the type of relationship it establishes between the governor and the governed. Whenever and wherever governance fails to be recognized as a service to fellow brothers and sisters, it becomes unpopular and unsustainable, no matter how plausible the ideological basis and philosophy of that government may appear to be. This is true whether of theocracy, socialism, republicanism, or liberal democracy. Good governance that guarantees development depends on the nature of relationship between leaders and citizens. And the duty of forming the adequate character for such public service

---

103. Quoted by Achebe, *There Was a Country*, 172. Similar sentiment was also expressed by Byrne in *Airlift to Biafra*.

104. See Ezeani, *In Biafra Africa Died.*

is one of the goals of evangelization. Forming good citizens is, hence, one of Christianity's tasks. Unfortunately, this is where Christianity has failed in the past and been often indicted and brought to disrepute for abusing its power over subjugated people. No religion whose votaries have conquered much of the globe in the hope of saving others (and presumably themselves too) can claim the privilege of a fundamental indifference to power. However, how such power has been exercised in promoting human well-being in various situations remains a fundamental question for theology. Christianity has often endorsed a particular style of management of subjugated peoples, a style marked by an unremitting search for unfair privilege. In the bid to favor tiny irreligious and corrupt elite that continue to milk resources and maintain itself in a position of undeserved affluence, whole nations have been impoverished. This is true not only of the history of colonialism but also of the history of Europe at the time when the Church was enjoying political privilege. Theology in Africa must not fail to denounce regimes in Africa under whose watch foreign companies have been able to transport to Africa the pollution and corruption of which the West has grown weary. Such foreign companies that prosper when the masses languish rightly deserve condemnation for colluding with members of the African ruling class, who amass scandalous personal fortunes through their collaboration with neo-colonial exploitation.[105] According to Ela,

> The notion of underdevelopment so dear to charitable institutions is the vehicle of an ideology that disguises the real nature of the neo-colonial condition predominating in black Africa. Actually, poverty in all of its forms is but the effect of the domination imposed on the great majority of Africans . . . Africa possesses immense riches. But they are exploited by the monied powers.
>
> One example among so many others is the geological scandal that is Zaire. Africa remains a reservoir of raw materials for the West. Its population is still cheap labor for foreign investors. The contemporary situation is marked by a division into two unequally privileged parts: an opulent West, wondering what meaning to ascribe to its society of abundance, and an impoverished, endlessly humiliated and exploited Africa, where an autochthonous club of haves is created to assist in the exploitation of masses groaning under the weight of their manifold privations.[106]

105. Ela, *African Cry*, 63–64.
106. Ibid., 64.

The 2004 Commission for Africa identified "the weakness of governance and the absence of an effective state" as one major factor that underlies all the difficulties caused by the interactions of Africa's history over the past 40 years.[107] The Commission defines bad governance here as "the inability of government and the public services to create the right economic, social and legal framework which will encourage economic growth and allow poor people to participate in it."[108] The question, however, is whether this "inability" is as a result of lack of knowledge of what to do or simply lack of the will to do the right thing due to selfishness. This is why I have made reference to Barack Obama's speech in Ghana. That reference is meant to underscore that leaders become true leaders only to the extent that they have come to appreciate their role as humble servants to their "brothers and sisters." This ideal of leadership remains in many cases in Africa still a forlorn hope. Hence, there is need to emphasize that the awareness of leadership as a call to fraternal responsibility is the first step to unlocking the potentials for development in Africa and everywhere.

The experience of military dictatorships and corruption in government in Africa in general is a clear testimony of the fact that the oppressor is not always to be found outside national boundaries. It is no longer the Whiteman alone that we must blame or fear. The enemy within is equally, if not more, dehumanizing in his operations and machinery as the enemy without. Recent history has been a testimony to the unholy alliances across national boundaries whose goal is to grease the machineries of oppression and exploitation in order to advance individual selfish ends. Successive governments in Africa have been indicted often for the unscrupulous conspiracy to hold their own people in perpetual bondage to poverty and misery. In Nigeria, for example, many years of military regime have come to be known proverbially as "years eaten by the locust."[109] Hence, the Igbo theologian is challenged to interpret O nuru ube nwanne agbala oso as an indelible inscription to be engraved on the consciences of political leaders and civil servants who wantonly abuse public offices and privileges, oblivious of the suffering they cause to fellow brothers and sisters. Accordingly, O nuru ube nwanne agbala oso encapsulates here a compact powerful appeal to a radical introspection whose result will be self-liberating as well as so-

107. Commission for Africa, *Our Common Interest: An Argument*, 23–24. Commission for Africa, chaired by Tony Blair, comprised of seventeen people, brought together to define the challenges facing Africa, and to provide clear recommendations on the changes that are needed to reduce poverty. The majority are Africans with experience in political leadership and public service.

108. Ibid.

109. Ehusani, *Nigeria: Years Eaten by the Locust*.

cially revolutionary. However, I fault the US president who thinks that the responsibility to unlock Africa's potential depends on Africans alone. On the contrary, it must be seen as a world-wide common endeavor in global solidarity.

As long as so many harsh realities weigh so heavily upon millions of Africans, we cannot pretend that decolonization has been achieved. But a genuinely lived faith can be a force for liberation, and so the Church must not only contribute to an awakening of the consciousness of the dozing masses but, most importantly, must herself become a sign of hope for those who live in hopelessness. The Church should work for respect of human rights wherever she sees such rights to be trampled. In political systems prevailing in Africa, the Church may be the only institution capable of speaking out and saving what is left of freedom.[110] She must be the torch-bearer to guide men and women to wherever the cries of anguish that demand their attention are discernible. As Pope Francis has recently demonstrated, the Church must be an enemy of "unbridled capitalism." It is the truth that oppression and violation of human rights have been rampant in Africa in regimes where large capitalist interests dominate. What Ela says about President Macias Nguema's long prevailing reign of terror in Equatorial Guinea, which caused the elimination of about 90 percent of the intellectual elite formed before independence, could be said about many regimes in African countries since independence.[111] The extent to which bad governance has adversely affected the lives of so great a number of poor Africans who are enslaved by a wealthy minority able to control the processes of orientation, regulation, and decision to their own advantage, is a cause for concern. This small group is aided and abetted by a trans-national capital that guarantees control of this fabulously wealthy continent. And a change to this status quo is not yet in sight. A Christian theology of fraternity should not be supine in the face of such socio-political injustice that is perpetrated by bad governance. Actions that go beyond pious homilies and communiqués are required as an aggressive but adequate response to the cries of powerlessness. The Church should be willing to build a coalition of politically conscious brothers and sisters at grassroots level and across ethnic borders who will engage themselves with strengthening the ties of brotherhood against corruption at all levels of socio-political life. Indifferentism will be a grave sin against humanity in such circumstances in African societies in which corruption in all of its forms is horrendous and such a source of revenue to the ruling classes and where social inequalities become starker by the day.

110. Ela, *African Cry.* 77.
111. See ibid., 71–72.

Bad governance in Africa evokes a heart-rending cry of anguish which cannot be ignored without compromising the gospel of Christ. As Ela puts it, "For the immense cohort of the frustrated, excluded from all growth and forming precisely the mass of *the wretched of the earth*, the problem of liberation remains. In black Africa, the glorious day of human development in every direction simply never arrived."[112] To be able to usher in that glorious day of human development it is, however, not enough that corruption be fought. Such ethnic or religious antipathies that gave rise to the Biafran tragedy have to be overcome through a fraternal love, openness and collaboration that make the society a home conducive for the human genius to thrive and prosper. For far too long, a "phantom, ambiguous Africa" has been followed by a "disenchanted, dispossessed Africa without a compass," the Africa of millions of human beings whose living conditions may be worse than before independence; human beings who are now the victims of a veritable "colonization of brother by brother." Such is the lament of passionate liberation theologians like Ela whose cry is now a testament bequeathed to the younger generations. To change or ameliorate this grim situation is the challenge of a theology of fraternity. In spite of the many forces of darkness that still exist we can with optimism say that we are already at the dawn of a socialization of the human consciousness at the global level—a socialization which holds the promise of a united peaceful world brought about by our willingness to carry each other with a fraternal love that fears no burden and creates no burden.

112. Ibid., 61.

5

The Secular and Theological Liberation Struggles in Africa

Liberation Movements of the Africans

It is important to note that Africans were not just passive sufferers under the crucibles that have impacted their being in the world. After the Second World War, Africa began to emerge politically in the world, albeit with some fairly serious handicaps. Without writing, populated by hundreds of tribes with multitudes of dialects, cut off from its past by a colonization one of whose many grave sins was to inculcate in Africans the idea that our forefathers were incapable of political organization and creativity, Africa needed urgently to know herself. As Mwalimu Julius K. Nyerere maintains, the history of Africa has not simply been one of deprivation, dispossession and exploitation but also one of resistance and struggle. At the center of this struggle has been the ardent quest for "re-membering" Africa, so brutally "dis-membered" by the "vultures of imperialism."[1] This struggle has assumed variously literary, artistic, political as well as theological dimensions. It found expressions in secular political ideologies like Négritude, African Nationalism and Pan-Africanism with the efforts of such great African visionary leaders like Julius Nyerere of Tanzania, Cheikh Anta Diop and Leopold Sedar Senghor of Senegal, Kwame Nkrumah of Ghana, Nnamdi Azikiwe and Obafemi Awolowo of

---

1. See Shivji, "Ngugi wa Thiong'o's Re-membering Africa."

Nigeria, Kenneth Kaunda of Kenya, Nelson Mandela of South Africa, just to mention a few. And in the area of theology, there emerged Black theology of South Africa, Inculturation and Women's liberation theologies. The various ways in which this "African Re-membering" was articulated by African authors constitute the Africans' attempt to give vent to the cumulative pains of their suffering brothers and sisters. They are the mouthpiece to the resounding echo of the *African Cry*.

Secular Liberation Struggles

Négritude

Négritude is one of the manifestations of the move towards cultural autonomy within Africa. Born as a movement in Paris during the 1930s, négritude was essentially an awakening of universal black consciousness; an awareness that African heritage and traditions united black peoples around the world. Within Africa négritude seemed to manifest itself as a more indigenous movement which, in Gerald Moore's view, "comes up in the insistence on African Socialism as the program of political and social action. And what goes with that—the attempt to feed into a new synthesis, into a new culture (a neo-African culture. . .) all those elements of African traditional civilization which are felt to be of absolute validity for the coming world in which Africa will pour its riches into a common pool."[2] Hence, it is part of a dream of a universal brotherhood in which racial and cultural otherness should be celebrated and not snubbed or vilified; where identity and alterity are both cherished as essential to society; where diversity is strength and strangeness is cherished as exotic rather than feared as threatening.

In a reference to L. Kesteloot, Bénézet Bujo observed that "the colonial powers were not content merely with replacing the African social system with another. They had recourse to every available means to impress upon the black people, in word and deed, that they were inferior to whites and, furthermore that the inferiority was due to the color of their skin. Black people had to be convinced that their inferiority was irreversible, unchangeable."[3] In fact négritude, which emerged out of such experience of racial discrimination, was then a form of cultural nationalism. It is a Pan-African idiom developed in francophone Africa and its diaspora, and often associated with the writings of the West Indian, Aimé Césaire and the African, Léopold Sédar Senghor. It is a parallel ideology to *African Personality* in Anglophone

2. Moore, "Politics of Négritude," 36.
3. Bujo, *African Theology in Its Social Context*, 41.

Africa. Bujo sees it as a kind of act of faith in Africa, in its past and in its destiny.[4] Négritude held that the rest of the world would benefit from an intellectual black renaissance, which would at last produce an environment where race, a core fact of our existence, and the negative baggage linked to its definition and meaning, would be effectively deemphasized, liberating the world's people to work together unencumbered.[5] Senghor, who is one of its pioneer authors, is known to have believed strongly "that there can be no political liberation without cultural liberation."[6] According to Frantz Fanon, therefore, "the concept of négritude . . . was the emotional if not the logical antithesis of that insult which the white man flung at humanity."[7]

However, critics have maintained that négritude is but a bourgeois ideology propagated by the African elite, a game embarrassingly akin to the game whites themselves play in regard to Africa. Allegedly, the ideology is meant to amuse Westerners captive to the notion of the noble savage.[8] Hence, it is vehemently rejected by new guard theologians, like Jean-Marc Ela, on the ground that it is an ideology of the African bourgeoisie, invented to present to foreigners an idyllic traditional life of exotic customs. An ideology that distracts attention from current situation by creating a mystique of vain expectation, and doing its best to check the revolt of the hungering masses by feeding them soporifics.[9] Ela is convinced, and is perhaps right, that négritude is an ideology whose strength is already spent and whose effectiveness has always been doubtful or marginal. According to him,

> The age of the black Orpheus, of sterile narcissism, has come to an end. In our confrontation with the great empires of finance and, those impregnable fortresses of capital, we need something more than music and dance, mask and smile. The quest for authenticity through rhythm can be a perilous pitfall for Africa. (. . .) No, we must search out a new manner of being in the world—in this age when the emergence of inner cities and industrial zones, the exodus to the city, and so on, are undermining the foundations of traditional family culture, and fostering an extraverted, alienating mass culture. African societies are being summoned to a global rethinking of their culture, to developing a new culture from a point of departure

4. Ibid., 48.

5. Achebe, *There Was a Country*, 164.

6. Senghor, *No Political Liberation without Cultural Liberation*, 71. Cited by Bujo, *African Theology in its Social Context*, 48.

7. Fanon, *Wretched of the Earth*, 212.

8. Young, *African Theology*, 16.

9. Ela, *African Cry*, 124–25.

in current challenges. These challenges provoke us to a cultural invention.[10]

I agree with Ela that the current need is that of rethinking our culture in such a way as to rise up to the challenges of today's global family. However, considering the historical context of négritude, we must not fail to acknowledge that it has been a worthwhile struggle against racial discrimination and alienation in a world dominated by white supremacy—a world in which the word *"fraternité"* ironically became a sacrosanct, but repudiated creed of a post-revolution era.

Pan Africanism

United by a shared interest in the *unification, empowerment,* and *liberation* of all black people, some African and African-American intellectuals fused ideas together and gave birth to the Pan-African movement of the early twentieth century that anticipated political independence in Africa. The pan-African spirit is actually traceable to the last decades of the nineteenth century and is seen in the liberating ideas and political philosophy of Edward Wilmot Blyden, whose "Pan-Negro" ideology has been described as "the most important progenitor of Pan-Africanism."[11] The movement seems to have reached its maturity with the series of pan-African congresses organized by W. E. B. DuBois from 1919 to 1945.[12] It is a movement across African national boundaries whose goal is to reaffirm African identity and sovereignty, achieve self-determination and emancipation, and oppose colonialism, racism and neo-colonialism. As Diop notes, "the cultural question can only be fully appreciated the day we will succeed through struggle and victory over colonialism in achieving national independence at the continental level."[13] Such independence was the goal of Pan-Africanism. But as a system of ideas, defining Pan-Africanism is onerous, for there are as many divergent strategies as there are differing thinkers behind the movement. However, its significance lies in its commitment to African liberation.

---

10. Ibid., 128.

11. Martey, *African Theology,* 10.

12. Ibid.

13. Diop, *Towards the African Renaissance,* 114.

African Nationalism

> Nobody can give you freedom. Nobody can give you equality or
> justice or anything. If you're a man, you take it.
>
> —Malcolm X

African nationalism emerged when the contradictions between Western-claimed democratic values and colonial autocratic oppression became apparent to Africans. Although a Western philosophy, it became an effective weapon in the hands of Africans in their struggle against colonialism. Born out of the pan-African spirit, nationalism became the chosen philosophy of the colonial independence movement. It was the Pan-African movement, especially its fifth congress in Manchester, which "provided the outlet for African nationalism and brought about the awakening of African political consciousness."[14] According to Martey, Christianity, in a sense, contributed both positively and negatively toward the rise of African nationalism in South Africa. On the one hand, it was the educated black Christians who became the "carriers" of the movement; they initiated it and gave it its ideological shape. For some of these black Christians, the new faith became a cohesive force in a society of ethnic diversity, and they saw its value as "a source of political ideas." Christianity on the whole "functioned as a guide for cultural, political and social judgments" and also provided blacks with "a language of protest."[15] This explains why Ethiopianism became one of the earliest expressions of African nationalism. African nationalism, however, differs radically from western nationalism, in that, "the two dominant motifs of African nationalism—liberation and consolidation—are the exact opposite of those of Western nationalism—colonialism and divisiveness."[16] These secular liberation initiatives represent the efforts of some of Africa's early visionary leaders to carry their own brothers and sisters. For it is through such acts of carrying the masses, that leaders become true brothers and sisters to their subjects, and history is transformed positively.

14. Nkrumah, *Ghana: Autobiography of Kwame Nkrumah*, 54. Cf. Martey, *African Theology*, 12.

15. Marjorie and Young, *South African Churches*, 36. Cited by Martey, *African Theology*, 21.

16. All-Africa Conference of Churches, *Africa in Transition: The Challenge and the Christian Response*, 66; cited by Martey, *African Theology*, 12.

Theological Currents in African Liberation Struggles

Black Theology of South Africa

The fight for African liberation was fought on the political as well as on the theological fronts. The development of Black theology of South Africa, for instance, is associated with the Black Consciousness Movement (BCM), which was a Movement for political emancipation that began in the early 1970s. During the era of the defunct white supremacist doctrine of the separation of the races, known as apartheid, the black majority, i.e., the so-called Bantu have been fourth class citizens with no franchise, providing cheap labor, and suffering, in the townships and hinterlands, the most impoverished conditions. Although black theology is peculiar to the southern part of the continent and does not reflect any specific experience of Igbo people, it has been influenced by the black theology of the United States and, therefore, articulates the common experience of black humanity. As a result, it is very important in any discussion about the African perspective to liberation theology. According to Steve Biko, the martyred leader of Black Consciousness Movement, the path to liberation required blacks to cleanse themselves of liberalism and its Christian expressions.[17] Blacks were to re-define the Christianity of white missionaries in terms of black theology, which ". . .seeks to relate God and Christ once more to the black man and his daily problems. It wants to describe Christ as a fighting god, not a passive god [sic] who allows a lie to rest unchallenged. It grapples with existential problems and does not claim to be a theology of absolutes. It seeks to bring back God to the black man and to the truth and reality of his situation."[18] Manas Buthelezi describes it thus:

> Blackness is an anthropological reality that embraces the totality of my daily existence: it daily determines where I live, with whom I can associate and share my daily experience of life. Life, as it were, unfolds itself to me daily within the limits and range of black situational possibilities. The word of God addresses me within the reality of the situation of blackness. I can only go to black churches and the only pastor who normally can minister to me is a black like myself.
>
> If I am a pastor, I can understand my ministry only within the context of a black flock. Christian brotherhood? Well, the only brothers with whom I can share daily the experience of

---

17. Young, *African Theology*, 36.
18. Biko, "Black Consciousness and the Quest for a True Humanity," 43.

Christ are black people like myself: Only with these can I listen to the word and receive sacraments.

This situation is neither a dream nor a mere fantasy: It is spiritual reality as it daily unfolds to me. Therefore, I have to take this seriously and try to understand the redemption in Christ within the context of my black experience.

As far as the question of redemption is concerned, traditional Christian theology has not addressed itself to my situation. It has left me with the impression that my blackness is a negative rather than a positive quality.[19]

Allan Boesak adds to this notion by saying that black theology is a "cry unto God" for the sake of the people. And this theology believes that liberation is not only "part of" the gospel, or "consistent with" the gospel; it is the gospel of Jesus Christ.[20] For Boesak, "black theology knows that it is not only people who need to be liberated; the gospel too, so abused and exploited, needs to be liberated . . . [And] for blacks, it is the discovery of the unique meaning of Jesus Christ in our lives; it is learning to say: *You're a Soul Brother, Jesus.*"[21] It seeks a community in which reconciliation with the black self and black brothers and sisters is of prime importance, but desires also to build a solidarity that encompasses not only Africans, but all the different groups in the black community.

However, the racial emphasis that was written into black theology's discourse was not without some demerits, for black theology eventually developed into a political theology that was split along ideological lines of partisan politics in South Africa. The Azania People's Organization (AZAPO)[22] and the National Forum (NF), for example, were inclined to a *Pan-Africanist* ideology reflecting an exclusive kind of nationalism and a strategy that excludes whites as participants in the revolutionary process.[23] Such ideology is reflected in the works of the black theologian, Takatso Mofokeng, for whom black and white reconciliation, and the non-racialism it implies, are premature goals in that they dissimulate the blacks' right to the land. As Mofokeng explains:

19. Buthelezi, "Toward Indigenous Theology in South Africa," 74.

20. Boesak, "Coming in out of the Wilderness," 76.

21. Ibid, 77; my emphasis.

22. Azania was the name envisioned by some political groups in the liberation struggle—groups whose agenda of reclaiming the black history and integrity included the vision of renaming South Africa into Republic of Azania.

23. See Goba, "Black Consciousness Movement," 57–70.

> Black people have been dispossessed of their land which is the basic means of all production and subsistence as well as a source of power. They have been turned into dispossessed workers whose only possession is their labor power. By identifying black people as workers [black] theologians have lifted our struggle beyond civil rights to human rights, from an exclusive struggle against racism to a social and national revolution.[24]

Some scholars defend Mofokeng against accusations of racism from critics, by insisting that his contention, that "non-racialism" is a political and thus ideological idiom, which dissimulates the human rights of the oppressed blacks, is not a racist argument. For them the equation, African nationalism = racism, appears specious.[25] Some of the critical questions that challenge such speciousness for Mofokeng are: How does one define and live a black theology that is itself the dynamic fruit of the liberation struggle? How will this struggle serve the humanizing agenda of black people? For Mofokeng, such questions are integral to the struggle for Azania.[26] But the lack of inclusiveness in its policy made "Azanianism"[27] very unpopular, and this is because the ideology repudiates, at least theoretically, the ideal of universal fraternity.

Parallel to "Azanianism" (i.e., the AZAPO and NF political tradition) is another line of black theology drawn from the camps of the African National Congress (ANC) and the United Democratic Front (UDF). Here, given the vilification of blackness in South Africa, Black Consciousness is a prerequisite for a democratic vision defined in terms of non-racialism. Blackness is a metaphor: all who love freedom and seek justice in South Africa are "black" by virtue of their identification with those who suffer most from the lack of basic freedoms.[28] "Black" then became a symbol of the struggle for racial and economic justice. For Allan Boesak, for example, who is one of the leading black theologians in the non-racialist tradition of the ANC and the UDF, blackness is "awareness, an attitude, a state of mind. It is a bold and serious determination to be a person in one's own right."[29] Many "Negroid" people, he argues, are not black; and many Caucasians, by virtue of their love for justice, are. So in Boesak's theology, oppressors partake of

24. Mofokeng, "Black Theological Perspectives," 109.

25. Cf. Young, *African Theology*, 37.

26. Ibid.

27. The term "Azanianism" and the idea behind it has been deplored as being inimical to Pan-Africanism, because it regards some Africans as more African than the others.

28. Ibid.

29. Boesak, *Farewell to Innocence*, 27.

true humanity as they overcome their contempt of the oppressed. The oppressed do so when, through a genuine establishment of universal fraternal consciousness, they shake off both their internalization of the oppressors' contempt and their hatred of the oppressor. For Boesak, then, the liberation of the oppressed involves the liberation of the oppressor; and both modes of liberation are integral to reconciliation between blacks and whites. In fact, the liberation of the whole of humanity consists in such a fraternal reconciliation between all racial, ethnic, sexual, social, and religious identities.

In this sense, black power is theologically justifiable since both oppressed and oppressor would attain liberation through the empowerment of blacks, just as both men and women are enriched in their relationship through the empowerment of women. For Boesak, black power mandates that whites accept "blacks as black persons, and give themselves in service to them [blacks]."[30] Thus, black power is a creative theological element as it fosters reconciliation. Black power is destructive, however, if it entails the apotheosis of blackness, which deforms black consciousness and precludes reconciliation. It is not surprising, then, that the ANC and UDF school of thought won immense popular support and acceptance politically both in South Africa and on the international level.

The lesson to be drawn from the Black Theology of South Africa and the whole of South African politics is that the acknowledgment of the universal brotherhood of all humanity and respect of the same is the beginning of peace. The Peace and Reconciliation Commission headed by Archbishop Desmond Tutu under the government of Nelson Mandela invested in this belief in order to steer the transition from apartheid in the right direction. Human beings are essentially driven by a passion to have a sense of belonging—a feeling of being treated as a brother or a sister. All oppressions, exploitations, and hatred have their origin in the failure of the ideal fraternal relation, and a lack of perception thereof. The end of apartheid reminds Africa and the world that no injustice can last forever. Hence, fighting injustice by providing the impulse that satisfies the human being's deep-seated need for a sense of belonging will be the goal of a theology that seeks to provide answers to the questions raised by black theology of South Africa. That context again resonates with the saying "O nụrụ ube nwanne agbala ọsọ" which imposes an obligation on us never to ignore the cry of the brother or sister because God would not ignore it.

30. Boesak, *Black and Reformed*, 15.

Inculturation Theology

Perhaps the most important theological effort at cultural authenticity and liberation in the African context, Inculturation theology is a type of evangelization involving translation of the Christian message into a form that can readily be assimilated by the native peoples of Africa. It is the theological counterpart to decolonization, permitting indigenous peoples to discover their own ways of internalizing and responding to the Christian kerygma. It represents the attempt from within Africa to move away from Eurocentric expression of the kerygma, and from abstract statements of dogma, to an African expression of the Christian truth. It is not an attempt to fashion Christ into an African (just as European theology cannot fashion him into a middle class European) but an attempt to show Christ as present in African history, culture and society. It represents, in other words, Africa's efforts at conceptualizing theology.[31] As such, it recognizes that the socio-political and historical contexts determine the way in which Africans answer questions about God's role in the playing out of human existence. This means that exegesis of the biblical message is accompanied by an equally important analysis of the social and cultural context in which the indigenous church tradition exists.[32] Inculturation could then be understood simply as the concretization of the good news of salvation in the cultural expression of the peoples of the world. P. Arrupe defines it as "the incarnation of Christian life and of the Christian message in a particular cultural context, in such a way that this experience not only finds expression through elements proper to the culture in question, but becomes a principle that animates, directs and unifies the culture, transforming it and remaking it so as to bring about 'a new creation.'"[33] Based on this notion of incarnation, Chinedu Amadi-Azuogu sees inculturation as "the *giving of flesh* to the message of the NT so that it is no more a set of abstract and foreign propositions having no real bearing on the experience of the people."[34] In this way the Jesus Christ event is made a tangible reality within a cultural milieu, thereby enabling people to hear with their own ears and believe (cf. John 4:42). Theology thus becomes a cultural expression. However, the best description of inculturation comes from Pope John Paul II in his Encyclical, *Redemptoris Missio*:

---

31. See Gary E. Gorman's definition of African theology in his Foreword to Young, *African Theology*, xi.

32. Ibid.

33. Arrupe, "Letter on Inculturation to the Whole Society of Jesus," 88. Quoted by Amadi-Azuogu, *Biblical Exegesis and Inculturation in Africa*, 37.

34. Amadi-Azuogu, *Biblical Exegesis and Inculturation in Africa*, 35.

Through inculturation the Church makes the gospel incarnate in different cultures and at the same time introduces peoples, together with their cultures, into her own community. She transmits to them her own values, at the same time taking the good elements that already exist in them and renewing them from within. Through inculturation the Church, for her part, becomes a more intelligible sign of what she is, and a more effective instrument of mission.[35]

By this and other similar statements of the Magisterium, the teaching authority of the Roman Church acknowledges that inculturation is an authentic Christian theology. But for African theologians in particular, especially for Edward P. Antonio, whose views about the discourse on culture I appreciate in a special way, inculturation represents the specifically religious or theological reassertion of African memory. It is the quest for the African identity which lies at the heart of the project of inculturation understood in this sense as the attempt by Africans to create a form of Christian self-understanding that is informed by an "anti-colonial" recuperation of their own varied cultural traditions. Its "anti-colonial" thrust and its location and largely implicit participation in the discursive practices of postcolonial theory, tie it to the history of colonialism.[36] Therefore, it is a theology of protest whose efforts is to rethink African identity and whose goal is to resist and displace the epistemic claims of a western inflected Christianity. Inculturation testifies to a crisis which "originated in the interrogation and devaluation of traditional modes of thought by and through the colonial project."[37] For, according to Antonio, "it is precisely in the realm of culture that the effectiveness of the colonial agenda is best evaluated, for it was there that new epistemic structures were created, new ways of being human were prescribed, new modes of perceiving and describing the world were preached and enforced and it was also there that the new myths of Christianity imposed a new moral consciousness and new forms of identity."[38]

Hence, inculturation is predicated upon racial consciousness because it takes as given that the dispute between Africa and the West is a racial dispute or at least one in which race epitomizes the essence of otherness and thus marks the parameters around which difference is contested and negotiated.[39] In other words, it is also a direct confrontation with the dispute that

35. John Paul II, *Redemptoris Missio*, 52.

36. Antonio, *Inculturation and Postcolonial Discourse*, 8.

37. Ibid, 12.

38. Ibid.

39. Ibid, 15.

has impeded good fraternal relation between Africa and the West. African theologians have consistently drawn attention to the contradictions and ambiguities of western ideas of the human which excluded the humanity of non-whites or modes of western social organization which lionized the individual often at the expense of community or, again, notions of western justice whose universality was part of philosophical and mainline political orthodoxy but whose conscious application was always carried out partially and in the interests of a few privileged colonialists.[40]

Inculturation theology is thus an ardent attempt to recuperate the goods of a repressed, subjugated and travestied indigenous cultural memory. This takes the form of a celebratory "return" to all the elements of the African past before the advent of colonialism. This return is necessitated by a posited primordial purity of the African heritage and justified through the uses to which it is put to critique and remedy the alienating effects of a colonial modernity.[41] One can say that inculturation theology is basically a theology of liberation except that it gives hermeneutical primacy to cultural meanings as opposed to dogmatic or philosophical meanings. It has been often alleged, and credibly too, that traditional theology is rather coy about or outright against inculturation and is only forced to tolerate it in order to diminish or at least accommodate Third World criticisms of theological and cultural imperialism. The question is continually being asked, why almost fifty years after the local churches were handed over to an indigenous clergy, are these churches still treated as spiritual colonies of a foreign religion? Is it because they are too timid in their initiatives and too discreet in the expression of their authenticity?[42] The dependence of African local churches has led to such paternalism, which invariably creates such situations whereby the convoking of an African Synod in Rome, for example, was ridiculed in the European Media, for it is neither foreseeable nor thinkable that Europeans would hold a European Synod in Africa. Through inculturation theology, therefore, it is hoped that the Church will invest the liberation project of the African man and woman with an evangelical cultural content. And as a discourse of protest against colonialism and alienation as well as an aspiration to authenticity, the inculturation project must amplify the *African Cry*, pointing out as it does that it is the cry of a brother in need of emancipation.

Again Antonio rightly observes that "again and again, new and foreign modes of rationality emphasized the difference and incompatibility of African and western cultures with the latter serving as the supreme norm for

40. Ibid, 16.

41. Cf. ibid., 17.

42. Ela, *African Cry*, 102–3.

civilization, development and progress—the goals of the colonial project. While it is not strictly true that this resulted in the total or unqualified destruction of African cultures, it did, nevertheless, institute on-going regimes of disruption, discontinuity and alienation in African self-understanding."[43] This fact is authenticated by the agenda of inculturation theology itself. Its aim is not the reinterpretation of African traditional thought for the sake of improving our understanding of its form and content, nor is it that of reconciling Christianity with the former; rather its aim is to reinterpret Christian categories in the light of traditional thought so that they make sense to Africans.[44] In the context of inculturation *Ọ nụrụ ube nwanne agbala ọsọ* typifies the light of traditional thought through which such Christian categories are illumined, that is to say, made more intelligible and culturally relevant to the Igbo and Africans in general. As a result, it is an epistemic expression of a theology that forges a synthesis of both liberation and inculturation in an Igbo context—a theology of fraternal global solidarity.

Women's Liberation Theology

The saying is true that one cannot build a free society on the back of slaves. And this fits arguably to the situation of many women in African society. However, the metaphor here is not meant to state categorically that Igbo or African women are slaves. No, it is rather meant to underscore that the unjust status quo of inequality that still exists between men and women in Igbo and African communities should be eradicated. The Nigerian Church even admits this when it observes that "traditional society has also its injustices against women like denial of inheritance rights, child marriage, widowhood rituals, and pariah status of a childless woman."[45] It also acknowledges that women are exposed to different kinds of oppression within the Nigerian society and Church.[46]

The role of African women has been very vital in the sustenance of a culture of love and community even in the midst of harrowing conditions. And the women folk hold the key to the future of the African continent if the project of women empowerment is taken seriously. On the increase in recent times are indigenous female voices that are vehemently questioning the traditional status quo and calling for a radical re-evaluation of the

43. Antonio, *Inculturation and Postcolonial Discourse,* 40.

44. Ibid., 43.

45. Catholic Secretariat of Nigeria (CSN), *Church in Nigeria: Family of God on Mission,* 51.

46. Ibid., 54.

anthropological self-understanding of the human person in Africa so that a new basis will be established for the transformation of the human relations in which it is assumed that the man takes precedence over the woman.[47] This should be seen as a positive sign of development. But beyond the euphoria of seeing women raise their voice in demanding for justice, is the more pertinent need to pause and ask ourselves: What is it that we have collectively overlooked for far too long? In Igbo society, for example, the identity of a woman is defined by her affiliation to a male *"souverain"* so much so that the fundamental transition in a woman's identity-journey is from *"whose daughter?"* to *"whose wife"?* Women and children are apparently part of what a man owns in African traditional society, such that the Igbo man calls his wife *"onye be m"* (a person of my household) or *"ndị be m"* (i.e., plural form when he includes the children). This expression appears to a good number of Igbo men and women as harmless because of its clichéd usage, but it betrays an unfair patriarchal mentality that subordinates women.[48] This is so even though, as Sofola and Obioma Nnaemeka argue, there is in African languages (to use Igbo and Yoruba as examples) no hint of the male chauvinism that is enshrined in the English language.[49] In spite of the fact that, linguistically speaking, the African perception of the gender question is more healthy and positive, and allows for a wholesome development of human society (Sofola),[50] patriarchy, nonetheless, prevails and lays a big burden on African women. Invariably then, in African patriarchal system, marriage is seen not as a bond of equal partners, but as the achievement of a man who has been able thereby to reach a milestone in self-actualization. In fact, women theologians have consequently identified marriage as a challenge to, rather than a fulfillment of, the personhood of a woman, more so than a man's.[51] This explicit and institutionalized claim of ownership over the woman has unconsciously sustained such evils like domestic violence

47. See Oduyoye, *Introducing African Women's Theology*, 67.

48. The fact that the woman cannot call her husband *"onye be m"* argues for this disparity and unfairness. She calls him *"di m"* (my husband); some use other names that denote her subordination, like *"ọga"* (boss). Actually the correct Igbo word for wife is *"nwunye."* Therefore, the predominant usage of *"onye be m"* is an index of institutionalized inequality.

49. See Nnaemeka, "Mapping African Feminisms," 33. Obioma and Sofola draw attention to the words "woman" and "female" as derivatives from masculine nouns *man* and *male* to which appendages "wo" and "fe" are prefixed. "And when it is necessary to specify her at all, the terms man and human are used to refer to both genders." This linguistic fixation on maleness, while referring to the human species, a thing that exasperate western feminists, is absent in African languages.

50. Ibid.

51. See Oduyoye, *Introducing African Women's Theology*, 71.

and other various forms of sexism to which women are the regular victims in many African homes and communities. A thorough linguistic analysis of the idioms or catch-phrases that are used to express the relationship between men and women in Igbo society gives us deeper insight into the inequality that characterizes that relationship. To avoid deviation, I do not want to delve into such an analysis in detail, but suffice it to mention some examples here: *"Ugwu nwanyị bụ di ya"* (a woman's pride is her husband). This is a popular saying mouthed even by many women, proudly and uncritically, believing that it is true. The glaring but unfortunate implication of this statement, however, is that a woman who for no fault of hers happens not to get married has lesser respect in the society because she has no husband.

Again, Rose Uchem complains about the exclusion of women from presiding over the Kolanut ritual in Igboland. According to her, there is the irony of turning the symbol of inclusion, communion and mutuality into a symbol of exclusion and subordination of women.[52] She is indeed right in this observation. The exclusively male presidency over the Kolanut ritual makes sense only as a patriarchal domination. Although this custom cannot be seen as oppressive, as Uchem purports, it nevertheless subordinates women unjustly.

In the light of the above, African Women's Theology seeks to offer an anthropology that would underline the fact that disrespect to women's humanity is disrespect to humanity and the God who made us woman and man. It is as if one were to say God made a mistake making one a woman.[53] Speaking with particular reference to the Asante culture of Ghana, Oduyoye blames the British bias for patriarchy as responsible for the marginalization of women in public affairs in West Africa. For example, no women's names appeared on the colonial chieftaincy lists. Thus, Westernization abolished the hitherto bi-focal political administration that had given women a measure of autonomy and enabled them to contribute to the general discussion of national issues. It undermined the traditional political role of such women like the *Ohemaa* (Queen mother) of the Asante, *Ọmụ* of the Igbo, and *Ịban Ịsong* of the Ibibio etc., and led to the strangulation of matrilineal heritage where it existed. The patriarchal systems introduced by the British in Ghana succeeded, according to Oduyoye, because they suited the Asante men.[54] And stretching the grim picture to a humorous level, Oduyoye says that since then women have been relegated to the kitchens where "their life-breath stimulated the wood fires that burned under the earthenware pots

---

52. Uchem, *Overcoming Women's Subordination*, 63.

53. Ibid., 77.

54. Oduyoye, *Daughters of Anowa*, 90–91.

of vegetables they had grown and harvested. And as long as the pot boiled, men remained blissfully innocent of whose life-breath kept the firewood burning."[55]

African Women Theology, therefore, rejects a narrative that is born out of uncritical nostalgia for or return to a past that is haunted by taboos and a glorification of domestic role and motherhood as the sole laudable function of womanhood. In an attempt to underscore the helplessness of women in the African societies and delineate the importance of more active role for them, Oduyoye appraises the life-loving tenacity of African women and deplores the contemporary socio-political status quo as she opines:

> [The] personification of Africa as a woman makes sense . . . , for if there is anything that characterizes the continent it is love and respect for life, of people and of nature. And yet, nothing seems to work. Africa continues to produce structures and systems barren of all creativity, not because her sons who run the affairs of the continent are intellectually impotent but because they use the strength of their manhood on what does not build a living community. Raped by the patriarchal manipulation of the North, Africa now stands in danger of further battering by home-grown patriarchies.
>
> . . . The daughters of Anowa sit, holding their bursting heads in their hands while their men mouth political or economic platitudes, speak the language of law and order, or pay lip-service to democratization. When their brothers have unburdened themselves of their many words, the daughters of Anowa pick up the old hoes and their wooden trays and go to the farm to gather the familiar harvest and the firewood so that the familiar soup may be ready. Meanwhile, the mindless talk about fruitless five-year development plans and multi-party elections continues. With quiet desperation, the daughters of Anowa try to apply ancient remedies.[56]

The unhappy experience, however, is that "ancient remedies" no longer work. But the new remedies must be based upon new forms of socialization that is mutually inclusive, for no free society can be built on the back of slaves. The liberation of African women from all possible constraints is a sine qua non for integrating the feminine genius that will enrich African society and foster development. This is not only socially just, but also evangelically imperative. In order to achieve this new socialization, a new anthropological perspective in relation to the gender question is necessary—a

55. Ibid., 2–3.
56. Ibid., 10.

perspective that epitomizes a fraternal response to the cry of incarcerated womanhood. Based on this new fraternal response which also finds expression in *Ọ nụrụ ube nwanne agbala ọsọ,* the married Igbo (African) woman ceases to be *"onye be m"* (a person of my household) and remains *"nwunye m"* (my wife). For the cause of gender disparity is traceable to the inability to perceive the woman primarily as a dear sister and a worthy daughter of one cosmic family made up of men and women whose equal and complementary sexuality constitutes the image of God as revealed by the Scripture: "in the image of God he created him, male and female he created them" (Gen 1:27). Humanity, therefore, will remain impoverished so long as women are forced to remain voiceless and supine partners in the divine mandate to vanquish the earth. African women theology positions itself aggressively against such an impoverishment and thus represents another loud cry that Christian theology should hearken to. And the theology best suited to respond to this need deserves the name, *theology of fraternity.*

PART III

Ọ nụrụ ube nwanne agbala ọsọ

Prolegomenon to a Theology of Fraternity
in the African Igbo Context

6

An Exigent Hermeneutic Shift

A Paradigm Shift from Liberation to Fraternal Solidarity

WITHOUT UNDERMINING LIBERATION THEOLOGY I presume, nonetheless, that there is an inherent limitation that weakens its prophetic ardor in some crucial circumstances and makes its message in such circumstances very controversial and questionable, consequently compelling a new socio-theological hermeneutics that augments the liberation hermeneutics without displacing it. Because liberation theology is primarily committed to the temporal needs of human beings in specific historical contexts, it is subject to new and ever shifting emphasis. With the ever changing phenomenon of our global social environment, which renders the possibility of a clear distinction between the oppressor and the oppressed more obscure, I do think that *enlightenment* rather than liberation suits better the emphasis of contemporary Christian theology. I use the word "Enlightenment" here according to a nuance borrowed from the Indian Jesuit priest Anthony de Mello.[1] Enlightenment thus implies a shading

1. To elucidate what I mean by Enlightenment, I want to retell a story told by the Indian Jesuit priest, Anthony de Mello, SJ. In one of his collection of short didactic stories titled *"The Song of the Bird,"* De Mello told a story of how a group of disciples grappled with the definition of this important concept: the disciples have often heard the Master use the word Enlightenment to describe the achievement of true knowledge. Perplexed about their inability to understand clearly what he meant by that word, they decided to ask him one day. "Master, what is enlightenment?" they asked after sitting at table with him. The Master threw a question back to them: "When do you realize at dawn that it is daybreak and the night is over?" The first disciple answered: "When I look out

of light on something for the purpose of a clearer vision. In this sense, the most important theological question is no longer that of liberation from who, but rather from what? The answer to this question consists in understanding, first of all, that we all need to be liberated from an interior blindness that obfuscates our perception of the ontological essence that unites us as human images of One God; a liberation that brings men and women to a new level of the appreciation of their *Dasein* in plurality. Armed with a new hermeneutic that "enlightens," that is, shades light on the mutual perception of men and women, a new perspective in catholic theology is expected to animate, refresh or revolutionize the religious and social pedagogy of all peoples so that a healthy mentality that realizes the hope of the kingdom of God could develop out of the spirit of a universal brotherhood. Such a mutual perception of ontological fraternal bond between all human beings is, in fact, apriori to any genuine commitment to liberation. The dictum "*Ọ nụrụ ube nwanne agbala ọsọ*" heralds such a new perspective in theology and aptly summarizes it in a very intelligible and compact *lecturé*.

Ọ nụrụ ube nwanne agbala ọsọ, in fact, recapitulates the *First Act* of the God of the Sinaitic covenant: "YHWH then said, 'I have indeed *seen the misery* of my people in Egypt. I have *heard them crying* for help on account of their taskmasters. Yes, I am well aware of their sufferings. And I have *come down to rescue them* from the clutches of the Egyptians and bring them up to that country . . .'" (Exod 3:7–8). In this Exodus-text YHWH sees the misery of His people, He hears their cry for help, and He comes down to rescue them. As we have already noted, *Ọ nụrụ ube nwanne agbala ọsọ* literally means "one who hears the cry of a brother/sister should not ignore it (i.e. walk away, or show apathy)." Invariably such a person is obliged to find out the cause of the cry and intervene by rendering brotherly help. YHWH's intervention in the book of Exodus demonstrates a historically divine precedence that authenticates this dictum, "*Ọ nụrụ ube nwanne agbala ọsọ*," raising it from the status of a mere idiomatic exhortation and qualifying it

---

of my window at dawn and see two trees standing on the adjacent lawn, and I am able to recognize that the one on the right is a mango tree and the one on the left an orange tree." The Master replied, "False." The second disciple answered similarly: "When I look out of my window and see two human beings walking along the street and recognize that the one on the right is a man and the one on the left, a woman." Again, the Master said no, and then answered: "It is when you look out of your window and see a human being walking on the street and recognize that he or she is your brother or sister. Then, and only then is the night over and the day has broken. That is Enlightenment, for Enlightenment is not about recognizing the differences, it is about recognizing the similarities." (*Note that my rendering is not a verbatim quote of the story*).

as a divine precept. In Old Testament biblical theology, YHWH's action in Exodus is by virtue of His relationship with Israel—an intervention that is analogous to the obligations of a senior uncle, גּאֹל—*goʾel* (Isa 43:14; 47:4; Jer 50:34). In this sense God is seen analogically as a supra-cosmic member of the family of Israel who is morally obliged to not abandon His family members to the mercy of their cruel persecutors. His intervention, therefore, does not only have a paradigmatic moral significance, but also a relational significance by virtue of its familial character. Over and above the need to render justice to Israel, His pathos was a *filial* pathos. This decisive exodus-event reveals to us an empathic God, a liberator and a kind of "Big Brother" who proverbially carries his people on eagle's wings[2] and delivers them to safety and prosperity. Through the exodus-event God invites us not just to acknowledge his mighty deeds as a liberator-God but above all to take after His example and intervene in those historical situations where the cries of need are earnestly calling for our attention and making urgent appeal to our humanity. This is what the theology of fraternal solidarity entails.

The term "solidarity" derives from the Latin noun—*solidus* which means the whole. In French language, *solidarité* implies also the whole, union, or fellowship arising from common responsibilities and interests, as between members of a class or a body of persons, or between classes, peoples or groups. It further signifies a community of interests, feelings, purposes, or actions.[3] When viewed as a philosophical concept, solidarity, in contrast to the two extremes of individualism and totalitarianism, is the most popular terminology used by almost all the philosophers in the neo-Thomistic school of thought and by official Catholic social teachers and thinkers to convey the moral unity between the metaphysical concept of the human person and of a community of persons. If black Africa hopes to successfully confront the immense problem of powerlessness and hopelessness in modern time and master the odds of their environment and the human sufferings that characterize that environment; if it will ever be able to throw off the yoke of indigence and other-reliance and achieve self-reliance and self-sufficiency, it must have to be united in fraternal solidarity. And the primordial model or locus of solidarity as a community of interests, feelings,

---

2. Exod 19:4; *Goʾel* is the Hebrew participle of the verb *gaal*, "to redeem." It is rendered in the *Authorized Version of the Bible* as "kinsman" (Num 5:8; Ruth 3:12; 4:1, 6, 8); "redeemer" (Job 19:25); "avenger" (Num 35:12; Deut 19:6, etc.) The Jewish Law gave the right of redeeming and repurchasing, as well as of avenging blood, to the next relative, who was accordingly called by this name. The word is often used of God, the Savior of his people and avenger of the oppressed. The early Jewish rabbis applied the term to the Messiah, and this probably induced St. Jerome to translate it as "Redeemer" (see *The New Jerusalem Bible*, Job 19:25, footnote g).

3. Ike, "Need for African Solidarity," 367.

purposes, or actions is the family. That means that any society that hopes to overcome the obstacles to human wellbeing must become a family in the true sense of that word. This, of course, is utopic but a comparative look at past history assures us that progress in such an achievement is possible. The focus here is not on the normative debate about what constitutes a true Christian family in a way that confronts such moral issues like same-sex marriage, divorce, care of children, etc. By family is meant to invoke the idea of affection, trust, equality, and mutual dependence. It is in the family that we learn to love without reservation, to quarrel without animosity, to forgive and be forgiven, and to give without counting the cost.

Writers on African history, art, literature, religion, sociology and anthropology (both foreign and indigenous) all agree on the assertion that the African tradition is characterized by the emphasis on community, family and progeny, and that wholesome human relations and hospitality are distinctive marks of the traditional African.[4] In Igbo society, therefore, where the fundamental structure of communal life is marked by a strong intra-family and inter-family bond,[5] the Church has a fertile ground where the message of the exodus-event provides a leaven for planting, promoting, nurturing and strengthening widespread Christian commitment to fraternity, solidarity and liberation. The Igbo use to say, "*Agbata-obi onye bụ nwanne ya*" (one's neighbor is his kin, i.e. his brother or sister). *Ọ nụrụ ube nwanne agbala ọsọ* illuminates and makes more comprehensible the precept of love of neighbor: I should love my neighbor therefore, because he or she is my brother or sister and we have the same God as Father. Whether we call that God "Chukwu," "Allah," or "YHWH" should not be an obstacle to our communion. However, my love is not to be expressed to my sister or brother only in terms of rendering material help in response to humanitarian disaster, but above all in various edifying attitudinal encounters with my

---

4. See Busia, *The Challenge of Africa*; Kaunda, *A Humanist in Africa*; Mbiti, *African Religions and Philosophy*; DuBois, *The Souls of Black Folk*; also DuBois, *The World and Africa*; Ottenberg, Simeon, and Phoebe eds., *Cultures and Societies of Africa*; Ritner, *The Death of Africa*; Nyerere, *Ujamaa—The Basis of African Socialism*; Sigmund, ed., *The Ideologies of the Developing Nations*; Abraham, *The Mind of Africa*; Ifemesia, *Traditional Humane Living Among the Igbo*; Ehusani, *An Afro-Christian Vision "ỌZỌVẸHẸ!"*

5. Amadi-Azuogu also citing the Igbo as an example recognizes the contrast between the African and European notion of family ties thus: "[T]he family in European usage strictly refers to the father, the mother and the child or children, as the case may be. The concept of *nwa-nne* is also restricted to this tiny 'nuclear' family, as they call it. So your brother or sister is strictly somebody from the same womb with you. But this is different in the African context. The Igbo contrasts the European mentality by affirming that *nwa-nne dị na mba*. That is to say, that even in a foreign land, there are still brothers and sisters to be found there. With this in mind, families in Africa are large enough." See *Biblical Exegesis and Inculturation in Africa*, 293–94.

neighbor that are characterized by mutual acceptance, respect and conviviality. And the identity of this neighbor of mine should not be determined by geographical proximity, but rather by the precept of universal love. The controversy and vagueness which bedevils liberation theology makes this shift to fraternal solidarity necessary. It is a shift toward the childlike innocence of carrying one another.

A Hermeneutic of Nwanne

Till now we have been using an Igbo pithy saying to analyze the historical context of theology in Africa from an Igbo perspective without yet an extensive explanation of the keyword in that saying. I have deliberately chosen to thematize first the shift that has become exigent in theology before delving into the translation of the word "*nwanne*"—a translation that may already have been presumed by the non-Igbo reader. Since a simple translation could be misleading, I think it is rather better to speak of hermeneutic in this respect. As the study of meaning, hermeneutic is important to all literary discourse in disclosing that wherein the intelligibility of something maintains itself.[6] The contextual meaning of the word "*nwanne*" in *O nuru ube nwanne agbala oso* would be crucial then in understanding the pithy saying and the spirituality it showcases. According to Heideggerian hermeneutics, the reciprocity of text and context in which the hermeneutic circle consists, would insist on the ontological and not merely epistemological meaning of the idiom. Hence, the word "*nwanne*" is not just meant to communicate knowledge of someone, but rather to state an existential truth of being (*facticity*) and, of course, motivate human action—"*being-for,*" or "*Dasein.*" Accordingly, *nwanne* is a *Dasein*, and the facticity of his or her being, which is expressed in the context of the above pithy saying, portrays him or her as the addressee and moral agent who is confronted with his or her "suffering other" and is thereby called to action. In this context, *nwanne* could be anybody, indeed everybody whose image of his or her "self" is authenticated in his or her empathy for a suffering other—i.e., his or her needy "*other self.*" To refuse to hearken to the anguished cry (*ube*) of this "other self" is to repudiate what it means to be *nwanne*. Africans (Igbo) sometimes register their disappointment with the West by saying: "*Bekee a bughi nwanne anyi?*"—"the Whiteman is not our brother!" Of course this is understandable only as an expression of annoyance. Thence empathy, ἐμπάθεια (*empatheia*, "*in passion,*" *suffering with*) as a necessary social and

---

6. Heidegger, *Being and Time*, 193.

moral duty is basic to the ontological facticity of *progeneration*, that is, the fact of being *ụmụnne*—children of the same mother or father.

In our hermeneutic discourse, the meaning we seek is the phenomenological basis wherein the word "*nwanne*" maintains its intelligibility in Igbo verbal communication. "Meaning," we should note, resides basically in the "in-here" of a concept or thing. This definition is without prejudice to Ricoeur's *The Rule of Metaphor*, which underscores the importance also of "resemblance" in the theory of interpretation and thus advances the positions of earlier thinkers. However, adopting the classical understanding of hermeneutics, meaning is that, which is *inherent* to the concept whose content is being disclosed in the hermeneutic process. And inherent to our concept of "*nwanne*" in Igbo linguistic morphology is primarily a sense of *shared origin*, and secondarily, a sense of shared *purpose, familyhood (ujamaa), togetherness, team work, friendship,* and *community.*

In an erudite study of this Igbo kinship terminology, albeit with a view to underscoring its matrifocal thrust, Joseph-Thérèse Agbasiere acknowledges that *nwanne* is a primary kinship idiom.[7] The word "*nwanne,*" which translates as "brother" or "sister," is actually a compound of two words, '*nwa*' (child) and '*nne*' (mother). From a purely lexical point of view, "*nwanne m,*" literally means "the child of my mother," and invariably "*nwanna m*" "the child of my father." The latter is usually used to designate members of the extended family, the kindred, clan, village, town, etc., although one can also refer to an extended family relative as *nwanne*. Agbasiere sees the notion of *nwanne* to be symbolic, in the sense that it is often manipulated in socio-economic and religious interactions. It also emphasizes Igbo propensity towards the orderly or appropriate. The concept is all-inclusive, it is not gender-specific and it is seen to operate as a means of asserting group membership.[8]

From the foregoing, the "inherent" meaning which the word "*nwanne*" communicates is the fact of a shared descent from one common progenitor. And from this attestation of a common biological descent and heritage, brotherhood in Igbo language and culture is linked inseparably with parenthood, so much so, that whoever rejects the one must necessarily reject the other. Accordingly, one cannot talk of *nwanne* status (brotherhood or sisterhood) in Igbo language without at the same time expressing the *filiation* that is the common denominator in the relationship. By implication, one cannot sever fraternal relationship without necessarily injuring maternal or paternal relationship and invariably jeopardizing the bond of the family and one's

7. Agbasiere, *Women in Igbo Life and Thought,* 80.
8. Ibid, 83–84.

own existential root. In this sense, it is easy to see deeper into the parable of the prodigal son and grasp why the father had to leave the feast in order to go and bring his elder son back to reconcile with his younger brother.[9] We shall come to this point later but suffice it to say here that theologically considered, when Christians recite the LORD's Prayer they profess exactly this bond which expresses both a vertical and horizontal dimension of the requirements for establishing the kingdom of God which is the object of petition in the prayer. Hence, the LORD's Prayer is, in fact, a profession of faith in a heavenly Father who is the source and foundation of an ecclesial communion that can only be sustainable through a transparent attitude of fraternity in solidarity. Christians invariably confess that God is the transcendent origin of fraternity. This unique position gives God the absolute right to judge and punish sins against fraternity as he judges and punishes Cain for murdering his brother Abel (cf. Gen 4: 9–12). We can then theologically relate the "*nwanne triangle*" to the Godhead in the sense that we are brothers and sisters because we have God as our Father. The *nwanne* catena will then look like this: *nwa↔nne/nna (Godhead) ↔mu*. The biological (*nne/nna*) or ontological (God) origin thus forms a necessary link that holds fraternal relationship intact.

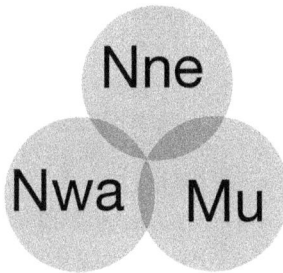

Figure 8: Nwanne Triangle

The "triadial" essence of *nwanne* (as in a *nwanne catena,* : the loving subject; the beloved subject; and the origin of love), also makes it an adequate theological resource for comprehending analogically the human participation in the Trinitarian economy, insofar as the immanent Trinity is understood as communicating the existence of community in the Godhead. There are some other African theologians who also maintain that we can try to interpret the mystery of the Triune God from the point of view of our domestic relationships. For these theologians, the notion of the "Church

9. Cf. Luke 15:14–32. I shall deal with this parable in more detail later.

as family" is a mystery of unity and communion which has its origin fundamentally in the Blessed Trinity.[10] And it is not by chance that the strong sense of family as the epicenter of all African social systems, which is entrenched in African culture, came to constitute the bedrock for the 1995 African synodal ecclesiology. The Vatican II ecclesiology of communion enunciated by the dogmatic constitution on the Church, *Lumen Gentium*, also speaks of the "mystery" of the Church and of her divine dimension, which proceeds from the Trinitarian missions of the Son and the Spirit in history. According to *Lumen Gentium*, the Church is seen as "a people made one with the unity of the Father, the Son and the Holy Spirit" (LG, 4). Cardinal Ouellet notes that "this Trinitarian vision of the mystery of the Church is not new. It belongs to the great tradition, but was obscured in modern times by a predominantly juridical approach to ecclesiology, that of the *societas perfecta*."[11] Theologians may have diverse approaches in articulating this mystery of the Trinitarian unity. What is unique or new here is that it is related to the duty of fraternal solidarity. In this sense, the implicit triad that is embedded in the word *"nwanne"* embodies community, whose primary expression of unity is the family. It could be seen as expressing, at least on the purely theoretical and Igbo linguistic level, a form of *"perichoresis" and "circumincession"* illustrated in the diagram above, insofar as *"nwanne m"* represents a triple interlocking relationship that is expressed in one word. It also symbolizes the Kingdom of God in its micro-phenomenal fullness, since to share in the life of the kingdom means to enjoy the community of saints—of men and women who are truly brothers and sisters to one another and who have lived out the perfect example of genuine fraternity on earth. Through baptism, being immersed in God, I am united to my brothers and sisters, because all the others are in God and if I am drawn out of my isolation, if I am immersed in God, I am immersed in communion with the others. To be baptized is never a solitary act of "mine," but is always necessarily a being united with all the others, a being in unity and solidarity with the whole Body of Christ, with the whole community of his brothers and sisters. This fact, that Baptism inserts me in community, breaks my isolation. And my personal faith in God makes no sense without the acknowledgement of this God as *"our God."* This idea of theistic anthropology is what Pope Benedict XVI insists we must keep present in our being Christians.[12] I cannot

---

10. Omuta, *From Vatican II to African Synod,* 97.

11. Ouellet, "Ecclesiology of Communion."

12. Stan Chu Ilo gave a good analysis of this theistic anthropology of Pope Benedict XVI in his (Ilo's) recent book, *The Church and Development in Africa* (2011). See also the address given by Benedict XVI in the Basilica of Saint John Lateran to conclude the pastoral year of the Diocese of Rome, JUNE 12, 2012. "By living the truth, the truth

address God in *The LORD's Prayer* without remembering that He is in fact "Our Father" and not "my Father" alone. Without the recognition of this all-embracing "we," human society, whether acting as individuals or as a community, risk being emptied of its essence. This helps to illuminate why this idiom, *Ọ nụrụ ube nwanne agbala ọsọ*, remains an important *repositum* for a theology of fraternal solidarity.

Ecclesiology of Liberation Theology

The hermeneutic of *nwanne* brings us back to the question of ecclesiology. As I suggested in chapter 1, ecclesiological skepticism reigns in South American theology, which we are using as heuristic tool, because the models and structure of the Church was imported from Europe and reproduces European archetypes. As a result there seem to be an absence of a fully developed ecclesiology of liberation theology in the sense of having a model or image to represent the Church. What we have is rather a critique and an offer of a new perspective for appreciating the life and mission of the Church in modern times. Gustavo Gutiérrez tells us that the Church's task must be defined in relation to social revolution. Its fidelity to the Gospel leaves it no alternative: the Church must be the visible sign of the presence of the LORD within the aspiration for liberation and the struggle for a more human and just society. Hence, "the Church is not a non-world; it is humanity itself attentive to the Word. It is the People of God which lives in history and is orientated toward the future promised by the LORD."[13] That future must be seen not only in relation to social, but also ethical revolution. Certain ecclesial themes that could be gleaned out of the works of Jon Sobrino include:

- the Church must always be contextually "merciful";

- the Church that is "merciful" practices a certain mutuality by listening to its people and responding to their needs;

- the Church that practices such mercy and mutuality serves the coming of the kingdom of God as well as those for whom the kingdom is primarily intended.[14]

Governed by this principle of mercy, the church of liberation theology will not only treat symptoms but also unmask causes. This may bring down persecution upon it, but without this persecution one is left with only "works" of mercy disconnected from one's context. Thus, "mercy" requires

---

becomes life." Zenit.org.

13. Gutiérrez, *Theology of Liberation*, 147–48.

14. Kelly, "Church Rooted in Mercy," 155–56.

not just the constructive work for the kingdom, the messianic voice, but also confrontation with the anti-kingdom, the prophetic voice. It requires a vehement rejection of bigotry, hatred, oppression, etc. The primary ecclesiological question for Sobrino is: "What is a Church that resembles Jesus?"[15] By taking this point of departure for his understanding of Church, it is clear that no church exists in and of itself—nor by itself—but only in reference to its founder and its context. However, it is always contentious which aspect of the founder is to be emphasized, and how can a church respond to its own particular context. This is what distinguishes one ecclesiological model from another, because the *sitz-im-Leben* (the *locus theologici*) is crucial for how revelation is received. It deeply affects what one chooses to emphasize or de-emphasize and how one appropriates what is important from the Gospels.

Accordingly, liberation theology in this case emphasizes the significance of the contextual determination of ecclesiological or Christological models. Sobrino sees the starting points for Christology, including those he would identify as "alienating," as emerging from different readings of revelation, "and the fundamental reason for the different readings was the place from which they were made."[16] This explains why "freedom" has been rediscovered in progressive Christologies as essential to the gospel, while these Christologies have not rediscovered "liberation"; why Latin American Christology has discovered "liberation" which was more or less absent from Christologies for centuries;[17] and why African theology now discovers "fraternal solidarity" and inculturation as also essential to its reading of the Gospel. In summary, the ecclesiology of liberation theology conceives of a Church that neither hates the rich nor preaches violent revolution to the poor. It embraces everyone in the universal love taught by Jesus and modeled in his ministry. This love is extended to all, but also generates the preferential option for the poor. The Church has not become Marxist, many liberation theologians will say, but it has questioned an economy that requires the armed forces to defend the privileges of a small number of families who controlled the vast majority of wealth in a country. Likewise, African ecclesiology questions the causes of Africa's woes,—causes whose range is wider and deeper than mere economic exploitation and or political oppression. Using the concepts of *"ujamaa," "ụmụnna,"* or *"nwanne dị na mba,"* theology in Igboland, in fidelity to its cultural and historical context,

15. Sobrino, *Principle of Mercy,* 15.

16. Sobrino, *Jesus the Liberator,* 24.

17. Ibid.

builds on the foundation of liberation theology and articulates an ecclesiology that meets the people's expectation of a church.

Owing to its specific socio-cultural context and values, ecclesiology in Africa finds its phenomenological expression in the family—the locus of the epiphany of the Church. Here theology questions the way in which men and women of the world have always related to one another and invites them to a thorough examination of conscience placing before them the evangelical mirror of *ujamaa* (familyhood) as an autochthonous ecclesial principle in Africa. I say this with the awareness and acknowledgement of the fact that such atrocities like the Holocaust and the Rwandan genocide are neither dependent on the failures of the Church's institutions nor on the errors of ecclesiological models in dogmatic teaching. We are the Church (the people of God) and we all bear the responsibility for the shortcomings of our world. As a cosmic family that desire to live in harmony, each and every member is obliged to commit herself or himself to the task of building the Kingdom of God by casting off all kinds of prejudices and "mental myopia" that obscure healthy human relationship and robs humanity of the chance for peace and integral development.

Nwanne dị na mba Ecclesiology

As I have already clarified, the concept of *"nwanne"* is not limited only to immediate brothers and sisters in a nuclear family. It could even go as far as being applied to an inter-continental friendship. The Igbo express this by saying that *"Nwanne dị na mba,"* meaning that a true kin can be a person of foreign origin. In other words, one can find a brother or sister abroad. He or she must not necessarily be a blood relation or fellow citizen. Agbasiere also corroborates this view where she says: "In a conflict situation even a stranger would be termed *nwanne*, if he or she has succeeded in helping to resolve the conflict. Often, this could lead to the establishment of a lifelong friendship and attachment between groups, not consanguineally related."[18]

This means that the *nwanne* relationship cuts across national, ideological, religious, racial or ethnic divide. Hence, the criteria for *nwanne* status is not only birth (even though it primarily refers to the biological fact of a shared maternity or paternity), but also an endearing behavioral attitude towards a person or group of persons. In a multi-ethnic environment that reflects Africa's socio-political landscape, an ecclesiology of *"Nwanne dị na mba"* demands special emphasis. Oliver Onwubiko has already tried creditably to articulate such an ecclesiology of communion with the concept of

18. Agbasiere, *Women in Igbo Life and Thought*, 83.

ujamaa.[19] *"Nwanne dị na mba"* indicates the inevitable evolution and ma-
turing of interpersonal relationship which reaches its superlative intensity
and significance in the messianic event. The Scripture itself testifies to the
fact that the quality of fraternal relationships is not static but rather changes
and progresses as human beings become more *enlightened.*[20] The history of
salvation is in a sense the history of the progressive maturity and expansion of human relationship. Mankind's first crime was the murder of the
younger brother by the elder. It would therefore follow that a major goal of
mankind would be to develop a spirituality by which brothers and sisters
can live in harmony. Civilization, which could be seen as the historical (i.e.
temporal) march to recuperate the lost grace of fallen humanity, will consist
in a gradual return to the plenitude of fraternal charity. *"Nwanne dị na mba"*
ecclesiology is an ecclesiology that focuses on tearing down the walls of
barrier that separates us from or pitch us against one another. The history of
salvation is a history of the gradual but inevitable growth in tolerance and
empathy that promotes familial, national and international unity and cooperation in which the way is paved for the realization of the Divine plan for
human salvation. This growth in cooperation is what is implied in *nwanne dị
na mba* ecclesiology. It is another way of expressing the *ujamaa* ecclesiology,
albeit bringing it nearer and making it more at home in the Igbo context.
Similarly, therefore, "it is opposed to all forms of discrimination, whether
racial or tribal. It insists on the equality of all peoples. It involves the entire
humanity since the extended family as considered in *ujamaa* embraces the
whole of mankind. *Ujamaa* builds on a classless society aiming at crushing
out the use of wealth to dominate others."[21]

Forging ideal relationships between brothers and sisters is the basic
ingredient for reaching the goal of the human enterprise. Through an ecclesiology of *nwanne dị na mba*, the Igbo urge themselves and all people to
constantly keep this ideal of uninhibited love in mind as the basis of their
praxis in interpersonal relationship. For the impulse which drives brothers
and sisters to rivalry and hatred is so strong and instinctive, but when it is
overcome, a fertile ground is thereby cleared for planting the seed of integral
human development and of the promised redemption of humankind.

In order to underscore the across-the-boundary dimension of
"nwanne" in Igbo semantic, the saying *"Nwanne dị na mba"* expresses
Igbo strong belief that the perfection of fraternal relationship transcends

19. Onwubiko, *Church in Mission*, 27–28.

20. See the first footnote of this chapter for my nuance of "enlightened."

21. Nwoko, *Basic World Political Theories*, 242. Cited by Onwubiko, *Church in Mission*, 33.

consanguineous and ethnic boundaries. This invokes the memory of the biblical human history, which begins with a conflict between two brothers that resulted in a tragic bloodshed. Hence, the first mortal sin of mankind was fratricide inspired by jealousy. And since then human history, epitomized in the African crucibles which I have dealt with in chapter 4, resonates with that inhuman retort: "Am I my brother's keeper?" (Gen 4:1–16). However, a reversal of Cain's envy, hatred, and murder of his brother Abel will later emerge in another biblical relationship between David and Jonathan who were not blood relations.

When we contrast Cain's fratricide with the narrative of the moving and dramatic saga of these two men, Jonathan the son of King Saul, and David the son of Jesse, each in line to be king of Israel, then we might begin to comprehend the true implications of *nwanne dị na mba* ecclesiology. Jonathan was a descendant of Benjamin, the son of Rachel while David was a descendant of Judah, the son of Leah. Each should have hated the other and each had ample reason to murder the other. But each rose above politics, pragmatism, family, succession, and reality, motives and aspirations typical of nearly all human beings. In a most dramatic and unexpected turn of events, these two outstanding individuals overcame self-interest, hatred, jealousy, and ego. Jonathan sublimated his dreams of royalty to serve a higher purpose—the establishment of the Davidic dynasty, from which the Messiah is destined to be born. The selfless and self-sacrificing behavior of Jonathan is the greatest such story ever told.

In 1 Samuel 18:1 it is written, "The soul of Jonathan was bound up with the soul of David and Jonathan loved David as he loved himself." The covenant of fraternal trust which bound the two men together was sealed when Jonathan removed his cloak and his tunic and gave them to David (1 Sam18:4). By renouncing voluntarily these symbols of royalty and kingship and also surrendering his military hardware to David, Jonathan declares both his affection and political loyalty to David,[22] thus acknowledging the providence and will of YHWH. Jonathan even endangered and ultimately sacrificed his life so that his arch-competitor would rule Israel in his father's stead. Ralph W. Klein agrees that Jonathan's gesture was "as if he were resigning his right of succession to David."[23] This overwhelming act of brotherly love and self-effacement made possible the emergence of the House of David, the vehicle for human redemption. Note that Cain and Abel, like David and Jonathan, struggled over the same prize: YHWH's favor (whatever this favor is in concrete terms). While Cain tragically solved

22. Schroer, *Die Samuelbücher*, 92.

23. Klein, *1 Samuel*, 183.

his challenge by eliminating his brother, Jonathan resolved his by offering up his life, not only so that David could live, but so that David would inherit his crown. This serves as a model for all human relationships. Jonathan and David aspired to and reached the highest level of human brotherhood. Indeed, when David learned that Jonathan had fallen in battle, he lamented over him as his beloved brother: *"Jonathan, by your dying I too am stricken, I am desolate for you, Jonathan my brother. Very dear you were to me, your love more wonderful to me than the love of a woman"* (2 Sam 1:26). There is admittedly a dearth of text-critical exegeses that emphasize the idea of exceptional fraternal bond made manifest in this passage. A. A. Anderson observes that some exegetes in recent times have in fact tried to suggest a possible Homosexual relationship between Jonathan and David.[24] But he quickly counters this argument based on the fact that the general attitude of the OT as a whole (see especially Lev 18:22; 20:13) seems to contradict this exegesis, and moreover, David's heterosexual relationships are well attested.[25] Far from licensing homosexuality, there is a compelling sense in which the eulogy in Second Samuel 1:26 is a superimposition of *philia* over *eros;* fraternity over sexuality. Without seeking further exegetical authentication, the text clearly presumes that Jonathan and David are brothers, at least in the sense in which all human beings are called to be sisters and brothers and to live up to that expectation. And the Church is the appropriate locus where the ideal of fraternal relationship is not only meant to be contemplated but above all actualized in our lives and daily activities.

The ecclesiology of the Church as the family of God illuminates this truth and makes it sacred. *Nwanne dị na mba* echoes and affirms it in the language of inculturation. Theology can only seek to appropriate this language and through the linguistic agency catapult the notion of filial love and solidarity beyond all possible barriers, in such a way that the distinction between love and sympathy is illuminated. For love knows no stranger. The Old Testament ecclesiology is clear on this. The Church of Deuteronomy celebrates God's blessings as to a family, and offers thanksgiving for the various events in its history. The liturgical guideline for this celebration stipulates "you and your family" (singular form, Deut 14:26; 15:20; plural form 12:7). The social and ecclesiological significance of this guideline is especially acknowledgeable where Deuteronomy further interprets it and gives the list of the liturgical participants, e.g., in Deut 12:18: "you, your son and your daughter, your serving man and serving woman, and the Levite living

---

24. Anderson, 2 *Samuel*, 19. Anderson is making reference to Horner, *Jonathan Loved David.*

25. Ibid.

in your community. . .."[26] The agenda to the offering of the "First Fruits" in Deut 26:11 adds the stranger to the list (the short historical creed of course narrates Israel's alienation in Egypt). This list expresses what the feast intends to communicate, namely, the stranger is integrated in the one family of God and is thereby adopted as brother or sister. He or she is no longer a stranger or alien. Hence, "*You must not regard the Edomite as detestable, for he is your brother; you must not regard the Egyptian as detestable, since you were once a foreigner in his country!*" (Deut 23:8).

This tearing down of the wall of national boundary is what is implied in *Nwanne dị na mba* ecclesiology. In fact, it is the meaning of Catholicism. It is an ecclesiology, which albeit articulated in the Second Vatican Council,[27] is nevertheless yet to find its actualization in the hearts of men and women of today. It is an ecclesiology that admonishes us to reach out beyond our cultural and racial diversities to that unity which has its root in the perfection of love in God. This ecclesiology appreciates the fact of the progressive maturity of love among human beings and seeks to promote and strengthen it.

In the New Testament plot, Jesus takes us to a new level of awareness of this supra-ethnic relationship in his answer to the question posed to him by a lawyer: "Who is my neighbor?" This lawyer obviously underscores the point that the traditional understanding of neighbor is not self-explanatory and therefore insufficient, hence the question. Jesus takes up this challenging question by leading us beyond our common sense notion of neighborliness with the parable of the Good Samaritan (Luke 10: 30–37). Concluding this parable, Jesus throws the question now back to the lawyer: "Which of these three, do you think, proved himself a neighbor to the man who fell into bandits' hands?" As the lawyer gave his answer, Jesus replied with words that are not short of a commandment: "Go and do the same yourself!" Hence, Jesus unequivocally commands us to become *"Nwanne dị na mba"*—brothers and sisters without borders. In the light of this ecclesiology, theology of fraternity assumes a universal character that is not limited to the boundaries of Africa, Latin America or any of the developing countries. *Nwanne dị na mba* admonishes us to cross the borders of ethnic, racial, religious, and sexual identities in order to experience the freedom of the children of God.

26. Braulik, *Kirche im alten Testament AT* (unpublished lecture), 10–11. The same list is given in plural form in Deut 12:12 where reason was given for the participation of the Levite in the liturgical meal, namely, "since he has no share or heritage of his own among you."

27. According to *Lumen Gentium*, 9, "Destined to extend to all regions of the earth, [the church] enters into human history, though it transcends at once all times and all racial boundaries."

In choosing to articulate *"Nwanne dị na mba"* as an authentic ecclesiological concept, I also bear in mind what Oliver Onwubiko has argued:

> . . . that good theologizing is often achieved with 'bilingual for-
> mation,' that is, the ability to express Christian teachings and
> meanings in a cross-cultural context so as to convey correct
> Christian concepts within a culture. It also implies the abil-
> ity to convey correct cultural meanings and understanding to
> the Christian community. In terms of inculturation, it implies
> bilingualism and biculturalism in the Pauline example. They
> are necessary for a transcultural theological orientation that
> is Christian. When a theology is transcultural, it means that,
> though rooted in one culture, it is not bound by and to that
> culture exclusively. If it is a Christian inculturated theology, it
> should be able to speak to people of other cultures in concepts,
> images, and, if possible, in a language intelligible to them, both
> to the Christians and the non-Christians of that culture.[28]

Should one wonder in what way *"nwanne dị na mba"* differs from *"ujamaa"* ecclesiology, I would say that the former makes explicit the rupture
with sterile clannish mentality and a subsequent expansion of all domestic
fraternal relationships in order to include a new global neighborhood in its
embrace. Unlike *"ujamaa"* which is merely a native concept that expresses
familyhood, the phrase *"dị na mba"* conveys additionally the far-reaching
extramural, inter-ethnic, inter-racial, inter-religious, international, and inclusive dimension of fraternity. In other words, *"Nwanne dị na mba"* simply
and compactly articulates an idiomatic theology of fraternal global solidarity whose intelligibility in systematic theological terms remains a task to
be explored further by theologians. The fertile rupture of familyhood and
filial friendship, which *"Nwanne dị na mba"* discloses finds a remarkable
New Testament biblical expression in Jesus' friendship with his disciples: "I
shall no longer call you servants,. . . I call you friends, because I have made
known to you everything I have learnt from my Father." (John 15:15). If
we admit, as I said earlier, that contextual ecclesiology depends on which
aspect of the founder one chooses to emphasize or de-emphasize, it is then
easy to see how John 15:15 constitutes the Christological fulcrum on which
"Nwanne dị na mba" ecclesiology is theologically validated. Jesus is by virtue
of his unreserved openness (*everything I have learnt from my Father*) the
divine *"Nwanne dị na mba"* (the celestial Big Brother) who humbled himself
rupturing the barrier between heaven and earth, adopting us into the divine
family, and thereby giving us an example to break down the barriers that

---

28. Onwubiko, *Church in Mission*, 30.

separate us from one another. But we cannot conclude this chapter without appreciating the Old Testament biblical hermeneutic which remains an invaluable fountain of the ecclesiology of fraternity.

The Church of the Old Testament and the Ecclesiology of Fraternity

As a people of God who have passed through the experience of slavery and liberation, the Church of the Old Testament gave its assent and evaluation of that experience especially in the book of Deuteronomy. The ethics which that book prescribes is to become normative for the social and liturgical life of the Israelites and subsequent people of God. No Old Testament book has exerted a greater influence on the formation and development of both Jewish and Christian thought and practice than Deuteronomy.[29] The book is a strong scriptural pillar that supports a theology of fraternity, for it possesses a richness of social ethics that, not only promotes harmony in the society, but more importantly unveils an underlying concept of society as a family of God. Coming after the book of Exodus in chronological order of the bible, one could say that this very important book attempts to give answer to the fundamental question: After liberation, what next? In this important and ineluctable question, one sees not only Deuteronomy's relationship with liberation, which the Exodus-Event highlights, but also its indispensable significance for a theology of fraternal solidarity; its intrinsic connection to YHWH's act of liberation in Exodus and its ethics of brotherhood (Deut. 15:1–18). After the ugly experiences of the transatlantic slave trade, colonialism, neo-colonialism, tribal wars and genocides—experiences that have left both the oppressor and the oppressed with shame and bitterness respectively, it is time for the whole world to unite in asking: Where forth? The Church of the Old Testament gives us the compass in the book of Deuteronomy. This compendium of narrative texts, homilies of exhortation, and social guidelines, which are interpreted as Moses' testament, recapitulates in retrospect the liberating actions of YHWH and sees in those actions the basis for a historical legitimation of an ethical demand for a just and free society (cf. Deut. 15:15; 24:18).

It is clear that Deuteronomy transcends the earlier charter of Israel in the covenant book in its social consciousness, and the inner logic of its appeal to brotherliness is based upon the liberation of Israel by YHWH. Like two faces of the same coin, therefore, liberation and fraternity constitute together the dominant motif of Deuteronomy, to be remembered as history, celebrated as liturgy, and lived out in community as social ethics. This

29. Brown, *Message of Deuteronomy*, 13.

humanistic motif becomes a norm that earmarks the people of God and distinguishes them from other peoples and cultures. The isolated legislations, which I cannot deal with in detail here, are in fact, reminiscent of the little lad mentioned in the introduction to this book, who, carrying his younger sister on his back, asserted to me that the weight is not heavy because she is his sister. Hence, one of the major lessons of Deuteronomy is the way in which it sharpens our perception of the poor or the less privileged as a brother or sister, and from the basis of this perception legislates against all forms of exploitation and promotes acts of solidarity. The weaker member of the society should never be seen as a burden that one may be unwilling to bear. By virtue of being a brother or sister, he or she may be seen as a challenge, but never as a burden.

Based on this perception Deuteronomy legislates provisions (Deut. 14:28f) and debt-relief (Deut. 15:7–11) for the poor, freedom of slaves (Deut. 15:12f), and against the exploitation of vulnerable women (Deut. 21:10–14). Deuteronomy even reiterates repeatedly that the blessings of YHWH are dependent on this act of solidarity with the poor (cf. Deut. 14:29; 15:10 & 18; 23:21; 24:13 & 19). In fact according to Georg Braulik, "Deut. 15: 1–18 offers a deuteronomic theology of liberation unto brotherliness, because it transforms the agrarian fallow-year into a social relief-year. God liberates the poor so that he can become a participant—an integrated brother again."[30] And the word "brother" is used in Deuteronomy more often than in any other book of the bible. The debt relief is geared towards eradication of poverty among God's people. As Braulik puts it, "*Affluence for all is not a human societal utopia; it is rather a demand from God. The scandal of poverty in Israel can be eradicated, and through Israel also among other nations.*"[31]

Simply put, fraternity is the soul of Deuteronomy and this unique way, of perceiving the needy primarily as a brother or sister, accentuates the humanitarian obligation towards him or her. Ọ nụrụ ube nwanne agbala ọsọ is hence an Igbo contextual norm of the deuteronomic social ethics. The welfare, which the poor has a right before God to demand for, determines the nature of the relationship between God and the economic prosperity of the faithful (cf. 1 John 3:17 & 22f).[32] With the images of malnourished African children haunting the living rooms of modern men and women, debt-relief has become a burning issue in the public square for the past few decades. If the world is prepared to take the deuteronomic injunctions seriously, the excruciating debt burden that hangs on African nations should

30. Braulik, *Deuteronomium*, 1:110–11.
31. Ibid., 1:112; translation and emphasis mine.
32. Ibid., 1:113.

move Western nations to rethink. Some Africans in this respect question the intentionality of the forces of globalization and ask:

> What does one understand as progress in a world where over twenty-two million children go to bed without food and 840 million people are starving; in a world where over a billion people lack water and 1.2 billion others lack adequate housing; where the wealth of three richest individuals on earth surpassed the combined annual GDP of the forty-eight least developed countries of the world; where fifteen richest individuals in the world enjoy a combined assets that exceed the total annual GDP of Sub-Saharan Africa. . .?[33]

Of course, the problem of debt burden, apart from appealing to the consciences of rich creditors, also makes a demand for responsible governance from African leaders who mortgage the future of African children while living in a state of scandalous affluence. The book of Deuteronomy legislates against such inequities and seeks to redress it wherever it exists. The Church of today is thus called to emulate that Church of the Old Testament in the relentless commitment to teaching the modern world that the poor is primarily a sister or a brother in need.

To conclude this chapter, given the above analysis of the social ethics of Deuteronomy, it will not be hyperbolic to say that the pithy saying *"Ọ nụrụ ube nwanne agbala ọsọ"* is the deuteronomic precept of the Igbo society. The "Church" of Deuteronomy is explicit that he or she who hears the cry of a brother or sister should not decline help (i.e. shy away from fraternal duty). The deuteronomic laws oblige the Israelites notably on the premise that they were once liberated from slavery and, therefore, must establish a just and egalitarian society. What this entails for the Igbo and blacks in general is that having been also freed from slavery and colonialism; having recovered from the bruises of several conflicts and civil wars, they too should embrace others in brotherly love and labor together for a just and harmonious society. A *Theology of Fraternity* cannot tolerate any longer excuses for the bad governance and corruption, hatred and bigotry that are exacerbating suffering in the African continent. It is the task of this theology to continue urging men and women, both Igbo and otherwise, to live up to the demands of the precept of *Ọ nụrụ ube nwanne agbala ọsọ.*

---

33. Kobia, *Courage to Hope*, 207.

7

Christology of Fraternity

A New Christology for the Igbo (Africans)

Jesu, Nwanne Otu Onye—Jesus the Brother

"Then the King will say to those on his right hand, 'Come, you whom my Father has blessed, take as your heritage the kingdom prepared for you since the foundation of the world. For I was hungry and you gave me food, I was thirsty and you gave me drink, I was a stranger and you made me welcome, lacking clothes and you clothed me, sick and you visited me, in prison and you came to see me.' Then the upright will say to him in reply, 'LORD, when did we see you hungry and feed you, or thirsty and give you drink? When did we see you a stranger and make you welcome, lacking clothes and clothe you? When did we find you sick or in prison and go to see you?' And the King will answer, 'In truth I tell you, in so far as you did this to one of the least of these brothers of mine, you did it to me. . ..'" (Matt 25:31–46)

WITH THE ABOVE WORDS, Jesus anticipated the last judgment and underscores God's definitive, irrevocable, liberating, and gratuitous glory which is present and actual in the world. This presence is hidden in His impalpable proximity to the hungry, the thirsty, the alien, the naked, the sick, and the impoverished, who he calls his "brothers" [and sisters]. Thus in the combat for human liberation, nothing less than the divine is at stake. What concerns humanity by that very fact concerns God: "LORD, when did we see you hungry and feed you. . .?" (Matt 25:37).

As I noted earlier, Christology of liberation builds upon two theoretical mediations: the social-analytic mediation and the hermeneutic mediation. In the hermeneutic mediation, the social-analytic text is read and understood in the light of Jesus Christ the Savior and the Word of revelation. The theology of fraternity appropriates these same mediations in its attempt at understanding the person of Jesus. It is evident that Christology derives ultimately from Jesus' witness to himself—from the manner in which he himself understood his task and mission, his cross, and, in these, himself. As Karl Rahner noted, a Catholic Christology can scarcely do without *communicatio idiomatum*, that is, the expression of unity (which does not mean an identity) between God's eternal Logos and the human reality of Jesus.[1] This unity is the point of convergence between "Christology from above" and "Christology from below." It establishes the mutual conditioning, the mutual inclusion, of that, what Jesus is in eternity and our incarnate experience of him in time. Attempting to explain the term "communication of idioms," Gerald O'Collins tells us that "it involves *naming* the *person* of Christ with reference to one nature (e.g., 'the Son of God') and *attributing* to him a property that belongs to the other nature ('died on the cross')."[2] This unity of faith in the divinity of Christ and the expression of our human and temporal experience of him is characteristic of all Christologies. As a matter of fact, African Christians and theologians, like all disciples of Christ, cannot evade the most fundamental christological question of all times: "But you, who do you say that I am?" (Mark. 8:29). Any response to this christological question must begin with the acknowledgment of concrete human experience. Whatever we can attribute to him in this instance must express what we believe about his human nature without negating his divine nature. Hence, the Son of God, the second person of the Trinity, is also the One, who a pious Igbo in his or her supplications addresses as "*Jesu, Nwanne otu onye.*" The choice of this christological title, which is widely used in Igboland, is very significant, even when it remains hitherto insufficiently explored theologically.

First, let us look at the meaning of "*Jesu, Nwanne otu onye.*" It is another example of an idiomatic "Christology from below." We know already that *nwanne* is a brother or sister. So what is *otu onye*? The saying that a translator is a traitor holds true here. "*Otu onye*" literally means "one person," "an individual," but this is not what it actually connotes in the title, "*Jesu,*

1. Rahner, *Love of Jesus and Love of Neighbor*, 31.
2. O'Collins, *Christology*, 173–74; O'Collins' emphases.

Nwanne otu onye." In this Christological title, *"otu onye"* is an idiom, which unearths and conveys a situation of abandonment, a feeling of alienation, and of helplessness in the face of insurmountable difficulties, a feeling of being in a world so populated with humans, and yet of being in a desperate struggle to overcome the void created by loneliness and forlornness. *"Jesu, Nwanne otu onye"* accordingly addresses Jesus as the Brother of the needy, the lonely, the dejected, the marginalized, the outcast etc. Jesus is thence *"Nwanne otu onye"*—the Brother of one who has no brother—because in Him the lonely and the marginalized find consolation and compassion; in Him all humans find help in moments of need.

Otu onye could also refer to a collective, a group of people whose collective experience of rejection compels them to languish on the margins of society. Hence, there is a sense in which the African people's experience in the world qualifies them to be *otu onye* in relation to other peoples of the world. That unique historical experience, the outline of which I have dealt with in chapter 3, invariably dictates a unique African perspective in Christology or any God-talk. Can anything good come out of Nazareth? (John 1:46). In order to give His answer to this derogatory question God became in Jesus Christ a Nazarene. In the same way He has become an African and a brother to us, to show that He comes from where we least expect Him. And it is by virtue of being seen first as a Brother to us, that Jesus is also seen as the Liberator of African people, and teaches us to view the whole of humanity from this perspective. In fact, it is the brother status of Jesus that precedes and lays the foundation to his liberator status. Jesus, who is Christ, hence personifies in himself the historical reality of the paradigm of brotherhood even as he represents the hidden image of God, who reveals Himself where He is most despised. He is the perfect fulfillment of the ideal of brotherly love in both its historical and eschatological dimensions. As the King and divine Judge of history, he rightly punishes those who sin against fraternity and who think they could escape or circumvent justice on earth. And he also rewards those whose brotherly commitment in the service of justice and solidarity is not duly rewarded on earth.

The incarnation finds its meaning only in the historical becoming-a-brother-to-us of Jesus Christ. The New Testament accounts of his birth situate it in the historical and sociological context of a human family. The letter to the Hebrews hence notes, "For it was not the angels that he took to himself; he took to himself descent from Abraham. It was essential that he should in this way become completely like his *brothers* so that he could be a *compassionate* and trustworthy high priest of God's religion" (Heb 2:16–17). And as high priest and consecrator of his people, he is of the same stock with the consecrated; "that is why he is not ashamed to call them *brothers. . .*"

(Heb 2:11). His birth narratives mention Mary and Joseph as his parents (Luke 2–3) and refer to other figures as his brothers and sisters (Mark 6:3). But beyond that, however, Jesus' teachings contained an express command to transcend the narrow boundaries of consanguinity in order to form a spiritual family of disciples uncluttered by blood ties (Mark 3:31–35; Luke 9:59–62). As a divine Brother in this spiritual family, he remains the refuge of all who suffer oppression and injustice, as well as the solace of all who grieve on account of having nobody as helper in times of need. Through his own "suffering-with"—"*com-passio,*" he restores to alienated individuals and groups whatever is lost in the broken communion between brother and brother and thus fills up the existential hiatus that has truncated fraternal love. And for this reason the Igbo call him "*Nwanne otu onye.*"

This christological portrait of Jesus as brother is not an Igbo phenomenon alone. It is an image that is very significant to many African Christians, as has been proved by a study made by Diane B. Stinton. It is an image that communicates the humanity of Jesus in a meaningful way, incorporating notions of intimacy and solidarity, contemporary presence and availability, protection from harm, and peace amid the hostilities of a divided humanity.[3] According to African Christians, the image of Jesus as brother clearly enhances one's understanding of the incarnation. Consequently, Africans with such perceptions of him claim to grasp the reality and significance of Jesus more deeply and personally, just as Irene Odotei attested. Asked who Jesus is for her, this Ghanaian lay woman answered, among other things:

> Jesus Christ for me today is God-made-man, who became man because of me, to know how I feel, to know how I think, and to die for me and go back up there [sic]. So then because he has become like me, he knows where I'm hurting. He knows and he, being there, intercedes for me to the Father. So to me Jesus is a representative who understands, I mean *a brother* . . .
>
> To me Jesus is real, more real than the Jesus I learned about, who wasn't interested in my pair of shoes or in all the mundane things of life. He's interested and he does everything well. So that's what Jesus is to me, *a big brother* and God made man.
>
> In the African context, having a brother means so much. So I suppose that's my Africanness—that's why I always want to think of Jesus as a brother, somebody close to me, *a big brother* who can take care of me, somebody I relate to. He's God, but he's also my brother.[4]

---

3. Stinton, *Jesus of Africa*, 151.

4. Irene Odotei spoke to Diane B. Stinton in an oral interview. Ibid., 148ff

Diane Stinton admitted that, in the oral interviews conducted by her, "no set question was asked regarding Jesus as brother. It is therefore interesting to note the extent to which respondents volunteered this image. In Kenya and Uganda, eight of the thirty individual respondents voiced this perception of Jesus as being meaningful to them personally. In Ghana, seven of the thirty-five individual respondents did likewise, and an additional two referred to the concept without explicitly advocating it."[5] We know also that prominent African theologians have argued about the theological validity of a similar image of Jesus as "Brother Ancestor" (Nyamiti) or "Proto-Ancestor" (Bujo). In contrast to the ancestors, however, an important facet of the christological portrait of Jesus as brother is particularly the emphasis on his being present and contemporary. Jesus' own reference to the Last Judgment in Matthew 25:31–46 clearly highlights this closeness to contemporary history, when he alludes to his intimate proximity to, if not identification with, the "least" of his brothers—the suffering poor. The christological image of Jesus as a brother is invariably the center and the driving force for a theology of fraternal solidarity. It is an image that is not only culturally relevant and dear to Africans; it has also ample biblical support. It is from this perspective of seeing Jesus as an intimate brother that Africans understand or seek to understand the theology of liberation. Such understanding could further be clarified by analyzing the parable of the prodigal son from a novel perspective.

The Parable of the Prodigal Brother

The parable of the prodigal son (Luke 15:11–32.) is one of the few sublime analogies that Jesus used to enable us understand more fully the mystery and essence of divine mercy, as a profound drama played out between the father's love and the prodigality and sin of the son. At least, this is how it has been hitherto understood in some of the official teachings of the Church.[6] However, this parable has more to say than about a father and his son. It is at the same time a parable of the prodigal brother, for it also brings into the narrative the disgruntled elder brother who could boast about himself not having been prodigal. I have intentionally renamed this parable here in order to emphasize the fraternal charity that was called into question in the narrative. The role of the first son in the parable is remarkable, because what will in the end emerge as scandalous in the parable is no longer the fact that the prodigal son lavished his wealth in reckless living, but rather

---

5. Stinton, *Jesus of Africa*, 147.
6. John Paul II, *Dives in Misericordia*, 5.

that his self-righteous elder brother would be willing to see him (as one might suppose) serve as a slave in his own father's house, or even be cast out entirely.

As we know, the parable narrates a story of squandered inheritance and a reckless, loose and empty life; of dark days of exile and hunger; but even more of lost dignity, humiliation and shame and then nostalgia for home; of the courage to go back, and the father's festive welcome.[7] Describing the miserable situation, the evangelist Luke tells us: The prodigal son *"would gladly have fed on the pods that the swine ate, but no one would let him have them"* (Luke. 15:16). This young man's loss of material goods consequently brought him to a deeper consciousness—the consciousness of the tragic loss of his own dignity. Hence, the parable, apart from referring ultimately to sin and forgiveness, is also emblematic of those miserable life situations where the suffering subject may be held culpable for having made wrong and foolish choices. As events unfold, the judgment of history becomes too harsh for the prodigal son to bear and he is ready to undergo the humiliation and shame of becoming a slave in his father's house, for he sees no better alternative. The obvious lesson, which emerges here, is that this humiliation is justifiable and even welcome by the prodigal son himself. The father, however, finds it intolerable and his mercy intervenes in the situation to prevent such a humiliation. The elder brother, who refuses to take part in the banquet, rebukes his younger brother for debauchery, and his father for the welcome given to the prodigal son. The father, however, prevails on his elder son to give up his indignation for reason of fraternity, arguing, "it was only right we should celebrate and rejoice, because *your brother* here was dead and has come back to life; he was lost and is found" (Luke 15:32). Pope John Paul II tells us that "to the extent that this brother, too sure of himself and his own good qualities, jealous and haughty, full of bitterness and anger, is not converted and is not reconciled with his father and brother, the banquet is not yet fully the celebration of a reunion and rediscovery."[8]

Jesus concludes the story, leaving it open-ended, probably to enable us draw a variety of personal meanings from the parable. And one meaning cannot be left out: that apart from the lesson about the Father's magnanimity (*dives in misericordia*), the conclusion of the parable opens a whole new perspective that informs the elder brother what his perception of his younger brother ought to be, namely, *"your brother,"* and not *"this son of yours."*[9]

7. John Paul II, *Reconciliation and Penance*, 5.

8. Ibid., 6

9. See Luke 15: 30. The elder son tends to distance himself from the prodigal by referring to him as "this son of yours." And he went even further to allege that his younger brother squandered his wealth with prostitutes, thus attempting to underscore why this

The lack of appreciation of this truth of a shared paternity in God is the root of resentments, hatred, oppression, exploitation, racism, ethnicism, and apathy in human history. Therefore, the task of restoring dignity to those sisters and brothers who have lost it through material poverty, whether it is their fault or not, is a noble and essential responsibility which humanity is called to fulfill. If poverty assaults the human dignity of any people, the dignity of all people is at the same time assaulted in every part of the world. Humanity cannot live in peace if a greater section of the world continues to live in inexcusable poverty. John Paul II goes further to remind us that when the parable evokes, in the figure of the elder son, the selfishness which divides the brothers, it also becomes the story of the human family: every human being is then also this elder brother. Selfishness makes him jealous, hardens his heart, blinds him and shuts him off from other people and from God. The loving kindness and mercy of the father irritate and enrage him; for him the happiness of the brother who has been found again has a bitter taste. From this point of view he too needs to be converted in order to be reconciled.[10] If the parable is read from the point of view of the elder son, it portrays the situation of the human family, divided by forms of selfishness that make us unwilling to carry our weaker siblings. It throws light on the difficulty involved in satisfying the desire and longing for one reconciled and united family. It therefore reminds us of the need for a profound transformation of hearts through the rediscovery of the Father's mercy and through victory over misunderstanding and over hostility among brothers and sisters.[11]

In his encyclical *Caritas in Veritate*, Pope Benedict XVI introduces a new principle in Catholic Social Teaching, the principle of gratuitousness, which he calls an expression of fraternity (*CIV,* 34). The paradox of the kingdom is such that by refusing to join the party organized by his father in order to welcome and honor his younger brother; by refusing to be gratuitous; it is the elder son who suddenly becomes the one in peril of being lost (by ostracizing himself from the feast of the kingdom). His reluctance to engage in a filial embrace posits an open question to individuals and groups in every generation and in various circumstances about their relationship with others. And whether this elder son eventually succumbed to his father's plea to join the party or not is left unanswered by Jesus. But wouldn't the Parable of the prodigal son be a story with an unhappy end, if the merciful father

---

son should be undeserving of honor. It is not seldom that one hears this kind of argument from the privileged in attempts to absolve themselves from guilt on the misery of the poor. Some of the arguments against universal health care in the USA are similar.

10. John Paul II, *Reconciliation and Penance,* 6

11. Schroer, *Die Samuelbücher.*

were to lose his elder son again simply because of his magnanimity to the younger son? Therefore, the "good news" in this parable can only consist in the fact that the father was able to bring his two sons together again (*the indignant* and *the lost*) to share the same patrimony as brothers. The elder son hence has to learn to be merciful as his father in order that he too shall obtain mercy (cf. Matt 5:7; Luke 6:36). It is in fact in this mercy that his righteousness will consist. Mercy in this case cannot only mean that implied in forgiveness, but also that implied in empathy and fraternal charity.

An unmistakable lesson could be gleaned out of this parable. Those who are unwilling to acknowledge the humanity of others are always the first to empty themselves of humanity without realizing it. Our fate and fortune are intimately tied and no nation on earth can demonstrate her greatness on top of the ruins of the anthropological poverty of her wretched and starving neighbors. An essential component of any civilization worthy of its name is how much respect and attention it gives to the weakest members of that society, and how it preserves and promotes the dignity of all its members and the common good. In this parable, the father's call to his disgruntled elder son to join him in restoring dignity to his younger brother is very significant. As much as it is a call to fraternal charity and mercy, which is divine, it is also a reminder of the fundamental humanism that is emblematic of the kingdom of God. In the end, whether we interpret this story in the light of a spiritual conversion of a sinner, or in the light of an exhortation to filial friendship, the significance of the story is enhanced by the metaphor with which Jesus concluded it: "[He] *was dead and has come back to life; he was lost and is found.*" With this metaphor, the celebration of the restoration of dignity to the poverty-stricken "lost brother" assumes a new dimension—the dimension of a new life and a new profit—a treasure lost but found. If the elder son fails to see his brother in this context as a personified treasure, then he has really missed the point and is himself in peril of becoming the loser. Yes, he is in peril of falling into a situation that is comparable to Ilo's concept of "homelessness"—a human condition deprived of any eschatological thrust, and without any firm and consistent ethics of love that moves human action beyond the merely self-satisfying goal of immediacy for one's self or group referent.[12] According to Ilo, "we are homeless when we deliberately try to exclude others because we unconsciously choose to live an exilic life, or shut ourselves from those who are not 'like us.'"[13] And this condition, which breeds violence and intolerance; nurtures anger and despair, can afflict Christians when they fail to manifest in their lives what they profess; or

12. Ilo, *Church and Development in Africa*, 116.

13. Ibid.

when they use religious practices and authority as cover for personal agenda or to advance a limited vision of God's kingdom that has no resemblance or relationship with the present and coming reign of God.[14]

Relating the parable of the prodigal son to our Igbo contextual Christology, I will say that the prodigal has lived through the experience of what it means to be *"otu onye,"* losing his dignity on account of loss of material possessions. However, the grace of Christ, *"Nwanne otu onye,"* brings him back home and reintegrates him into the community where through divine compassion he is clothed with a new dignity. Homelessness is thus dispelled here by that divine compassion and reconciliation which places an obligation on all followers of Christ to value and cherish fraternal solidarity, to seek and find the lost brotherhood. In this sense, this parable, which is also known as the parable of mercy, provides an answer to such "apparently" inexcusable situations which validly question the call for solidarity based on the reason that the poor man or woman is indeed responsible for his or her miserable life. Jesus teaches us then that even in such situations the duty to solidarity remains meaningful and morally binding. Here the theology of solidarity teaches us not to despise and castigate others for their failures, but to help them on the path to new life in all ramifications of what "new life" could entail, both spiritually and materially. However, in addition to the above personal and contextual interpretation, I intend also to demonstrate how African idioms could be used to explore the depth of the Christian message and enrich theological pedagogy both for Africans and non-Africans.

14. Ibid.

8

Mysticism of Compassion

Christianity and African Culture: On the Resonance of the Christian Message

THE SIXTEENTH CHAPTER OF Chinua Achebe's famous novel, *Things Fall Apart*, ends with a remarkable episode that gives us a clue to the secret of the success of Christian mission in Africa. It relates the subtle but powerful appeal which missionary preaching made on young indigenes during the early evangelization of Igboland:

> It was not the mad logic of the Trinity that captivated him [i.e. Nwoye, Okonkwo's first son]. He did not understand it. It was the poetry of the new religion, something felt in the marrow. The hymn about *brothers* who sat in darkness and in fear seemed to answer a vague and persistent question that haunted his young soul—the question of the twins crying in the bush and the question of Ikemefuna who was killed. He felt a relief within as the hymn poured into his parched soul. The words of the hymn were like the drops of frozen rain melting on the dry palate of the panting earth. Nwoye's callow mind was greatly puzzled.[1]

Nwoye's eventual conversion to the "new religion" in Achebe's fiction explains the point of convergence between Christianity and Igbo culture. It is precisely the humane countenance of Christianity, not its dogma that is

---

1. Achebe, *Things Fall Apart*, 128; my emphasis.

its most valuable asset. And it is the latent presence of such evangelical humanism in African culture that enabled the Africans to see in Christianity a religion worthy of embrace. It was this humanism that emboldened the first converts of the nascent Church into accepting a faith that welcomes outcasts (*osu*), believing that "there is no longer Jew or Greek, no longer slave or free, no longer male or female" because all "are one in Christ Jesus" (Gal 3:28).

Probably the desire to eliminate all kinds of discrimination was already simmering in the hearts of young Igbo indigenes. This desire is arguably not yet fully realized. Hence, given this backdrop, Christianity in Africa must deplore and reject all kinds of discrimination against the weak. It must also shun clericalism and undue clerical privilege. In fact, one can say that the cultural compatibility of African culture and the Christian kerygma is what makes the theology of solidarity in the African and especially Igbo context comprehensible. The saying that *"Igbo ama eze"* (the Igbo knows no king) delineates the fact that the Igbo does not condone autocracy or domination. This unique cultural-anthropological characteristic enabled the Igbo culture to be a fertile ground for Christianity to thrive. For instance, speaking about the people of her rural community, Ibi, majority of whom were resistant to externally imposed changes, Agbasiere informs us that the women and men alike expressed identity by self-conscious adherence to what they held to be appropriate behavior, compatible with their past, accepting only such changes as could be accommodated within pre-existing value patterns.[2]

Indeed there are basic humanistic elements and values that are present in both the gospel and Igbo culture, which make a nuptial bond between them a theological desideratum. Unfortunately, these humanistic values are gradually but effectively being eroded by an egotistic, materialistic modern culture, so much so that Elochukwu Uzukwu noted that the root of our problem is cultural. To effect an enduring change, Uzukwu aptly contends that a radical cultural action is imperative. We are both the victims and agents of the negation of our fundamental cultural values, which are the resources we bring into our encounter with other groups of people and which may still constitute viable resources for the transformation of the African continent.[3] Ọ nụrụ ube nwanne agbala ọsọ, in this sense, voices not only a theology of fraternal solidarity (i.e. seen as an Igbo perspective to liberation theology), it is, in fact, in itself an inculturation theology. It is a cultural and evangelical call urging Igbos and Africans in general not to derail from the path of genuine African humanism. The ultimate aim of this cultural prompting is to liberate; to free women and men in the continent

---

2. Agbasiere, *Women in Igbo Life and Thought*, 37.

3. Uzukwu, *Listening Church*, 6.

from servitude—servitude to others and servitude to their own individual parochialism (or narrow-mindedness) that is dividing us. Ours is not a culture that should produce such atrocities like the Rwandan genocide and the numerous bloodbaths in ethnic, religious and political conflicts.

To buttress this argument, Uzukwu presents us the Nri civilization which does not tolerate holy wars, crusades, or jihads—a society where religion is at the service of humane living.[4] *Ndị Nri* is a village-group among the Igbo of Eastern Nigeria who distinguished themselves for presenting the strongest principled action against slavery and against the cheapening of human life in those difficult times. No slaves were bought or sold in Nri markets or in the markets of Nri colonies. To practice such a trade in Nri markets would be an abomination.[5] Also, the priest-king of Nri decries war and sends priests all over Igboland to persuade people to live in peace and to purify the earth polluted by violence. This does not mean that violence is totally eschewed by the Nri. On the contrary, but throughout the turbulent period of slavery and colonization, it is on record that only once in Nri history did an Nri king take up arms to fight a war. The aim of that war was to resist the Abam mercenaries who were hunting for slaves for the Aro group.[6] In a modern world marked by a clash between "the culture of death" and "the culture of life,"[7] our societies need to be reconstructed anew on the sound ethical principle that any attack on human life, no matter how well such attack may be disguised, is an offence against the earth, against the owner of the earth, and against the inhabitants of the earth.

Theological Authenticity of the Igbo Perspective

> We believe that African theology must be understood in the context of African life and culture and the creative attempt of African people to shape a new future that is different from the colonial past and the neo-colonial present . . . African theology must reject, therefore, the prefabricated ideas of North Atlantic theology by defining itself according to the struggles of the people in their resistance against the structures of domination. Our task as theologians is to create a theology that arises from and is accountable to African people.[8]

4. Ibid, 26.
5. Ibid, 25.
6. Ibid.
7. Cf. John Paul II, *Evangelium Vitae*, 24.
8. EATWOT II, "Final Communiqué," 193.

Indeed one of the goals of this book is to demonstrate that creating "a theology that arises from and is accountable to African people" involves essentially using African idioms to articulate theology. Perhaps the question may (or may not) arise, whether we can legitimately consider our Igbo saying here as a valid theologoumenon. Such a validity of an idiomatic approach can neither be questioned nor adjudged inadequate. In fact, it finds counterparts in western thought. The word *"Da-sein,"* for example, is a German idiom with which Martin Heidegger developed his metaphysics of existence. *"Ich werde immer für dich da sein"* is a German statement that expresses: "You can always count on me" (e.g. for moral or material support). This banal promise of solidarity became, for Heidegger, the foundation and compact nucleus of his philosophy. Only the human being can make such a statement. Thus, invariably the human being is, for Heidegger, the tangible and concrete expression of "Being" as "Being-there" (*Dasein*). In fact, only the human being *exists*, all other things *are*. Hence, the theological validity of *Ọ nụrụ ube nwanne agbala ọsọ* for a theology of fraternal solidarity is comparable to "Dasein" as a German idiom in Metaphysics.

Having said that, let me return to the above statement of the Pan-African Conference of Third World Theologians which asserts the notion that "Inculturation" and "liberation" in African theological discourse are essential hermeneutic procedures that seek to interpret the gospel of Jesus Christ to the contemporary African in the light of the African condition.[9] They are hermeneutic procedures that seek both the understanding of the African cultural-political reality and interpretation of this reality in the light of the gospel of Jesus Christ, so as to bring about radical transformation of the oppressive status quo.[10] These hermeneutic models evolved as a result of the African Christian's search for intellectual clarity and comprehensibility of the Christian faith. They are attempts to disengage from the basic Western theological frameworks, orthodoxy, liberalism and neo-orthodoxy. They evolved as a response to what the Pan-African Conference of Third World Theologians has described as Africa's need for "a new theological methodology that is different from the approaches of the dominant theologies of the West."[11]

The Igbo perspective articulated here in idiom is, as I said, a valid theological approach or model that responds to the hope of EATWOT theologians. This perspective bears in mind Kwame Nkrumah's apt affirmation that before any social revolution can take place it must, first of all,

---

9. Martey, *African Theology*, 55.

10. Ibid.

11. EATWOT II, "Final Communiqué."

have "standing firmly behind it an intellectual revolution, a revolution in which our thinking and philosophy are directed towards the redemption of our society."[12] *Ọ nụrụ ube nwanne agbala ọsọ* calls for such a mental and ethical revolution. It adopts African epistemological language and breaks from Western metaphysical, theological methodology. This idiomatic approach to theology is nearer to the Scriptures, comprehensible and more authentic than the abstract and philosophical approach of many medieval and contemporary theologies of the West, for the common man is less interested in suffering himself at understanding such nebulous concepts like "*hypostase*," "*homousios*," "*perichoresis*," etc. than he or she is in seeking to know how the Gospel of Jesus Christ should be translated into daily life. The fundamental aim of education in Africa is to ground and initiate the young into an authentic sense of *familyhood*. It is only with such genuine and functional sense that anyone can attain his or her genuine cultural personhood.

Idioms, no less than myths or cultural fictions, become undoubtedly efficacious means of human communication of social and cultural values in the community, and thus powerful instruments of education. And such idioms as *ube nwanne* and *ujamaa* are good examples. The all-embracing and fundamental principle which underlies and guides all the traditional African educational and economic systems is the individual person's freedom to choose, as well as work for the good of the family which involves the good of herself or himself. The good of the family is the primary purpose of all African social interaction. It provides the Africans with the best possible basis of freedom for all.[13] Speaking about the significance of *ujamaa* socialism, for instance, Julius Nyerere argues:

> It is opposed to capitalism, which seeks to build a happy society on the basis of the exploitation of man by man; and it is equally opposed to doctrinaire socialism which seeks to build its happy society on a philosophy of inevitable conflict between man and man.
>
> We, in Africa, have no more need of being 'converted' to socialism than we have of being 'taught' democracy. Both are rooted in our past—in the traditional society which produced us . . . Our recognition of the family to which we all belong must be extended yet further—beyond the tribe, the community, the nation, or even the continent—to embrace the whole society of mankind.[14]

12. Nkrumah, *Consciencism*, 78.

13. Egbujie, *Hermeneutics of the African Traditional Culture*, 85.

14. Nyerere, *Ujamaa: Essays on Socialism*, 12.

This global embrace (not just liberation) is the ultimate destination of theology. No other apologetic defends better the authenticity of the African perspective to humanism, or the theological relevance and wisdom of African idioms in articulating such humanism. Once speaking about "the most difficult and central problem in creating African theology," Charles Nyamiti sees the problem as consisting in the effective adoption of African elements into sacred science. According to him, among the reasons for deficiency in African theological essays are a lack of intrinsic employment of cultural themes and a narrowness of approach to the factors involved. Hence, African ideas far from entering internally into the theological elaboration of revelation so as to form an organic part of it are rather used as a mere propaedeutic providing exterior illustrations or subjective preparations.[15] Nyamiti then singled out the theme of family as an example—a theme that is emphasized in both African and western communities, albeit in distinct ways.

To appreciate fully the African originality of the category "family," Nyamiti counsels that the themes it evokes should in their turn be examined in the light of the African context. This means that, although the formal content of the category "family" is identical in Africa and in the West, the mode of its integration in its cultural contexts is different. And it is particularly in this concrete mode of integration, i.e., in the local coloring of the cultural themes, that the originality of the African themes has to be sought.[16] Such originality or uniqueness of African idioms, however, does not make African theology irrelevant to Western theology, nor can it make it incomprehensible to Western readers. In fact, African theological idioms serve for the cultural enrichment of Western theology and vice versa. Since both currents of theology have a common point of departure as *fides quaerens intellectum*—faith seeking understanding, the two theological genre intersect in many ways and complement each other. This fact is attested in the next section when we shift our gaze on the political theology that has become popular in Western Europe through the writings of Johann Baptist Metz. The preponderance of such themes like suffering, justice, solidarity, and compassion in these theologies indicates how close we are in sharing common problems, even if in different magnitudes, contexts and idioms.

15. Nyamiti, "Approaches to African Theology," 41.
16. Ibid., 39.

A Mysticism of the Open Eyes

The metaphor of the "open eyes" captures adroitly the soul of fraternal solidarity and the spirituality of compassion that is so aptly articulated in the saying "*Ọ nụrụ ube nwanne agbala ọsọ*." Culled from the political theology of Johann Baptist Metz, *Mystik der offenen Augen*[17] is a metaphor used by the German theologian in reiterating the fundamental theme of his theological thesis. In that theology, "the cry" (*der Schrei*) and "the mysticism of compassion" are dominant themes, which are very relevant to any theological discourse on solidarity or fraternity. The problems which Metz grappled with in his theology do not only establish a firm resonance of *Ọ nụrụ ube nwanne agbala ọsọ* with European political theology, but also demonstrates the pivotal role of fraternal solidarity in contemporary theology. For Metz, any theology worth its name cannot be indifferent to, or disconnected from the individual history of suffering in the world, for it is in its sensibility to human suffering that theology exercises its function as fundamental theology. If suffering belongs to the fundamental experience of human beings, theology is then obliged to posit and give answers to the questions about the place and role of God in the face of contingent evil. Mysticism of the open eyes, as I said, is the metaphorical reference to the obligation imposed by Christian spirituality which should compel people of faith not to close their eyes or ears to the ever present cries of suffering humanity. This central theme of Metz's political theology—the cry (*der Schrei*)—typifies the harrowing experiences of unjust crucibles which Metz sought to interpret in the light of the fundamental question of Theodicy—a question about the presence of evil in the world and of the goodness of God in the face of such an abysmal history of suffering in a world, which ought to be His world after all. Exceptionally remarkable about Metz's formulation of the theodicy question is the personal history he brings into this discourse. As a child soldier who had a traumatic experience of the Second World War—an experience whose immediate reaction was an engulfing shock that could only find vent in a silent scream (*ein lautloser Schrei*),[18] as he would call it, Metz sees such an experience as representing the immanent presence of the passion of Christ, which is ever actual. It was an experience that turns childhood dreams into nightmares leading one to ask: *Where is God, and why does He allow this to happen?*

The traditional theology of the Church Fathers had sought to answer this question by saying that God is not answerable for evil, because evil is

17. Metz, *Mystik der offenen Augen.*

18. Metz, *Memoria Passionis*, 93–94.

the consequence of the abuse of human freedom (St. Augustine). For Metz, however, this traditional answer is not sufficient, God should take some responsibility. But God's response consists in the positing of the question, because it is in the cry of lament which questions God's presence and action in the world that God's answer is mysteriously made manifest. In line with this explanation, the theodicy question becomes a personal as well as collective challenge, understood in terms of the need for a compelling effort to salvage the human character of modern rationalism. And for Metz, one must have fought with all the means available to one's disposal before one should ask the theodicy question. Hence, theodicy will always be seen in the light of the actions of solidarity we have brought to bear on the sufferings of humanity in such a way that those actions of ours constitute God's answer to and His loving intervention in the face of earthly predicaments. Theodicy is hence leaving our eyes open to see the injustice, pains and misery that challenge our humanity and Christian spirituality. It cannot be overemphasized that the often grim and ungodly realities of human history lays a burden of responsibility on all those in earnest search of the kingdom of God, i.e. those seeking through works of mercy and evangelization to establish such a kingdom on earth. Metz sees the imperative of the kingdom and indeed the whole of Christian spirituality, including prayer, in what he calls the mysticism of compassion, i.e., to put it in other words, in Ọ nụrụ ube nwanne agbala ọsọ—in the ability to recognize in prayer a petition, "asking God for God," giving or finding oneself in the mystique of God's passion and compassion. It is not a mysticism of the closed eyes, but rather a mysticism of the open eyes.[19] It is this mysticism of the open eyes that motivated the abolitionists of the eighteenth century, the fathers of African independence, and the many theologians of liberation. Here again, the pertinent question asked by a Muslim theologian is ad rem: What could have been the inner state of the Lutheran bishops who refused to struggle against Hitler's regime? Can one compromise so fully with evil, and still be capable of prayer? It is for the modern Christian to explain to the world how such a conjunction might be imaginable, let alone achieved.[20] The mysticism of the open eyes hence presupposes that one cannot refuse to struggle against evil and still remain capable of prayer. Metz also asked: What is the experience of one who, assessing his being (Dasein) is compelled to admit that only ruins stand on the path of his life—ruins of people who are destroyed by his own selfishness?[21] The social relevance of any theology and of Christian

19. Ibid., 105.

20. Akhtar, Final Imperative, 62–63.

21. Metz, Memoria Passionis, 99.

spirituality in the modern time can only be determined by its preoccupation with these questions.

The spiritually open eyes are eyes that see in other human beings, their own brothers and sisters, the image of God with which these brothers and sisters are imbued. For, the moment we see anything less than human in others, in that moment is history bound to take a tragic turn. Remembering the indictment of the history of the past twentieth century, therefore, what Metz cautions against is the warped perceptions that lead men and women to live up to the worst instincts of the human species. It is a caution against the danger of the eyes that see in fellow human beings "a pest" (*Ungeziefer*, as in the Nazi propaganda) or "a cockroach" (as in the Rwandan propaganda). Accordingly, it is only when we see, or listen to, other human subjects as brothers and sisters can humanity in general be really able to rise up to the challenges that suffering, poverty, greed, intolerance, discrimination and hatred present to us in this world. That is what makes a theology after Auschwitz, Rwanda or Biafra very important. Auschwitz, Biafra and Rwanda remind us of the incredible and ignominious bestiality and inhumanity which the human species is capable of, and which could be best described as an eclipse of humanism. Metz, quoting Elie Wiesel puts it radically: "Every thoughtful Christian knows that in Auschwitz it is not the Jews, but rather Christianity that died."[22] Similarly, some African authors believe that in Biafra Africa died.[23] It may sound hyperbolic, but this is meant to underscore what is actually at stake, namely the question, if there is indeed such a God who we can pretend to worship while turning our back to such horrors.[24] In this sense, *Ọ nụrụ ube nwanne agbala ọsọ* calls for the opening of our eyes to the harrowing conditions of fellow brothers and sisters through a theistic anthropology whose humanistic thrust is profoundly rooted in a genuine understanding and appreciation of the fraternal charity of the kingdom of God. With the spirituality of the open eyes we see no longer merely the human sister or brother but rather mystically, we see a suffering God: "*LORD, when did we see you hungry and feed you, or thirsty and give you drink? When did we see you a stranger and make you welcome, lacking clothes and clothe you? When did we see you sick or in prison and go to visit you?* (Matt 25:37ff.). In this sense, Metz's conviction, which is shared by several other theologians of liberation and which I generously affirm, is that in the mysticism of compassion the authority of God manifests itself in the authority of the suffering human being, in that single authority under

---

22. Ibid., 36; translation is mine.

23. Ezeani, *In Biafra Africa Died*.

24. Metz, *Memoria Passionis*, 38.

which Jesus brings the whole of human history in his famous parable of
the Last Judgment. Although the suffering human beings should not as a
result be considered as earthly equivalents of God, they, nonetheless, represent earthly manifestations of His proximity.[25] In this understanding, the
traditional idiomatic expression of African theology of fraternal solidarity
finds a non-negligible echo in the West, in the political theology of Johann
Baptist Metz.

But Metz radicalizes the notion of the cry in his discourse on the cry
of Jesus on the cross. The Paschal Mystery reveals to us a Son of God who is
no longer merely a brother to the suffering (*Nwanne otu onye*), but indeed is
the *suffering brother* himself and whose New Testament identification with
the "Suffering Servant" of Deutero-Isaiah (Isaiah 52:13—53:12; see also
Matt 20:18–19; Mark 10:33–34; Luke 18:31–33) makes a compelling appeal
on behalf of solidarity. Condemned by the religious hierarchy of his time,
abandoned by his friends; mocked by the crowd, tortured and crucified by
the imperial powers, the heart-rending cry of this God, Jesus, constitutes
the *locus theologicum* for understanding suffering and giving an adequate
response to it. The cry of anguish then becomes, in general, a prayer addressed to God seeking an answer to the theodicy question: "God, where
are you?" Jesus Christ, the mediator between God and human beings, addresses this prayer in his cry of Good Friday. For Metz, this cry itself is God's
answer. But this God's answer to our prayer is conceivable only as a call to
action addressed to men and women inviting them to be willing to commit
themselves to the works of fraternal solidarity. This commitment to solidarity is the mysticism of compassion for the least of Jesus' brothers and sisters
which is articulated in *Ọ nụrụ ube nwanne agbala ọsọ*. Jesus gathers in his
cross and death the experiences of the sufferings of all humankind uniting
them in his passion and articulating them as a desperate and agonizing cry
to the Father: "*Eloi, eloi, lama sabachthani,*"—"My God, my God, why have
you forsaken me?" (Matt 27:46; Mark 15:34). Therefore, the cross of Christ
imposes an obligation through the mysticism of the open eyes by which humanity is invited to contemplate the sufferings of Christ through the lens of
the sufferings of fellow brothers and sisters. Fundamental theology becomes
therefore a call to participate in the *Memoria Passionis et resurrectionis*. For
Metz, sin, understood as a conscious or willful separation from God, will
then consist, in what Jesus sees as a refusal to participate in the sufferings
of others. Sin will then be a rejection of the need to look beyond the dark
horizon of one's own experiences of suffering; what St. Augustine calls
"self-distortion of the heart." Sin becomes a self-surrender to the hidden

25. Ibid., 106.

narcissism of the creature.[26] Sinful will be the condition of a soul so preoccupied with its own selfishness and vainglorious worries that it ignores the cry of *nwanne.*

The Conciliar Orientation for Inclusive Humanism

The 50th anniversary of Second Vatican Council has led to renewed studies of the content of that land-mark event in the life and mission of the Catholic Church. It has called our attention back to reflect on how the Church understands herself and her pastoral mission in the modern world. And in one of the most important document of the Council, the Constitution on the Church in the Modern World, *Gaudium et Spes,* we see the acknowledgement that the earth has not yet become the scene of true brotherhood (*GS,* 37). Fifty years after the Council, that apt observation still remains valid and the Church is still asking how this unhappy situation can be overcome. In seeking an answer to this important question, the council Fathers turned to the Word of God, which became man. It is He, who "assures those who trust in the charity of God that the way of love is open to all men and that the effort to establish a universal brotherhood will not be in vain" (*GS,* 38). Keeping the flame of this hope alive is admittedly one of the major goals of Christian theology. The very questions that motivate the theology of fraternal solidarity as propounded in this book arise from this hope. By using an idiomatic hermeneutic for interpreting the Scripture, I have come to the conclusion that fraternal solidarity is an aspect of theology that demands special attention today. The very heart of this theology is the Word of God itself. The excursus in political theology serves merely to affirm the fundamental motif of solidarity and liberation as imperative of the kingdom of God.

According to Ela, "In African reading of the Bible, there now wells up out of the life of black communities a protest that the parent churches have never dared to make heard. The missions have slain in African men and women the message of liberation in the revelation of the God of the exodus."[27] This and similar assertions are viewpoints, which the theology of fraternal solidarity articulated here modifies. The message of liberation is not dead in African men and women. This new perspective to liberation theology demonstrates this assertion, but it is a perspective that does not seek to jubilate over the demise of "Pharaoh's Egypt,"[28] but rather hopes

26. Ibid., 163.

27. Ela, *African Cry,* 50.

28. Pharaoh and Egypt here are symbols and have nothing to do with the political

to celebrate the humanization of Pharaoh. Pharaoh in this sense could be seen as a prototype that may stand for anybody or any institution, from an ordinary husband who prides himself to be superior to his wife and other women, to a corrupt politician who impoverishes his people through exploitation, or still more to the global economic "imperium" of the West which denigrates Africa while exploiting her natural and human resources. Therefore, what this discourse represents is a perspective that lays a genuine humanistic and theological foundation for the "universal brotherhood" which *Gaudium et Spes* envisions.

The historical and theological analysis of the "African cry" which I have made in chapters 4 and 5 is an indispensable tool in making a critique of the present. We must learn to create a present that recognizes the necessity of inclusive humanism. The project of Christianizing culture or of inculturating Christianity in Africa cannot and should not in any way ignore the unsustainability of extolling a culture that still subordinates women and discriminates against "*osu*" (*Homo sacer*—outcasts). African theologians who engage in inculturation must then bear in mind that culture is more than the arts. It is about shared patterns of identity. It is about how social values are transmitted and individuals are made to be part of a society. Culture is how the past interacts with the future. Culture is all about "*onye aghala nwanne ya*" (let no one abandon his sister or brother), and is always essentially communitarian. Without this understanding of culture, inculturation as an expression of protest against "theological imperialism" becomes meaningless. In one notable criticism of Inculturation theology, for instance, Bénézet Bujo casts aspersion on it as a pompous irrelevance and a truly ideological superstructure at the service of the bourgeoisie. For Bujo, it may be a cause of some satisfaction that the African hierarchy has adopted a theology of incarnation as its official policy. So far, however, there have been more words than actions and one cannot help wondering how serious is the commitment of the bishops of Africa to a truly effective incarnation of Christianity in Africa.[29] Bujo's criticism indeed follows from an alleged discontent of an African student who questions the relevance of a God that is extolled in ancestral traditions and customs while the sufferings of millions of refugees are ignored. This criticism stimulates our awareness of the fact that the African continent reminds us that the future belongs to those who will have found a way to give present generations reasons to live and hope.[30]

---

and geographical entity that is known as Egypt today.

29. Bujo, *African Theology*, 66.

30. Ela, *African Cry*, 104.

Also in the wake of unprecedented brutal expressions of religious intolerance in our time, theology in Africa earnestly needs inclusive models in
doctrinal hermeneutic. Such models are supposed to eliminate barriers to
dialogue in the search for truth, and build inter-religious and inter-denominational bridges in which proclamations of faith will respect the primordial
transcendence of universal fraternity and communion. Jude Uwalaka has
once proposed that such an inclusive humanism is the basis of a sound
socio-political order for Africa. It is a theory which asserts that "no one
or group in society should be treated in any way that would constitute any
real threat to their security and survival, unless such an individual or group
wants to deny to others such similar security or survival."[31] This entails
building an African society that can live out successfully the national and
international demands of the twenty-first century. Uwalaka maintains that
"inclusive humanism takes the African man and society as he is perceived
today, as man or society which no longer belongs to a past that is no longer,
but belongs to a present brought about by many cultural and historical experiences and encounters, which have shaped the African man and society
in some cases irreversibly."[32] We carry the burden of a history that compels
us to seek ways of overcoming all forms of barriers and engaging in efforts
that strengthen brotherly love and solidarity.

Furthermore, it will be more and more difficult for Christians to live
their relationship with God, as Ela consistently invokes, in cozy isolation
from questions dealing with rising prices and speculation in real estate in a
capitalist economy, or with the problem of the recrudescence of tribalism.
The very nature of the problems we face today, therefore, calls for a re-examination of who we are, that is, how we see ourselves and our common destiny. This is the fundamental basis for finding lasting solution to eradicating
sins against humanity. This inward-looking is not only exigent; it is also very
promising and potentially fruitful. And it feeds on a perspective that enables
us to see in man-made poverty and misery not just a pitiable condition, but
above all an unjust crucifixion of a brother or a sister. Inclusive humanism
in this case, refuses to abstract the African man's encounter with history in
order to reach a so-called African social and political originality.[33] It equally
refuses an iconoclastic attitude which sees nothing good that could be recovered from the African traditional past. It is the meeting point between the
past and the present, identity and alterity, diversity and unity, liberation and
reconciliation. It is the point where exclusion is overcome by fraternal em-

31. Uwalaka, "Inclusive Humanism," 95.
32. Ibid.
33. Ibid., 96.

brace. Hence, all that have been said here are not based merely on a politics of liberation struggle, whether political or cultural, but more importantly on the view of a necessary engagement with the truth and challenges of the history of salvation. A truth that calls on us to see in the myriads of the problems already dealt with in this book an Africa whose beauty is marred by misery and injustice and whose cry cannot be ignored within and outside her borders. The theological task which this cry engenders is not that of a cultural or social-political Puritanism, but rather that of building a civilization of love where carrying one another is no longer a burden but a fraternal duty that is soul-satisfying; where *joys and hopes* are multiplied, while *grief and anguish* are diminished through acts of solidarity.

9

Conclusion

Philadelphia in Ecclesiae

POPE FRANCIS' APOSTOLIC EXHORTATION, *Evangelii Gaudium*, reminds us that the New Jerusalem, the holy city (cf. Rev 21:2–4), is the goal towards which all of humanity is moving. And God's revelation tells us that the fullness of humanity and of history is realized in a city. For God's presence accompanies the sincere efforts of individuals and groups to find encouragement and meaning in their lives. He dwells among us, fostering solidarity, fraternity, and the desire for goodness, truth and justice. This presence must not be contrived but found, uncovered.[1] This reiterates Pope Benedict XVI's views in the encyclical, *Caritas in Veritate*, which maintains that, "Man's earthly activity, when inspired and sustained by charity, contributes to the building of the *universal city of God*, which is the goal of the history of the human family. In an increasingly globalized society, the common good and the effort to obtain it cannot fail to assume the dimensions of the whole human family, that is to say, the community of peoples and nations, in such a way as to shape the earthly city in unity and peace, rendering it to some degree an anticipation and a prefiguration of the undivided city of God."[2]

---

1. Francis, *Evangelii Gaudium*, 71.

2. *CIV*, 7; emphasis mine.

This city of God is just a figure of human society that is bound together by brotherly love, and whose expression could be seen in such mode
of relating to one another that the ancient Greek philosophers referred to
as *philia*, hence, the idea of *Philadelphia*, the city of brotherly love. This city
is a spiritual edifice that has nothing to do with an urban metropolis in
the United States of America. The concept of *Ubuntu* in African worldview
best expresses the ideal of this *city of God*, which subsists in the *city of man*.
No man is an island, and that is why a Zulu proverb says: *umuntu ngu-
muntu ngabantu, "a person is a person through other persons."* Archbishop
Desmond Tutu of South Africa has used this concept of *Ubuntu* to argue for
reconciliation and healing of the wounds of apartheid. For him, it is *Ubuntu*
that constrains many to be magnanimous and ready to forgive, rather than
to demand retribution or wreak vengeance.[3] *Philadelphia* as a symbolism
of brotherly love and community is thus the sacrament of the city of God
in which the consciousness of *Ubuntu* helps men and women of diverse
identities to become aware of their ontological unity as *ụmụnne*—brothers and sisters. God's being—*ntu*—is the metadynamic (active rather than
metaphysical)[4] principle or light that enlightens that awareness and lays the
foundation for the city of brotherly love.

Empirically, the city is the archetype of human achievement in civilization. It is the exhibition center for the *Genius* of the Homo-Sapiens.
Ironically it is also a curious abode of contradictions between good and
evil; affluence and squalor; culture and crime; industry and exploitation;
scientific progress and moral depravity; the beautiful and the ugly. If God
has decided to build a city, then it is for the reason that the human yardstick
for measuring progress needs to be displaced and dislocated, in order to
usher in genuine civilization. Such a civilization hinges on the recognition
of human society as a global family, a cosmic city, where *philia* or *Ubuntu*
abides as the cohesive principle. Commitment to fraternity involves the recognition of the absolute importance of this nature of love which in German
language is called *"entgrenzende Liebe,"* that is, a love that erases boundaries, especially consanguineous, racial, ethnic or religious boundaries. It is
for this reason that I have chosen to conclude this work with a reflection
on *philia*.

One of the basic assumptions of a theology of fraternity is that the
effort at transforming the human society into one cosmic *"Philadelphia"* is
a divine imperative. It is a sacred duty which begins with a thorough examination of conscience and an honest evaluation of our own perceptions and

3. Tutu, *No Future without Forgiveness*, 31.

4. Battle, *Reconciliation*, 39.

judgments of other people. And it is only a heart that says "no" to exclusion, a heart that is open to universal friendship and has situated itself in the context of a family of loving hearts that will be capable of exercising this sacred duty. This requires a true and fundamental *enlightenment* about who we are in relation to one another. Today the fortunes of the richest people in the richest countries are tied irrevocably to the fate of the poorest people in the poorest countries of the world, even though they are strangers and will probably never meet each other. This interdependence forms the basic substratum for our appreciation of the world as one cosmic family bound together by *philia* in solidarity. *Philia,* understood often in the private level as the love of friendship, and of fellowship shuns the boundaries of blood ties. Its main thrust is in mutual sharing of confidence, just as Jesus Christ expressed to us, his disciples: "I call you friends, because I have made known to you everything I have learnt from my Father" (John 15:15). And after saying this he added: *"My command to you is to love one another"* (John 15:17). Hence, Jesus loving relationship with his disciples is based on his sharing his Father's patrimony with them and from this sharing arises also his appeal, or better, express injunction to love one another.

The kingdom of God which Jesus preached and for which he sacrificed his precious blood is undoubtedly a *"Philadelphia in Ecclesiae"*—a truly mystical city of brotherly love, which subsists, according to the Second Vatican Council, in the Church, understood not merely as the Roman Catholic Church, but rather as the people of God. The Church's essence as a community of children of God and the immanent structure of that kingdom imposes on it the vocation and mission to preach and live out brotherly love both to believers and unbelievers alike. Jesus' avowal of total openness to his disciples in John 15:15 hence indicate to us that an uninhibited appreciation of others is the basis of the friendship that nurtures the life of the kingdom. This is a truth which the global campaign against poverty should recognize and cherish. It is no longer the act of giving aid to the poor that matters most, but rather the act of sharing intimate divine truth about the human person and human dignity. It is the fact of cherishing the poor for who she is, namely, my sister or brother whose beauty has been marred by suffering and deprivation. For this reason Pope Francis has lambasted the global economic imperium that has developed a globalization of indifference whose sole interest is to sustain the selfish ideal and a lifestyle which excludes others from economic justice.[5]

Philia (φιλία) which is known as a dispassionate virtuous love, is a concept developed by Aristotle, and according to this ancient Greek

---

5. Francis, *Evangelii Gaudium*, 54.

philosopher, it includes loyalty to friends, family, and community, and requires virtue, equality and familiarity. In ancient texts, *philos* denoted a general type of love, used for love between family, between friends, a desire or enjoyment of an activity, as well as between lovers.[6] It is a love that is not restricted by definition. *Philia* is thus a strong bond existing between people who share a common interest or activity. And one of such common interests which all people share is the desire for a peaceful, just and egalitarian human society where opportunities for progress are rife for everybody. Built on the ruins of the exploited and *wretched of the earth*, the *city of man* often fails to provide these opportunities and has to be displaced by the *city of God* that is built on the foundation of universal love. This universal love expresses itself as *philia*. In his treatise on *The Four Loves*, C. S. Lewis sees *philia* as the least *natural* of loves, in the sense that, it is not biologically necessary to progeny like either *storge*, affection, (rearing a child), *eros* (procreating a child), or *agape*, charity (providing for a child). It has the least association with impulse or emotion. In spite of these characteristics, it was the belief of the ancients, (and Lewis himself), that it was the most admirable of loves because it looked not at the beloved (like *eros*), but towards the purpose of love—that thing because of which the relationship was formed. This freed the participants in this friendship from self-consciousness.[7] Lewis believes that, to the Ancients, this kind of love is the happiest and most fully human of all loves; the crown of life and the school of virtue. But the modern world ignores and does not value it, because only few experience it.[8]

In Modern Greek as also in Aristotle's *Nicomachean Ethics, philia* (φιλία) is usually translated as "friendship," though in fact Aristotle's use of the term is much broader, as I have pointed out. As Gerard Hughes notes, in Books VIII and IX of the NE, Aristotle gives examples of *philia* including: "young lovers (1156b2), lifelong friends (1156b12), cities with one another (1157a26), political or business contacts (1158a28), parents and children (1158b20), fellow-voyagers and fellow-soldiers (1159b28), members of the same religious society (1160a19), or of the same tribe (1161b14), a cobbler and the person who buys from him (1163b35)."[9]

All of these different relationships involve getting on well with someone, though Aristotle at times implies that something more like actual liking is required. The notion of *philia* must be mutual, and thus excludes relationships with animals. It requires, according to Aristotle in his *Rhetoric*, τò

---

6. http://en.wikipedia.org/wiki/Greek_words_for_love

7. Lewis, *Four Loves*, 56.

8. Ibid., 55.

9. Hughes, *Aristotle on Ethics*, 168.

φιλεῖν: "wanting for someone what one thinks good, for his sake and not for one's own, and being inclined, so far as one can, to do such things for him [or her]" (1380b36–1381a2). According to John M. Cooper, this indicates that the central idea of φιλία is that of doing good to someone for his or her own sake, out of concern for him or her and not, or not merely, out of concern for oneself. The different forms of φιλία, as listed above, could hence be viewed just as different contexts and circumstances in which this kind of mutual well-doing can arise.[10] Aristotle takes *philia* to be both necessary as a means to happiness: "no one would choose to live without friends even if he had all the other goods" (1155a5–6), and as noble or fine (καλόν) in itself.[11]

It is an existential truth that we are not isolated individuals, who happen to live side by side, but rather people who are dependent on one another, and whose life's fulfillment lies in the quality of our relationships. But what is the meaning of fellowship among individuals and peoples; what is the meaning of solidarity and friendship, in the context where misery and oppression are rife in human society? This is an important question which the Church and the entire humanity must confront itself with. Hence, the real meaning of fraternity and friendship will be seen as a radical change of attitude from the individual person who has surrendered his or her will to the authentic humanism that enables an enlightened and healthy anthropological vision of humanity that sees beyond the ephemerals and the accidentals of human existence. What animates a Christian's faith is the perception of an unfinished world placed in our hands by God. The world is not to be saved, but reinvented by the power of the gospel. Faith impels us to toil in order that all reality become, in Jesus Christ, a new creation.[12] At the dawn of the first creation, the human species received a mandate from God to be master of creation and to rule over the earth (cf. Gen 1:28f). The person of faith is a person of creation. His or her mission is to build through a preponderance of embrace a dis-alienated society, a *civitas Dei*, a city of brotherly love—*Philadelphia*; a city of peace—*Dar es Salam*; a society in which all women and men find it possible really to live. Faith is witness to a God who takes up the cause of those who cannot defend themselves. To believe is to have a role to play in the changes demanded by the kingdom of God, which means an end of suffering for the poor and the liberation of the oppressed (Matt 11:4–5). It means to refuse to ignore the cries of anguish and injustice; it means to receive a divine vocation and awaken to the challenges and gospel imperative envisaged in *Ọ nụrụ ube nwanne agbala ọsọ.*

10. Cooper, "Friendship and the Good," 302.

11. See http://en.wikipedia.org/wiki/Philia.

12. Ela, *African Cry*, 92.

Bibliography

Abraham, K. C., ed. *Third World Theologies: Commonalities and Divergences*. Maryknoll, NY: Orbis, 1990.

Abraham, Willie E. *The Mind of Africa*. Chicago: University of Chicago Press, 1962.

Achebe, Chinua. *Hopes and Impediments: Selected Essays*. New York: Doubleday, 1989.

————. *There Was a Country: A Personal History of Biafra*. New York: Penguin, 2012.

————. *Things Fall Apart*. London: Everyman's Library, 1992.

Ade Ajayi, J. F., ed. *General History of Africa*. Vol. 6, *Africa in the Nineteenth Century until the 1880s*. Abridged ed. Berkeley, CA: University of California Press, 1998.

Adekunle, Benjamin. *Stern Magazine*, West Germany, August 18, 1968.

Adichie, Chimamanda. "The Danger of a Single Story." Talk delivered at TEDGlobal 2009. http://www.ted.com/talks/chimamanda_adichie_the_danger_of_a_single_story.

Afigbo, A. E. *The Warrant Chiefs: Indirect Rule in South-eastern Nigeria 1891–1929*. London: Longman, 1972.

Agbasiere, Joseph-Thérèse. *Women in Igbo Life and Thought*. London: Routledge, 2000.

Aguilar, Mario I. *The Rwandan Genocide and the Call to Deepen Christianity in Africa*. Eldoret, Kenya: AMECEA, 1998.

Akhtar, Shabbir. *The Final Imperative: An Islamic Theology of Liberation*. London: Bellew, 1991.

Alao, Shittu. *Washington Post*, June 7, 1969.

Amadi-Azuogu, Chinedu A. *Biblical Exegesis and Inculturation In Africa In The Third Millennium*. Enugu, Nigeria: Snaap, 2000.

Anderson, A. A. *2 Samuel*. Word Biblical Commentary 11. Dallas: Word, 1989.

Anderson, Gerald, and Thomas Stransky, eds. *Mission Trends No. 3: Third World Theologies; Asian, African and Latin American Contributions to a Radical, Theological Realignment in the Church*. New York: Paulist, 1976.

Antonio, Edward P., ed. *Inculturation and Postcolonial Discourse in African Theology*. New York: Lang, 2006.

Appiah-Kubi, Kofi, and Sergio Torres, eds. *African Theology En Route*. Maryknoll, NY: Orbis, 1979.

Arinze, Francis A. *Lenten Pastoral Letter*. Onitsha, Nigeria: Tabansi, 1973.

Arrupe, Pedro. "Letter on Inculturation to the Whole Society of Jesus." *Indian Missiological Review* 1, no. 1 (1979) 87–95.

Assaf, Andrea Kirk. "Nun Speaks of African-American Catholics: Untold Stories." *ZENIT*, March 2, 2011, http://www.ewtn.com/library/CHISTORY/zaframcath. HTM.

Awolowo, Obafemi. *Financial Times*, London: June 26, 1969; *Daily Telegraph*, London: June 27, 1969.

Battle, Michael. *Reconciliation: The Ubuntu Theology of Desmond Tutu.* Cleveland: Pilgrim, 1997.

Bediako, Kwame. *Christianity in Africa, The Renewal of a Non-Western Religion.* Maryknoll, NY: Orbis, 1995.

———. *Jesus and the Gospel in Africa, History and Experience.* Maryknoll, NY: Orbis, 2004.

Benedict XVI, Pope. "By Living the Truth, the Truth Becomes Life." (Pope's Address on Baptism at Opening of Rome's Ecclesial Congress.) Translation by Zenit. org. Rome, June 12, 2012. http://www.zenit.org/en/articles/pope-s-address-on-baptism-at-opening-of-rome-s-ecclesial-congress.

———. *Caritas in Veritate.* Encyclical Letter. Rome: Vatican, June 29, 2009.

———. *Deus Caritas Est.* Encyclical Letter. Rome: Vatican, December 25, 2005.

Biko, Steve. "Black Consciousness and the Quest for a True Humanity." In *The Challenge of Black Theology in South Africa,* edited by Basil Moore, 36–47. Atlanta: John Knox, 1973.

Bishops of Peru "Justice in the World." In *Liberation Theology: A Documentary History.* edited by Alfred T. Hennelly, 125–36. Maryknoll, NY: Orbis, 1990.

Boesak, Allan. *Black and Reformed: Apartheid, Liberation and the Calvinist Tradition.* Maryknoll, NY: Orbis, 1984.

———. "Coming in out of the Wilderness." In *The Emergent Gospel: Theology from the Underside of History,* edited by Sergio Torres and Virginia Fabella, 76–93. Maryknoll, NY: Orbis, 1978.

———. *A Farewell to Innocence: A Socio-ethical Study on Black Theology and Power.* Maryknoll, NY: Orbis, 1977.

Boesak, Willa. *God's Wrathful Children: Political Oppression and Christian Ethics.* Grand Rapids: Eerdmans, 1995.

Boff, Leonardo. "Eine kreative Rezeption des II. Vatikanums aus der Sicht der Armen: Die Theologie der Befreiung." In *Glaube im Prozess. Christsein nach dem II. Vatikanum,* edited by Elmar Klinger and Klaus Wittstadt, 628–54. Freiburg: Herder, 1984.

———. *Jesus Christus, der Befreier.* Translated by Horst Goldstein and Karel Hermans. Freiburg: Herder, 1986.

Boff, Leonardo, and Clodovis Boff. *Introducing Liberation Theology.* Maryknoll, NY: Orbis, 2002.

———. "Methodology of the Theology of Liberation." In *Systematic Theology, Perspectives from Liberation Theology,* edited by Jon Sobrino and Ignacio Ellacuria, 1–19. Maryknoll, NY: Orbis, 1996.

Braulik, Georg. *Deuteronomium.* 2 vols. Die Neue Echter Bibel, Kommentar zum Alten Testament mit der Einheitsübersetzung. Würzburg: Echter, 1986–92

———. *Kirche im Alten Testament, AT. Biblische Theologie.* Unpublished handout, Uniwien, Winter semester 2003/04.

Brown, Raymond. *The Message of Deuteronomy.* Leicester: InterVarsity, 1993.

Bujo, Bénézet. *African Theology in Its Social Context.* Nairobi: Paulines, 1992.

Busia, K. A. *The Challenge of Africa*. New York: Praeger, 1962.

Buthelezi, Manas. "Toward Indigenous Theology in South Africa." In *The Emergent Gospel: Theology from the Underside of History*, edited by Sergio Torres and Virginia Fabella, 56–75. Maryknoll, NY: Orbis, 1978.

Byrne, Tony. *Airlift to Biafra, Breaching the Blockade*. Dublin: Columba, 1997.

Catechism of the Catholic Church, The (CCC). Translated by *AMECEA* Nigeria. Ibadan, Nigeria: Liberia Editrice Vaticana, 1992.

Catholic Secretariat of Nigeria (CSN). *Church in Nigeria: Family of God on Mission*. Lineamenta for the First National Pastoral Congress. Lagos: CSN, 1999.

CBCN. "Nigeria in Distress—The Way Out." *Communiqué*, September 11, 1993.

———. "Prolonged Distress of the Nigerian Nation." *Communiqué*, September 16, 1994.

Cesear, Aimé. *Discourse on Colonialism*. Translated by John Pinkham. New York: Monthly Press Review, 2000.

Chimezie, Bright, and Zigima Sound. "Ube Nwanne." http://www.youtube.com/watch?v=qO4ZR1xjvzI.

Commission for Africa. *Our Common Interest: An Argument*. London: Penguin, 2005.

Cooper, John M. "Friendship and the Good in Aristotle." *Philosophical Review* 86 (1977) 290–315.

Corelli, Marie. *Sorrows of Satan*. Philadelphia: Lippincott, 1895.

Cornwall, Andrea, ed. *Readings in Gender in Africa*. Bloomington: Indiana University Press, 2005.

Davidson, Basil. *The African Slave Trade: Precolonial History, 1450–1850*. Boston: Little, Brown, 1961.

Demaison Michel, "Die Wege der christlichen Utopie." *Concilium* 6 (1970) 617–26.

Diop, Cheikh Anta. *The African Origin of Civilization, Myth or Reality*. Edited and translated by Mercer Cook. Chicago: Hill, 1974.

———. *Precolonial Black Africa*. Translated by Harold Salemson. Westport, CT: Hill, 1987.

———. *Towards the African Renaissance: Essays in Culture and Development 1946–1960*. Translated by Egbuna P. Modum. London: Karnak House, 1996.

Dorr, Donal. *Option for the Poor: A Hundred Years of Vatican Social Teaching*. Dublin: Gill and Macmillan, 1992.

———. *The Social Justice Agenda*. 1991. Reprint, Ibadan, Nigeria: Ambassador, 1994.

DuBois, W. E. B. *The Souls of Black Folk*. Greenwich, CT: Fawcett, 1961.

———. *The World and Africa*. Cambridge, MA: Harvard University Press, 1962.

Dulles, Avery. *Models of the Church*. New York: Image, 2002.

EATWOT II. "Final Communiqué" (1977). In *African Theology En Route*, edited by Kofi Appiah-Kubi and SergioTorres, 192–93. Maryknoll, NY: Orbis, 1979.

Egbujie, Ihemalol I. *The Hermeneutics of The African Traditional Culture: An Interpretative Analysis of African Culture*. Nyangwe, Zaire: Omenana, 1985.

Ehusani, George Omaku. *An Afro-Christian Vision "ỌZỌVẸHẸ!" Toward a More Humanized World*. Lanham, MD: University Press of America, 1991.

———. *Nigeria: Years Eaten by the Locust*. Ibadan, Nigeria: Kraft, 2002.

———. *A Prophetic Church*. Ibadan, Nigeria: Provincial Pastoral Institute. 1996.

Ela, Jean-Marc. *African Cry*. Translated by Robert R. Barr. Eugene, OR: Wipf and Stock, 2005.

Ellacuria, Ignacio, and Jon Sobrino. eds. *Mysterium Liberationis: Fundamental Concepts of Liberation Theology.* Maryknoll, NY: Orbis, 1993.

Enaharo, Anthony. *Daily Mirror,* London: June 13, 1968.

Equiano, Olaudah. *The Interesting Narrative of the Life of Olaudah Equiano or Gustavus Vassa, The African: Written by Himself.* London: Wilkins, 1794.

Ezeani, Emefiena G. B. *In Biafra Africa Died.* London: Veritas Lumen, 2012.

Fanon, Frantz. *The Wretched of the Earth.* New York: Grove Weidenfeld, 1986.

Fiorenza, Francis Schüssler. "Liberation Theology." In *New Catholic Encyclopedia,* 8:544–46. 2nd ed. Washington, DC: Catholic University of America Press, 2003.

Fiorenza, Francis Schüssler, and John P. Galvin. *Systematic Theology: Roman Catholic Perspectives.* Vol. 1. Minneapolis: Fortress, 1991.

Flannery, Austin. ed. *Vatican Council II.* Vol. 1, *The Conciliar and Post-Conciliar Documents.* Northport, NY: Costello, 1998.

Francis, Pope. *Evangelii Gaudium.* Apostolic Exhortation. Rome: Vatican, November 24, 2013.

Gheddo, Piero. *Why Is the Third World Poor?* Maryknoll, NY: Orbis, 1973.

Gibellini, Rosino, ed. *Handbuch der Theologie im 20. Jahrhundert.* Regensburg: Pustet, 1995.

———. *Paths of African Theology.* Maryknoll, NY: Orbis, 1994.

Goba, Bonganjalo. "The Black Consciousness Movement: Its Impact on Black Theology." In *The Unquestionable Right to be Free,* edited by J. M. Itumeleng and Buti Tlhagale, 57–70. Maryknoll, NY: Orbis, 1986.

Gowon, Yakubu. Interview by Tom Burns. *Tablet,* London, December 7, 1968; *Spectator,* London, December 27, 1968.

Grillmeier, Alois. "Jesus Christ: Christology." In *Sacramentum Mundi: An Encyclopedia of Theology,* edited by Karl Rahner et al., 3:186–92. Basel: Herder and Herder, 1969.

Gutiérrez, Gustavo. *Aus der eigenen Quelle trinken: Spiritualität der Befreiung.* Mainz-Münich: Grünewald, 1986.

———. "Option for the Poor." In *Mysterium Liberationis: Fundamental Concepts of Liberation Theology,* edited by Ignacio Ellacuria and Jon Sobrino, 235–50. Maryknoll, NY: Orbis, 1993.

———. *The Power of the Poor in History.* London: SCM, 1983.

———. *A Theology of Liberation: History, Politics and Salvation.* Maryknoll, NY: Orbis, 1988.

Hammond, Dorothy, and Alta Jablow. *The Africa That Never Was; Four Centuries of British Writing about Africa.* New York: Twayne, 1970.

Heidegger, Martin. *Being and Time.* Translated by John Macquarie and Edward Robinson. New York: Harper & Row, 1962.

Hegel, G. W. F. *The Philosophy of History.* Translated by J. Sibree. In *Great Books of the Western World,* 46:151–369. Chicago: Encyclopaedia Britannica, 1984.

Henry, Michel. *I Am the Truth: Toward a Philosophy of Christianity.* Translated by Susan Emanuel. Stanford: Stanford University Press, 2003.

Herodotus. *The Histories.* Translated by Aubrey de Sélincourt. England: Penguin, 1954.

Horner, T. *Jonathan Loved David: Homosexuality in Biblical Times.* Philadelphia: Westminster, 1978.

Horton, Robin. *Patterns of Thought in Africa and the West: Essays on Magic, Religion and Science.* Cambridge: Cambridge University Press, 1997.

Hughes, Gerard J. *Aristotle on Ethics*. New York: Routledge Philosophy GuideBooks, 2001.

Ifemesia, Chieka. *Traditional Humane Living among the Igbo: An Historical Perspective*. Enugu, Nigeria: Fourth Dimension, 1979.

Ike, Donatus. "The Need for African Solidarity: An Issue of 21st Century Survival." In *Africa, Philosophy and Public Affairs*, edited by J. Obi Oguejiofor, 366–78. Enugu, Nigeria: Delta, 1998.

Ikenga-Metuh, Emefie. *God and Man in African Religion: A Case Study of the Igbo of Nigeria*. 2nd ed. Enugu, Nigeria: Snaap, 1999.

Ilo, Stan Chu. *The Church and Development in Africa: Aid and Development from the Perspective of Catholic Social Ethics*. Eugene, OR: Pickwick, 2011.

———. *The Face of Africa: Looking Beyond the Shadows*. Bloomington, IN: AuthorHouse, 2006.

Itumeleng, J. M., and Buti Tlhagale, eds. *The Unquestionable Right to Be Free: Black Theology from South Africa*. Maryknoll, NY: Orbis, 1986.

J. S., I. B., and L. P. "Rewarding Work." *The Economist*, July 15, 2013, http://www.economist.com/node/21011894/2013/07/daily-chart-12.?page=1.

John Paul II, Pope. *Dives in Misericordia: On the Mercy of God*. Encyclical Letter. Rome: Vatican, 30. Nov. 1980.

———. *Ecclesia in Africa*. Post-Synodal Exhortation. Yaoundé, Cameroon, September 14, 1995.

———. *Evangelium Vitae*. Encyclical Letter. Rome: Vatican, March 25, 1995.

———. *Redemptoris Missio*. Encyclical Letter. Rome: Vatican, December 7, 1990.

———. *Reconciliation and Penance*. Post-Synodal Apostolic Exhortation. Rome: Vatican, December 2, 1984.

———. *Solicitudo Rei Socialis*. Encyclical Letter. Rome: Vatican, December 30, 1987.

Kalilombe, P. A. "The Presence of the Church in Africa." In *The Emergent Gospel: Theology from the Underside of History*, edited by Sergio Torres and Virginia Fabella, 22–30. Maryknoll, NY: Orbis, 1978.

Kasper, Walter. *Christologische Schwerpunkte*. Düsseldorf: Patmos, 1980.

Katsina, Hassan Usman. *Times*, London, June 28, 1969.

Kaunda, Kenneth. *A Humanist in Africa*. Nashville: Abingdon, 1966.

Kelly, Thomas M. "A Church Rooted in Mercy: Ecclesial Signposts in Sobrino's Theology." In *Hope and Solidarity: Jon Sobrino's Challenge to Christian Theology*, edited by Stephen J. Pope, 155–70. Maryknoll, NY: Orbis, 2008.

Klein, R. W. *1 Samuel*. Word Biblical Commentary 10. Waco, TX: Word, 1983.

Kobia, Samuel. *The Courage to Hope*. Geneva: World Council of Churches, 2003.

Law, Ian. "Immigration and the Politics of Ethnic Diversity." In *Policy-Making in Britain: An Introduction*, edited by Maurice Mullard, 233–47. London: Routledge, 1995.

Leo XIII, Pope. *Rerum Novarum*. Encyclical Letter. Rome: Vatican, May 15, 1891.

Lewis, C. S. *The Four Loves*. London: Fontana, 1960.

Lois, Julio. "Christology in the Theology of Liberation." In *Mysterium Liberationis: Fundamental Concepts of Liberation Theology*, edited by Ignacio Ellacuria and Jon Sobrino, 168–94. Maryknoll, NY: Orbis, 1993.

Lugard, Fredrick. *The Dual Mandate in British Tropical Africa*. London: William Blackwood, 1923.

Maimela, Simon, and Dwight Hopkins, eds. *We Are One Voice: Black Theology in the USA and South Africa*. Braamfontein, South Africa: Skotaville, 1989.

Mandela, Nelson. *Long Walk to Freedom: The Autobiography of Nelson Mandela*. Boston: Back Bay, 1995.

Marjorie, Hope, and James Young. *The South African Churches in a Revolutionary Situation*. Maryknoll, NY: Orbis, 1981.

Martey, Emanuel. *African Theology: Inculturation and Liberation*. Maryknoll, NY: Orbis, 1995.

Marx, Karl. *A Contribution to the Critique of Hegel's Philosophy of Right* (1843). http://www.marxists.org/archive/marx/works/1843/critique-hpr/intro.htm.

Masanja, Patrick. "Neocolonialism and Revolution in Africa." In *The Emergent Gospel: Theology from the Underside of History*, edited by Sergio Torres and Virginia Fabella, 9–21. Maryknoll, NY: Orbis, 1978.

Mazrui, Ali. *Cultural Forces in World Politics*. London: Currey, 1990.

Mbiti, John. *African Religions and Philosophy*. London: Heinemann, 1970.

Meredith, Martin. *The Fate of Africa: From Hope of Freedom to the Heart of Despair*. New York: Public Affairs, 2005.

Metz, Johann Baptist. *Memoria Passionis*. Freiburg: Herder, 2006.

———. *Mystik der offenen Augen: Wenn Spiritualität aufbricht*. Freiburg: Herder, 2011.

Mofokeng, Takatso. "Black Theological Perspectives, Past and Present." In *We Are One Voice: Black Theology in the USA and South Africa*, edited by Simon Maimela and Dwight Hopkins. Braamfontein, South Africa: Skotaville, 1989.

Moore, Basil. ed. *The Challenge of Black Theology in South Africa*. Atlanta: John Knox, 1973.

Moore, G. "The Politics of Négritude." In *Protest in African Literature*, edited by Cosmo Pieterse and Donald Munro, 26–42. London: Heinemann, 1969.

Morrison, Jago. "Imagined Biafras: Fabricating Nation in Nigerian Civil War Writing." *ARIEL* 36, nos. 1–2 (2005) 5–25. http://www.ariel.ucalgary.ca/ariel/index.php/ariel/article/viewFile/362/358.

Mveng, Engelbert. "Impoverishment and Liberation: A Theological Approach for Africa and the Third World." In *Paths of African Theology*, edited by Rosino Gibellini, 154–65. Maryknoll, NY: Orbis, 1994.

Nash, Ronald H., ed. *Liberation Theology*. Grand Rapids: Baker, 1988.

Nebechukwu, Augustine. "Third World Theology and the Recovery of African Identity." *Journal of Inculturation Theology* 2, no. 1 (1995) 20–32.

Neuhaus, Richard John. "Liberation Theology and the Cultural Captivity of the Gopel." In *Liberation Theology*, edited by Ronald H. Nash, 215–36. Grand Rapids: Baker, 1988.

———. "The New Orleans That Was." *First Things* 157 (2005) 10–12.

Nkrumah, Kwame. *Consciencism: Philosophy and Ideology*. New York: Monthly Review, 1970.

———. *Ghana: The Autobiography of Kwame Nkrumah*. New York: International, 1957.

Nnaemeka, Obioma. "Mapping African Feminisms." In *Readings in Gender in Africa*, edited by Andrea Cornwall, 31–41. Bloomington: Indiana University Press, 2005.

Norman, Edward. "The Imperialism of Political Religion—Jesus as Subversio de Nazaret." In *Liberation Theology*, edited by Ronald H. Nash, 121–38. Grand Rapids: Baker, 1988.

Novak, Michael. "Liberation Theology and the Pope" (June 1979). In *Liberation Theology: A Documentary History*, edited by Alfred T. Hennelly, 173–89. Maryknoll, NY: Orbis, 1990.

Nwoko, M. I. *Basic World Political Theories: Ancient-Contemporary*. Owerri, Nigeria: Claverianum, 1988.

Nyamiti, Charles. "Approaches to African Theology." In *The Emergent Gospel: Theology from the Underside of History*, edited by Sergio Torres and Virginia Fabella, 31–45. Maryknoll, NY: Orbis, 1978.

———. *Jesus Christ, the Ancestor of Humankind: Methodological and Trinitarian Foundations*. Vol. 1 of *Studies in African Christian Theology*. Nairobi: Catholic University of Eastern Africa, 2005.

———. *Jesus Christ, the Ancestor of Humankind: An Essay on African Christology*. Vol. 2 of *Studies in African Christian Theology*. Nairobi: Catholic University of Eastern Africa, 2006.

Nyerere, Julius. "Ujamaa—The Basis of African Socialism." In *African Socialism*, edited by William Friedland and Carl G. Rosberg, 238–47. Stanford: Stanford University Press, 1967.

———. *Ujamaa: Essays on Socialism*. Dar es Salaam: Oxford University Press, 1968.

O'Collins, Gerald. *Christology: A Bibilical, Historical and Systematic Study of Jesus*. New York: Oxford University Press, 2009.

Oduyoye, Mercy Amba. *Daughters of Anowa: African Women and Patriarchy*. Maryknoll, NY: Orbis, 1995.

———. *Hearing and Knowing*. Maryknoll, NY: Orbis, 1986.

———. *Introducing African Women's Theology*. Cleveland: Pilgrim, 2001.

Oguejiofor, Obi J., ed. *Africa: Philosophy and Public Affairs*. Enugu, Nigeria: Delta, 1998.

Ojukwu, Emeka. *The Ahiara Declaration (The Principles of the Biafran Revolution)*. http://www.biafraland.com/Ahiara_declaration_1969.htm.

Okafor, Ikenna Ugochukwu. "O nuru Ube Nwanne Agbal Oso, A Theology of Fraternal Solidarity: An Igbo Perspective to Liberation Theology." *Bulletin of Ecumenical Theology* 24 (2013) 5–39.

———. "Proclaiming the Gospel of Salvation to a Nation in Distress: A Call to Liberation Theology in Nigerian Context." Master's thesis, University of Vienna, 2005.

Okpehwo, Isidore. *Myth in Africa: A Study of Its Aesthetic and Cultural Relevance*. Cambridge: Cambridge University Press, 1983.

Olisa, Michael S. O., and Odinchezo M. Ikejiani-Clark, eds. *Azikiwe and the African Revolution*. Onitsha, Nigeria: African-FEP, 1989.

Olson, Roger E. *The Story of Christian Theology*. Downers Grove, IL: InterVarsity, 1999.

Omuta, Patrick Eloka. *From Vatican II to African Synod: Catholic Social Teaching in African Context*. Onitsha, Nigeria: Tansi, 2004.

Onwubiko, Oliver A. *The Church in Mission in the Light of Ecclesia in Africa*. Nairobi: Paulines, 2001.

Orobator, A. E. *The Church as Family: African Ecclesiology in Its Social Context*. Nairobi: Paulines, 2000.

Ottenberg, Simon, and Phoebe Ottenberg, eds. *Cultures and Societies of Africa*. New York: Random House, 1960.

Ouellet, Marc. "The Ecclesiology of Communion, 50 Years after the Opening of Vatican Council II." Address given at the opening of the International Theology Symposium, Maynooth, Ireland, June 7, 2012. http://www.zenit.org/en/articles/cardinal-ouellet-at-international-theology-symposium.

Paul VI, Pope. *Populorum Progressio*. Encyclical Letter. Rome: Vatican, March 26, 1967.

Pieterse, Cosmo, and Donald Munro, eds. *Protest in African Literature*. London: Heinemann, 1969.

Pindiga, Habeeb I. "Nigerian Lawmakers Top Salaries Chart." *Daily Trust*, July 22, 2013, http://allafrica.com/stories/201307221471.html.

Pontifical Council Cor Unum. *World Hunger a Challenge for All: Development in Solidarity*. Nairobi: Paulines, 1996.

Pope, Stephen J., ed. *Hope and Solidarity: Jon Sobrino's Challenge to Christian Theology*. Maryknoll, NY: Orbis, 2008.

Rahner, Karl. "Jesus Christ: History of Dogma and Theology." In *Sacramentum Mundi: An Encyclopedia of Theology*, edited by Karl Rahner et al., 3:192–209. Basel: Herder and Herder, 1969.

———. *The Love of Jesus and the Love of Neighbor*. Translated by Robert Barr. New York: Crossroad, 1983.

———. *Schriften zur Theologie*. Vol. 14. Einsiedeln: Benziger, 1980.

Ratzinger, Joseph. "Liberation Theology." http://www.christendom-awake.org/pages/ratzinger/liberationtheol.htm.

Ritner, Peter. *The Death of Africa*. New York: Macmillan, 1960.

Rowland, Christopher, ed. *The Cambridge Companion to Liberation Theology*. Cambridge: Cambridge University Press, 1999.

Sacred Congregation for the Doctrine of the Faith. *Libertatis Conscientias, Instruction on Christian Freedom and Liberation*. Rome: Vatican, March 22, 1986.

———. *Libertatis Nuntius, Instruction on Certain Aspects of the Theology of Liberation*. Rome: Vatican, August 6, 1984.

Sanneh, Lamin. "The Horizontal and the Vertical in Mission: An African Perspective." *International Bulletin of Missionary Research* 7, no. 4 (1983) 165–71.

Schall, James V. "Ratzinger on the Modern Mind." Ignatius, http://www.ignatius.com/Magazines/hprweb/schall_10-1997.htm.

Schroer, Silvia. *Die Samuelbücher*. Neuer Stuttgater Kommentar—Altes Testament 7. Stuttgart: Katholisches Bibelwerk, 1992.

Scott, Peter. *Theology, Ideology and Liberation*. Cambridge: Cambridge University Press, 1994.

Segundo, Julian Luis. *The Historical Jesus of the Synoptics*. Vol. 2. Maryknoll, NY: Orbis, 1985.

———. *Liberation of Theology*. Translated by John Drury. Eugene, OR: Wipf and Stock, 2002.

———. *The Shift within Latin American Theology*. Toronto: Regis College Press, 1983.

Setiloane, Gabriel. "I Am an African." In *Third World Theologies*, edited by Gerald H. Anderson and Thomas F. Stransky, 128–31. Mission Trends 3. New York: Paulist, 1976.

Shivji, Issa. "Ngugi wa Thiong'o's Re-membering Africa" (October 2, 2009). http://www.langaa-rpcig.net/+Ngugi-wa-Thiong-o-s-Re-membering+.html.

Sigmund, Paul E., ed. *The Ideologies of the Developing Nations*. New York: Praeger, 1967.

Sobrino, Jon. *Jesus the Liberator, A Historical-Theological Reading of Jesus of Nazareth*. Translated by Paul Burns and Francis McDonagh. Maryknoll, NY: Orbis, 1993.

———. *The Principle of Mercy: Taking the Crucified People from the Cross*. Maryknoll, NY: Orbis, 1994.

———. *The True Church and the Church of the Poor*. Translated by Matthew J. O'Connell. London: SCM, 1985.

Sobrino, Jon, and Ignacio Ellacuria, eds. *Systematic Theology: Perspectives from Liberation Theology*. Maryknoll, NY: Orbis, 1993.

Sogolo, Godwin. *Foundations of African Philosophy*. Ibadan, Nigeria: Ibadan University Press, 1992.

Soyinka, Wole. *The Man Died: Prison Notes of Wole Soyinka*. New York: Noonday, 1972.

Stinton, Diane B. *Jesus of Africa: Voices of Contemporary African Christology*. Maryknoll, NY: Orbis, 2004.

Stride, G. T., and C. Ifeka, eds. *Peoples and Empires of West Africa*. Lagos, Nigeria: Thomas and Nelson, 1978.

Taiwo, Olufemi. "Exorcising Hegel's Ghost: Africa's Challenge to Philosophy." *African Studies Quarterly* 1, no. 4 (1998) 3–16. http://www.africa.ufl.edu/asq/v1/v1_i4.htm.

Torres, Sergio G. "The Future of Liberation Theology in Latin America." In *Ethical Issues in the Struggle for Justice*, edited by Daniel Chetti and M. P. Joseph. Tiruvalla, India: Christava Sahitya Samiti, 1998. http://www.re,igion-online.org/showchapter.asp?title=1571&C=1498.

Tutu, Desmond. *No Future without Forgiveness*. New York: Doubleday, 1999.

Uchem, Rose N. "Overcoming Women's Subordination in the Igbo African Culture and in the Catholic Church: Envisioning an Inclusive Theology with Reference to Women." PhD diss., Graduate Theological Foundation, 2001.

Ukpong, Justin. "Theological Literature from Africa." *Concilium* 199 (1988) 65–79.

Uwalaka, Jude. "Inclusive Humanism: The Basis of a Sound Socio-political Order for Africa." In *Africa: Philosophy and Public Affairs*, edited by J. Obi Oguejiofor, 94–113. Enugu, Nigeria: Delta, 1998.

Uzukwu, Elochukwu. *A Listening Church: Autonomy and Communion in African Churches*. Maryknoll, NY: Orbis, 1996.

Volf, Miroslav. *Exclusion and Embrace: A Theological Exploration of Identity, Otherness, and Reconciliation*. Nashville: Abingdon, 1996.

Walsh, J. J., and P. Loewe. "Christology." In *New Catholic Encyclopedia*, 3:559–60. 2nd ed. Washington, DC: Catholic University of America Press, 2003.

Walvin, James. *The Trader, the Owner, the Slave: Parallel Lives in the Age of Slavery*. London: Vintage, 2008.

Weigel, George. "*Caritas in veritate* in Gold and Red." *National Review Online*, July 7, 2009, http://www.nationalreview.com/articles/227839/i-caritas-veritate-i-gold-and-red/george-weigel.

———. "Just War and Iraq Wars." *First Things* 172 (2007) 14–20.

———. "World Order: What Catholics Forgot." *First Things* 143 (2004) 31–38.

Williams, Walter L. *Black Americans and the Evangelization of Africa (1877–1900)*. Madison: University of Wisconsin Press, 1982.

Young, Josiah U. *African Theology: A Critical Analysis and Annotated Bibliography*. Westport, CT: Greenwood, 1993.

Index